DEFENDING LINCOLNSHIRE

DEFENDING LINCOLNSHIRE

A Military History from Conquest to Cold War

MIKE OSBORNE

First published 2010

The History Press
The Mill, Brimscombe Port
Stroud, Gloucestershire, GL5 2QG
www.thehistorypress.co.uk

© Mike Osborne, 2010

The right of Mike Osborne to be identified as the Author
of this work has been asserted in accordance with the
Copyrights, Designs and Patents Act 1988.

All rights reserved. No part of this book may be reprinted
or reproduced or utilised in any form or by any electronic,
mechanical or other means, now known or hereafter invented,
including photocopying and recording, or in any information
storage or retrieval system, without the permission in writing
from the Publishers.

British Library Cataloguing in Publication Data.
A catalogue record for this book is available from the British Library.

ISBN 978 0 7524 5399 6

Typesetting and origination by The History Press
Printed in Great Britain

Contents

	Acknowledgements	7
	Abbreviations	8
	Introduction	11
ONE	Fortifications in Lincolnshire prior to 1066	13
TWO	The Early Medieval Period (c.1000–1300)	25
THREE	The Later Medieval and Tudor Period (c.1300–1600)	54
FOUR	The Stuart and Georgian Periods (c.1600–1815)	81
FIVE	The Victorian Period (c.1815–1914)	104
SIX	The First World War (1914–18)	119
SEVEN	Preparing for the Next War: Rearmament (1919–38)	145
EIGHT	The Second World War (1939–45)	161
NINE	The Cold War (1946–93)	227
	Bibliography	247
	Index	251

Acknowledgements

Grateful thanks are due to the following who have generously made information available: Adrian Armishaw, Roger Audis, Group Captain Ross Bailey and Flight Sergeant Mike Ullyatt (RAF Digby), Malcolm Baxter, Mark Bennet (Lincolnshire HER), Deborah Bircham (Museums Collections Officer, Grantham, Stamford and Coningsby), the management at Fiskerton former ROC HQ, Sue Burden, Peter Chambers, Eric Cubbin, Terry Hancock, John Herridge and Phil North (Lincoln City Council Heritage Dept), Mike Hodgson, Tim Hudson, Lincolnshire Archives, Lincolnshire Libraries, Henry Meir, Charles Parker, Eric Sharpe (Lincolnshire Army Cadet Force), David and Margaret Sibley, Stewart Squires, Mike Suttill (East Midlands RFCA), Sam Thompson, Robert Walker (East Lindsey DC Planning & Regeneration Dept), Alison Williams and Mike Hemblade (North Lincolnshire Museum Scunthorpe), and Peter Wright. My wife Pam has, as ever, provided constant support, particularly in unearthing interesting archive material. My apologies to anyone I may have missed.

Abbreviations

AA	anti-aircraft
AAOR	anti-aircraft operations room
ACF	Army Cadet Force
AEW	Airborne Early Warning (aircraft)
AMES	Air Ministry Experimental Establishment (early radar site)
Ants. Jnl.	Antiquaries Journal
APS	Auxiliary Patrol Service (RN)
ARP	Air Raid Precautions
A/S	anti-submarine
ASR	air-sea rescue
AT	anti-tank
AWACS	Airborne early warning (AEW) operations and control
BABS	Blind (later Beam) Approach Beacon System
Bde.	brigade
BEF	British Expeditionary Force
BMEWS	Ballistic Missile Early Warning System
Bn.	battalion
BRO	British Resistance Organisation (auxiliary units)
BYM/S	British Yard Minesweeper
CASL	Coastal Artillery Searchlight (Second World War)
CD	Civil Defence
CH	Chain Home (radar)
CH(E)L	Chain Home (Extra) Low (radars)
CO	Commanding Officer
CPRE	Council for the Protection of Rural England
CSG	Castle Studies Group
DEL	Defence Electric Light (First World War coast defence searchlight)
Div.	division
DFW3	Directorate of Fortifications and Works, Dept. 3 (War Office)
DL	defended locality
EFTS	Elementary Flying Training School
EH	English Heritage
FAA	Fleet Air Arm
FIDO	Fog Investigation & Dispersal Operation OR Fog, Intense, Disposal Of

FOIC	Flag Officer In Charge (RN base/sector commander)
FRIBA	Fellow of the Royal Institute of British Architects
GCI	Ground Control Interception (radar)
GDA	Gun Defended Area (AA defence)
GL	Gun-laying (radar)
GNR	Great Northern Railway
HAA	Heavy anti-aircraft
HAS	Hardened aircraft shelter
HCU	Heavy Conversion Unit (bomber training)
HER	Historic Environment Record (formerly SMR)
HMSO	Her Majesty's Stationery Office
hp	horse-power
HSL	High speed launch
ICBM	Inter-Continental Ballistic Missile
IFF	Identification Friend or Foe
IRBM	Intermediate-Range Ballistic Missile
ITC	Infantry Training Centre
LAA	light anti-aircraft
LAC	Leading Aircraftsman
LCT	Landing Craft, Tank
lmg	light machine gun
LMS	London Midland Scottish (railway company)
MAD	Mutually-assured destruction
MAFF	Ministry of Agriculture, Food and Fisheries
MAP	Ministry of Aircraft Production
MCU	Marine Craft Unit (RAF)
mg	machine gun
MFV	motor fishing vessel
MGB	Motor Gun Boat
MGC	Machine-Gun Corps
ML	Motor Launch
MM/S	motor mine-sweeper
M/S	minesweeper
NAAFI	Navy Army & Air Force Institutes
NATO	North Atlantic Treaty Organisation
OB	Operational Base (auxiliary unit hide)
OCTU	officer cadet training unit
OTU	Operational Training Unit (RAF)
PAD	Permanent ammunition depot
PoW	prisoner of war
PBX	private telephone exchange
QF	quick-firing (gun)
QRA	Quick Reaction Alert (Cold War interceptor aircraft)
RAF	Royal Air Force (after 01.04.1918)

RASC	Royal Army Service Corps ('Royal' after First World War)
RCHM(E)	Royal Commission on Historical Monuments (England)
RE	Royal Engineers
REME	Royal Electrical & Mechanical Engineers
RFA	Royal Field Artillery
RFC	Royal Flying Corps (up to 31 March 1918)
RFAC	Royal Fine Arts Commission
RFCA	Reserve Forces and Cadets Association
RGA	Royal Garrison Artillery
RML	Rifled muzzle-loader (Victorian heavy gun)
RMS	rendering mines safe (operation)
RNAS	Royal Naval Air Service (up to 31 March 1918)
ROC	Royal Observer Corps ('Royal' from 1941)
RSG	Regional Seat of Government
RSJ	rolled steel joist
SFTS	Service Flying Training School
S/L	searchlight
SLHA	Society for Lincolnshire History and Archaeology
SMR	Sites and Monuments Record, now Historic Environment Record
SRHQ	Sub-Regional Headquarters (Cold War)
TA	Territorial Army (1920–39, and 1947–present)
tb	temporary brick (single brick construction with buttresses)
TDS	Training Depot Station (RFC/RAF)
TF	Territorial Force (1908–1920)
UDC	Urban District Council
UKWMO	United Kingdom Warning and Monitoring Organisation
USAAF	United States Army Air Force (Second World War)
USAF	United States Air Force (post-Second World War)
VAD	Voluntary Aid Detachment
VCR	Visual Control Room (on watch office)
VHF	Very high frequency
VP	vulnerable point
WAAF	Women's Auxiliary Air Force
WD	War Department
WLA	Women's Land Army
WRAF	Women's Royal Air Force
WRNS	Women's Royal Naval Service
W/T	Wireless/Telegraphy

Introduction

Lincolnshire with the Humber Estuary in the north, the Wash to the south, and a western boundary following the River Trent, has an obvious geographical integrity. Its long coastline however has at times attracted the wrong sort of visitor, or has been seen as vulnerable to such invasions. In more recent times its position, particularly enhanced by the Lincoln Cliff, has provided a springboard for offensive operations, real or potential. This book sets out to record the buildings and other structures within the boundaries of historic Lincolnshire that have purely military purposes, military connections, or mere fleeting appearances on the military stage. These include forts and castles, strong houses and moats, fortified ecclesiastical precincts, coast defence batteries, pillboxes and gun-emplacements, barracks and drill halls, military airfields, missile sites, air defence systems and radar, munitions factories and supply depots.

Historic Lincolnshire (Holland, Kesteven and Lindsey), though neatly delineated, has a wide variation of landscape. The ridge of high ground stretching from the Humber to Stamford and known as the Lincoln Cliff has a gap below Lincoln cut by the River Witham; the high land of the Wolds stretches from the Humber to Horncastle; an extensive coastal strip of fenland, all under 5m but much of it actually below sea-level, was gradually drained through the middle ages and into the seventeenth century, meaning that the Roman coastline was very different from the one we see now, although in some places, the sea is once more reclaiming the land; finally, around Sleaford is a large area of heath-land. Lincolnshire has one of the highest densities of villages reflecting its agricultural predominance in both arable and livestock farming, and its towns once counted amongst the largest and wealthiest in the land. These factors have encouraged exploitation and development as the rich and powerful have sought to maintain their dominance both political and economic. Sometimes this has led to actual conflict, at other times being prepared for, or appearing to be prepared for the possibility of conflict has been enough.

It is unsurprising that one has only to scratch the surface to uncover the wealth of heritage below. During the First World War, Anglo-Saxon burials were unearthed in Riby Park by troops of the Manchester Regiment practising entrenching. When Kirmington airfield was under construction in 1941 finds associated with a Roman fort were revealed. Whilst Tattershall and Lincoln castles are well known across the country, many other such historical monuments can be visited. More recent events have spawned an Aviation Heritage industry which includes the Battle of Britain Memorial Flight at Coningsby, flourishing museums at East Kirkby, Cranwell,

Tattershall Thorpe, Sandtoft, Scampton, Metheringham and The Lawn in Lincoln, and organised tours and trails leaflets available in tourist information centres, particularly North Kesteven's in Sleaford. Digby's perfectly preserved Battle of Britain operations block is open to the public, and many other airfields are visible with the buildings of Hemswell and Manby remaining both well preserved and easily accessible. Most airfields have memorials on site, and the listings of the Department of Culture, Media and Sport reflect the importance of Lincolnshire in the development of the RAF. Clearly not everything can be saved and recent demolitions at Fulbeck and Bracebridge Heath underline the vulnerability of tired structures. On balance however, the county enjoys the finest portfolio of aviation heritage assets anywhere in Britain.

This interest in aviation heritage spreads across the globe. During the First World War, there were US fliers at Killingholme, and Australians at Harlaxton and South Carlton, but throughout the Second World War, a vast family of allies served here. There were Canadians, Belgians and Czechs at Digby and Coleby Grange; Australians at Binbrook; Americans at Fulbeck, Goxhill, North Witham, and Folkingham; Poles at Faldingworth and Ingham; Australians and Poles at Swinderby; New Zealanders, Poles, Australians and Americans at Kirton-in-Lindsey; and Free French naval and air force pilots from 7SFTS, Peterborough trained on *Oxfords* at Sutton Bridge. In 1952, the Rhodesian No. 44 Squadron flew their *B29s* from Coningsby.

Lincolnshire RAF units took part in all the key operations of the twentieth century, from the anti-*Zeppelin* patrols of the First World War, to the 'Dambusters' Raid of the Second World War, to the bombing of Port Stanley by *Vulcans* from Waddington during the Falklands War. In 2009, Lincolnshire remains a major operational base for the RAF, with aircraft still flying from Barkston Heath, Coningsby, Cranwell, Scampton and Waddington, whilst Woodhall, Digby and Kirton-in-Lindsey are home to ground-based units with gliding taking place at the latter station. The constant threat of terrorist activity has seen the return of the *Yarnold sangar* to airfield perimeters and a general awareness of the need for tight security.

This book also highlights the contribution of the other services to the life of the county. The Royal Anglian Regiment, descended from the 'Poachers', recently marched through Lincoln on its return from overseas service. The Royal Navy has left its mark on the ports of Grimsby and Immingham, and a ghostlier image at Skegness. Sadly, it has been left to outsiders to commemorate Newton's contribution to military science in the fields of optics and mechanics with the REME Depot being located in Isaac Newton Road, Arborfield Garrison, Berkshire.

The first chapter outlines the history of fortifications in Lincolnshire prior to the Norman Conquest, and successive chapters trace the development of defensive arrangements through the Medieval period, the Civil War, the Napoleonic Wars, the Victorian age and the world wars of the twentieth century, showing how military activities and operations have contributed to the rich fabric of Lincolnshire's heritage.

Mike Osborne, August 2009, Market Deeping

one

Fortifications in Lincolnshire prior to 1066

PREHISTORIC FORTIFICATIONS

An archetypal feature of the Iron Age landscape, especially associated with the southern Downlands, is the hill fort, such as those at Maiden Castle in Dorset or Cissbury Ring in West Sussex. They also appear throughout the country from the Welsh border (Old Oswestry) to Northumbria (Old Bewick). The form they usually take is an enclosed area with a number of concentric banks and ditches, entered through an often complex entrance with dog-legs and gates. The banks were usually topped by a palisade and reinforced by storm-poles. The usually large interior was occupied by huts for living and working, and space to keep animals at night or in time of danger. It is still a matter of debate as to whether such forts were permanently occupied, or were used only as refuges. Whilst hill forts are not a common feature of the Lincolnshire landscape, there are a number of locations in the county where clusters of habitation sites are associated with what have traditionally been taken for Iron Age forts. There are examples of such juxtapositions around Ulceby and Kirmington with the neighbouring Yarborough Camp, and around Ancaster with Honington Camp nearby. However, the apparently significant settlements of Dragonby and Old Sleaford, and the vanished South Ferriby, appear not to have had earthwork defences. Other possible forts of the period may exist at Ingoldsby (Round Hills), at Careby near Bourne, and at Tattershall Thorpe where a ploughed-out fort has been found.

Honington Camp consists of a sub-rectangular enclosure of under two-thirds of a hectare, bounded by double banks and ditches entered through a gap in the eastern side. Iron Age finds have been made here as well as Roman coins, which may point to further occupation. It has also been suggested that its shape is similar to that of some Roman farmsteads identified by aerial photography. The larger enclosure at Ingoldsby has a single bank and ditch. Careby Camp, slightly larger again, has concentric banks and ditches, but 40m apart. Yarborough Camp, in woodland, only a kilometre from the Iron Age site at Kirmington, is largely obscured by vegetation, but boasts the discovery of items of prehistoric and Romano-British material. It would appear that while the balance of probability would suggest that these sites may well be of Iron Age origin, nothing about their use is certain.

From the very end of this period, Colsterworth provides us with an example of a late Iron Age defended site. Here, surrounded by a ditch 20ft (6m) wide and 8ft (2.5m) deep, the enclosed area contained a number of circular huts. Finds from the 1942 excavation date the settlement to the early years of the first millennium. There must have been dozens of small settlements such as that found in 1978 at Weelsby Road, Grimsby, where an Iron Age round house is surrounded by a ditch, 11ft (3.5m) wide and 4ft (1.2m) deep with an inner bank. Whether this was for defence, drainage, or for confining or excluding animals is unknown. It is possible that a site to the south of Brayford Pool in Lincoln may represent an earlier settlement pre-dating Roman Lindum, but there is no evidence for defences. The large settlement at Dragonby has been suggested as an oppidum of the Corieltauvi tribe, occupied and still expanding, into the late Iron Age. Castle Hills Wood Camp, also referred to as Danes Camp, at Thonock near Gainsborough was once listed by the RCHM(E) as a possible Iron Age camp, but this has now been assigned to the time of the Danelaw, with a later history as an earthwork castle dating from the second quarter of the twelfth century.

ROMAN FORTIFICATIONS

There are a number of fortified sites from the later Roman period but the major one began much earlier. It is probable that there was an Iron Age settlement south of the River Witham by Brayford Pool or thereabouts, and that the invading Romans located their first fort, possibly on South Common in *c*.AD 47–50, in this strategic location on the Fosse Way. This was designed to defend the frontier that had been consolidated for a while at the Humber, with other forts and settlements along the lines of Ermine Street and King Street. Subsequently, around AD 60, a highly-defensible site on the top of the hill was chosen as a strong base for first the 9th *Hispana* and, after *c*.AD 71, the 2nd *Adiutrix* Legions. This legionary fortress may have replaced a smaller, more temporary fort on part of this site. Within a few years, following the defeat of the Iceni, the army advanced northwards, moving its legionary fortress from Lincoln to York. On the redeployment of the *Adiutrix* to Chester in AD 78, the fortress was replaced by the *colonia*, a settlement for discharged legionaries, which ultimately expanded down the hill to the river. As well as this major fortified base, there were Roman town defences at Ancaster, Caistor and Horncastle, and earlier forts at Kirmington and Old Winteringham, and possibly Hibaldstow and Louth as well, all securing routes north to the Humber crossings. Kirmington was built over an Iron Age settlement. Old Winteringham began life as a military supply base at the top of Ermine Street. Excavations have uncovered evidence of timber military buildings from this time, but the later civil settlement was unfortified (***Fig. 1***).

Fortification in Lincolnshire prior to 1066　15

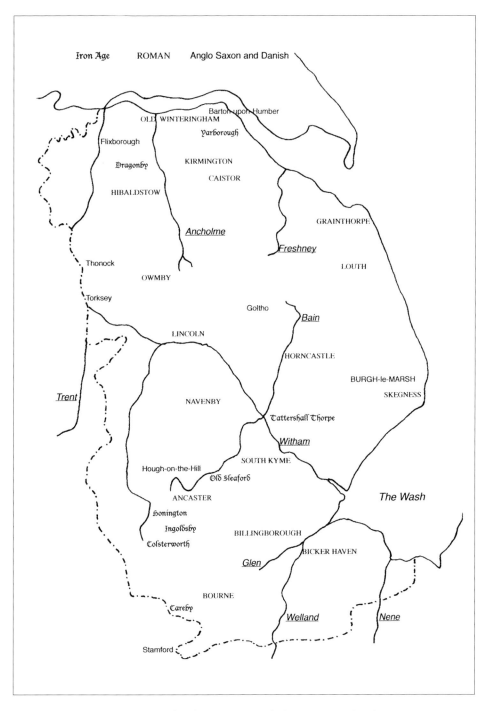

Fig. 1 Map to show pre-Conquest fortifications in Lincolnshire mentioned in the text

ROMAN LINCOLN

The Roman legionary fortress on the hill above the River Witham began life with earthwork and timber defences, which enclosed a roughly square area of around 40 acres (16 hectares). It had the familiar characteristics of Roman forts with north–south and east–west internal roads crossing in the centre where a headquarters building stood, along with the commander's house. The earthen rampart, revetted in timber on both faces, was reinforced by internal timber towers at intervals, and had a single ditch in front. The four roads exited the fort through timber gateways with fighting platforms above. During the fifty years after the military had gone, the town was largely rebuilt in stone. The military headquarters building was replaced by a grand forum, part of which, known as the Mint Wall, survives in the Westgate/Bailgate area. By the end of the second century AD, the town had been extended down the hill to the river, enclosing a further 56 acres (22.5 hectares). The upper town's defences were strengthened by being rebuilt in stone to a thickness of 5ft (1.5m) and a height approaching 20ft (6m) with a ditch around 80ft (24.5m) wide and 25ft (7.5m) deep, creating formidable defences. The four gates were also enlarged and rebuilt in masonry.

There remain a number of survivals from these stone defences, and excavations have revealed aspects of both main fortification phases. There was, from the first, a ditch around the fort, but its small scale suggests that at the very least, a second ditch, such as that whose inner lip has been found near the East Gate, would have

1 LINCOLN: the Newport Arch, the north gate of the Roman upper city dating from after AD 200; it consisted of a central arch flanked by pedestrian arches and D-shaped towers

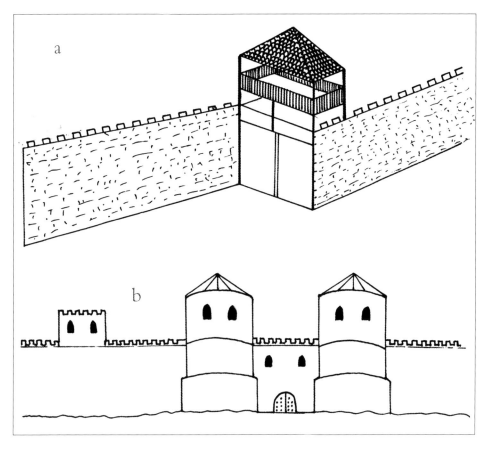

Fig. 2 Roman Lincolnshire. 2a: conjectural view of one of Horncastle's possible off-set gates; 2b: view of a gate and wall-tower of Lincoln's upper city walled around AD 200

surrounded the whole site. The original earth bank, formed from the spoil from the ditch(es), was laid on a continuous log raft, and was wide enough to accommodate a palisade and sentry-walk. At some time whilst still in military occupation, it appears that projecting timber interval towers were added to the wall, with their forward wooden supporting posts embedded in what had been the inner ditch, but had now largely been filled in. Each gate, one in the centre of each wall, probably had a projecting tower inserted next to it as the evidence at East Gate would suggest. The next phase in the development of the defences was the construction of a stone wall around the new *colonia*, probably begun around the beginning of the second century AD. By using the former inner ditch as a base for this new stone wall, 5ft (1.5m) thick, resting on a stone plinth, the builders were able to utilise the earlier, existing bank as an inner rampart by which the new wall might be supported. A stretch of this wall may be seen between Chapel Lane and Cecil Street behind Lillicrap Court.

Whereas the earlier, timber towers had been added to the outside of the wall, new stone towers were built against the inside face of the wall. The locations of

2 LINCOLN: a postern gate in the western wall of the Roman lower city, built in the fourth century AD; it stands next to City Hall off Orchard Street

two of these towers found on the northern wall would suggest that there were originally three between each gate and the fort's corner, making twenty-four in all. The wall and the base of an internal rectangular tower survive in East Bight. What may possibly have been an external circular corner-bastion has also been found at the north-east angle, suggesting the possibility of a further phase of construction, perhaps much later in the site's history, into the fourth century.

Much of the strength of the fortress lay in the gates. The impressive remains of the Newport Arch (*1*), or North Gate, represent a central arch through which ran the main north–south road, with a pedestrian walkway alongside. The missing elements are the corresponding western pedestrian arch, and the two massive flanking towers shaped as elongated 'D's, the base of the western one still visible. The central part of the gate was over 30ft (9m) wide, and 24ft (7.5m) deep. The East Gate, as rebuilt in the third century, was even more massive. Two wide roadways, without pedestrian arches, were flanked by towers 26ft (8m) square with additional rounded fronts to them. It was fronted by a ditch, 80ft (25m) across. The lowest stages of the north gate-tower may be seen at the bottom of East Bight in front of the Lincoln hotel. The West Gate was a smaller construction, with a single arch over a roadway, found buried in the castle earthworks in 1836. The South Gate, located at the top of the precipitous Steep Hill, appears likely to have had just two pedestrian walkways, flanked by similar, but smaller, towers to the other gates (***Fig. 2***).

The extension of the *colonia*, down the hill to the river, was also provided with stone defences. On the west, an external rectangular tower has been found in The

Park, and may represent a fortified gate. There was probably a corresponding gate on the east where Monks Road exits the city, and the South Gate would have stood very close to where the Stonebow now stands. Several remnants of the stone wall still remain in Temple Gardens, Lindum Road, Beaumont Fee and The Park. A substantial stretch of wall and a postern gate (**2**), built well into the fourth century, may be seen off Orchard Street under the entrance to City Hall. It would appear that parts of this wall were strengthened at some later date by having a mass of rubble and mortar added to the inside of the rampart. The walls of the *colonia*, a circuit of over a mile (1.6km), were rebuilt in the fourth century, possibly to underline the town's status as a provincial capital.

ROMAN FORTS AND FORTIFIED SETTLEMENTS

Two significant Roman forts lie just outside the county's boundaries. The fort at Newton-on-Trent (Nottinghamshire) was in use for only a short time during the first-century AD campaign to subdue the region. At about the same time, a fort at Great Casterton (Rutland) was built to guard Ermine Street and the crossing of the river Gwash. Unlike Newton, this fort grew into a town, given permission to have town defences, modest ones at first, but strengthened in the fourth century, with thicker walls, external bastions for mounting artillery, and a very wide outer ditch.

In Lincolnshire itself, there are three defended Roman towns. Ancaster stands on Ermine Street, and was a settlement from Iron Age times. A Roman fort preceded the establishment of a town that was walled towards the end of the second century. Like Casterton, the town was an irregular polygon astride the road. A wide ditch may have succeeded an earlier weaker one, and external bastions were added to at least one of the angles of the wall in the fourth century. On the south, the defences are still visible as earthworks. Other sites straddling Ermine Street may have had defences, but none has been traced. Whilst connected to each other by the prehistoric trackway known, for this part of its length, as Caistor High Street, neither Horncastle nor Caistor, the other two defended towns in the county, appears to have close connections with the region's major Roman roads.

Caistor is another irregular polygon of 7-8 acres (2.5 hectares) surrounded by walls, small pieces of which are visible in several places. It was furnished with external semi-circular bastions, possibly at a date after the wall's initial construction. One of the southern bastions (Coopers) was solid and may have been added in order to accommodate artillery. Fragments of others near the Grammar School and near Bogs Lane may indicate the presence of two more such bastions. The North Bastion could have been part of a gateway, and walling in a cellar on Bank Lane may represent part of one of the East Gate's gate-towers. The footings of the wall were recorded by Rahtz in 1959 as being around 11ft (3.3m) wide. There is a wholly different situation with two distinct settlement areas at Horncastle. The larger area was un-walled, but the other, of only 5 acres (2 hectares), sandwiched between the rivers Bain and Waring, was a trapezoidal enclosure of the late third century or later, walled in stone. This wall was 13ft (4m) thick, sitting on a foundation raft 18–22ft (5.5–6.5m) wide, with an internal rampart heaped up against it. At least three of the angles had external bastions, generally shown by bonding, to have been contemporary with the wall. No traces of gates, or even their undisputed locations, have been found. Logically, a North Gate would have allowed the High Street trackway to exit the town, and a South Gate would have facilitated communication with the rest of the settlement outside the walls. The alignments of both the eastern and western walls seem to point to the existence of postern gates dog-legging through the walls. This design was intended to enable defenders on the wall-walk to overlook the gateway without having to construct projecting towers, whilst also making the gate less vulnerable to a frontal rush (**Fig. 2**).

The defence of the coasts against raiders from northern Europe in the fourth century was effected by a fleet, supported by a chain of shore forts on both sides of the English Channel, and extending around the North Sea coast as far as Brancaster (Norfolk). Other forts such as Brough-on-Humber, serving a similar function, have been located further north, but no certain examples have been identified in Lincolnshire, although Poor Farm at the top of the road through Horncastle and Caistor to the Humber has been suggested as a site where German mercenaries were stationed to guard the ferry to Brough. Additionally, Whitwell has suggested three possible sites for such forts. The first is a possible end-point for the track, the Salters Way, used in Roman times, which crosses the southern part of the county from the Fosse Way at Sixhills running east as far as Donington. It could thus have connected Leicester, the cantonal capital, with a fort near Bicker Haven. Similarly, Whitwell argues, either or both of the roads that run east from Lincoln, could have led to a fort on the coast.

There is a strong tradition that there was an ancient fort at Skegness, whose supposed site now lies under the sea a mile off shore. This would also have provided a convenient terminus for a postulated ferry across the Wash from Brancaster, at the top of the Peddars Way. The north-eastern road from Lincoln would have crossed the Wolds to hit the coast around Grainthorpe Haven. A further possibility is added by Field and Hurst, who point out that Horncastle was much closer to the coast in late Roman times than it is now. They also show that beyond the similarities in shape with several shore forts, the specific design of Horncastle's East and West gates is shared with both Burgh Castle, the Roman shore fort in Norfolk, and by Brough, the fort on the Humber, and that this similarity may be more than coincidental. Horncastle could have formed part of a wider coast defence system, protecting the Lincoln hinterland. Added to this notion is the suggestion that Bourne, Billingborough, South Kyme or Burgh-le-Marsh, all coastal settlements at the time, might have filled the gaps in the defence system so visible in adjacent East Yorkshire and Norfolk. A possible candidate for filling the gap between Caistor and Horncastle is Louth. Owen argues that the area of Northgate could well be based on the outline of a fort, with a side of 650ft (200m) located on the old Louth Street trackway.

ANGLO-SAXON AND DANISH FORTIFICATIONS

After the departure of the Romans it is likely that the upper city in Lincoln continued in occupation, since the Roman defences survived into the early medieval period and beyond. Evidence exists for the importance of the settlement into the seventh century when a Christian church was built, and the local Anglo-Saxon kingdom of Lindsey ultimately derived its name from Lindum. Other tribal groups had their own centres, an example being Billingborough – the fort or burh of the Billingas. Although the county was the scene of several significant battles, these appear to have been the exception rather than a commonplace.

In 616, Aethelfrith, King of Berenicia, was defeated in battle by Raedwald, King of the East Angles, who was supporting the claim of Edmund, the exiled heir to Deira. This battle took place by the river Idle, some 20 miles (32km) along the Roman road from Lincoln to Doncaster, on the present border with Nottinghamshire. In 679, Lindsey was returned to the kingdom of Mercia, and enjoyed a long period of peace that lasted until the Viking raids of the second quarter of the ninth century. Few fortifications, apart from the walls of Lincoln that survived, presumably in a state of continuous deterioration, may be traced from this period. The settlement at Flixborough, where twelve or more buildings within a strong ditch has been excavated, suggests a combination of lordly and monastic centres in the Middle Saxon period. Other survivals include a site with ditches, banks and palisades to the east of the Saxon church of St Peters at Barton-upon-Humber, protecting a residential site, and a palisade with ditch combination, apparently dating from the reign of Alfred, under a later pottery kiln at the western end of the Stamford Castle site.

The origins of the Barton-upon-Humber site are unclear. It could be an Iron Age fort; it could be an early-Christian monastery site; it could be a Danish laager for over-wintering the army; or it could be a lordship site similar to Goltho/Bullington. There are arguments for and against them all, but the fact that the church, built between AD 960–1000 is superimposed over one edge, and the later manor house is contained within the enclosure, may lend weight to that fourth interpretation. Only additional excavation can supply an answer. There is an oval enclosure measuring roughly 200 x 150 yards, about 5 acres (2 hectares) in area. There was a ditch, 16ft (4.8m) across at its top, and 8ft (2.4m) deep. An interior bank was topped by a timber palisade. This would appear to be much bigger than any of the other local Iron Age forts, and the bank and ditch would seem much stronger than those normally found in a monastic context. The case for a Danish laager is plausible as it is known that such structures would have been raised somewhere along the Trent, perhaps at Torksey and/or Gainsborough. The Viking raiders would have benefited from such a semi-permanent base at Barton, particularly in an area with rich pickings.

Warlike times, however, were soon to return. A raid on Lindsey was recorded in 841, but this was probably only one of many. A Viking fleet sailed up the Humber and into the Trent in 872, the army wintering at Torksey into 873. From 877, Viking settlement became permanent, with the five boroughs of the Danelaw including

Lincoln and Stamford in Lincolnshire. This was reversed by Edward the Elder who, in 918, built a burh on the south side of the Welland at Stamford, as a base for threatening the Viking one on the north. Despite Edward's successes, within twenty years the five boroughs were once more granted to the Danes under Olaf, by Athelstan's brother Edmund. After Edmund's death, his brother Eadred continued the struggle, although many of these ups and downs were achieved peacefully by negotiation, or simply by recognising that one party's position was, if only temporarily, unassailable. Eadred may have defended his manoeuvres with a fort on the Trent at Newark. Both Lincoln and Stamford functioned as mints during these years. In 993 a Viking push up the Humber led to a reversal when the English in Lindsey were defeated.

A period of peace came at the price of buying Danish protection out of Lindsey's healthy revenues. In 1013, Swein Forkbeard invaded, landing his army at Gainsborough. His base for this expedition has traditionally been held to be the earthwork fort at Thonock near Gainsborough, apparently now confirmed by excavation. It consists of a central mound surrounded by a double bank and ditch, the whole covering 11 acres (4.5 hectares). Swein and his son Cnut took over Lindsey, rather too easily for Aethelred who returned to exact retribution on those who had placed survival and profit before loyalty to their king. A year later Cnut was back, demanding the loyalty of all those holding power locally, creating earldoms that ultimately resulted in a unified England under a single king.

Much of the evidence for fortified places is tied to place-names. A number of sites in Lindsey have been suggested as forts that may have been connected with Danish settlement, or with defence against Viking raids. These include Burgh on Bain, Burgh-le-Marsh, Ludborough, and Stallingbrough. Gainsborough may have defended a crossing of the Trent, and Coningsby may be the king's fort (*cyninges burh*), but all this is speculative and awaits corroboration. The word 'burh' usually tends to be associated with urban settlements as seen in Alfred's Wessex, but its origin lay in the private, often fortified residence of a thegn. So some of Lincolnshire's putative fortifications in this period may have been private residences as at Goltho/Bullington, whilst others may have been communal defences, and others nothing at all.

In the ninth and early tenth centuries, Lincoln thrived under Danish rule. The upper town accommodated the ruling aristocracy and the church, whilst artisans' workshops and other commercial enterprises flourished in the lower town and south of Brayford Pool. Stamford was about a third of the size of Lincoln, with the Danish burh occupying a roughly rectangular area north of the river and east of the present Market Place. We have already noted the defensive position on the west of the market later to be occupied by the castle, and this may represent either an earlier Danish fort, or a Saxon enclosure containing a hall and a church. South of the river, Edward the Elder's burh most probably occupied a rectangular site on the top of the hill that overlooks the river, possibly giving Burghley House its name. It would have been very different from the traditional model of Alfred's Wessex burhs that protected the populace and their livelihoods. This was a much smaller enclosure designed to provide a base for a force embarking on a military operation.

Fortification in Lincolnshire prior to 1066   23

3 BARTON-upon-HUMBER: the tower of St Peter's church, built AD 960–1000 and possibly representing a defensive feature in a fortified lordship residential site

If the purpose and scale were different, the basic defensive elements were similar. All these fortifications would have been surrounded by earthen banks, ditches, and timber palisades. Gates would have been defended by timber wall-walks carried over the gate passages, perhaps forming a tower. Gates themselves would have been strengthened by iron studs, and may have been covered in hides that could have been dowsed in water, if under attack, in order to reduce the risk of fire. Given the need to delay the attackers' approach to the walls for as long as possible in order to maximise the efforts of defending archers, it is likely that multiple ditches were employed where possible to enlarge the killing ground. Torksey constituted a third civil settlement strategically located to command the Foss Dyke linking the Witham with the Trent, forming one of Lincoln's main trade outlets, and providing easy access for raiding fleets. The army which wintered there in 872–3 would probably have constructed a simple bank and ditch around its encampment. A permanent settlement then developed, with churches, houses and a mint, but toward the end of the Anglo-Saxon period, the dyke silted up, not to be reopened until 1121.

One site of national importance stands out from this period as being almost unique, and that is Bullington, or Goltho as it is more generally known. Its importance stems from its status as a fortified thegn's house, probably of the tenth century, rather than earlier in the ninth, as was initially thought. Very few sites in England – Eynsford (Kent) and Sulgrave (Northamptonshire), for example, and Goltho itself – provide archaeological evidence of Anglo-Saxon fortified thegns' houses. Goltho consisted of an enclosure bounded by a bank and ditch, containing timber halls, weaving sheds, detached kitchen and bower, later having a Norman motte and bailey castle built over the top of it. It is likely that the bank and ditch were added to protect pre-existing buildings. Beresford has suggested that the rampart was 18–20ft (5.5–5.6m) wide, with a defensive ditch deeper than one for drainage would have been. A number of Anglo-Saxon references suggest that landowners of sufficient means were entitled, if not actually required, to announce their status by building themselves defensive dwellings, and Goltho may represent such a *burh-geat*, named for the gate-tower.

It has also been suggested that the dislocation of castle studies from mainstream architectural commentary over the last 100 years has resulted in possible connections being lost. A case in point would be the possible significance of the Anglo-Saxon stone tower of St Peter's church at Barton-on-Humber (*3*) as the defensive element of a manorial enclosure with bank and ditch containing both hall and church. Whilst the tower dates from 970–1030, it may have replaced an earlier belfry, perhaps of timber. It may simply have been a means by which the Abbey of Peterborough, its mother-church, sought to underline its dominance on the local landscape after its rebirth under Aethelwold in 971.

The west tower of All Saints church, Hough-on-the-Hill, similar in age and style to Barton, but with a semi-circular stair projection, is surrounded by the defensive ditch of the earthwork castle. Although one thinks of Viking raids as providing ample incentive to fortify one's dwelling, there were also more localised conflicts as the laws involving *wergild* and *burh-bryce* demonstrate. This last involved breaking through the defensive hedge or fence surrounding a private residence, and was looked on with official disapproval.

two

The Early Medieval Period (*c.*1000–1300)

This chapter will examine the evidence for a range of buildings that shared defensive characteristics. Some were out-and-out fortresses, and some were domestic structures with an eye to security. It will look at a number of issues connected with castles and castle-building, with the various conflicts which provided a backdrop to early medieval life, and with the life-span of those buildings which fell under a very broad definition of fortifications.

EARLY CASTLES

It has long been believed that the castle was a phenomenon imported into Britain by the Normans under William the Conqueror. The precedents that were used to prove this rule were the small group of earthwork castles constructed, mainly in the Welsh Marches, by Norman favourites of Edward the Confessor, prior to the Conquest. The apparent novelty of the castle as a tool of military subjugation was underlined by the network of fortresses put up by William at strategic points throughout his new kingdom to ensure that thoughts of resistance were discouraged. However, this simplistic picture is now considered misleading. We have already seen places such as Stamford, Barton-upon-Humber and Goltho where Anglo-Saxon thegns had built fortified residences for themselves independent of any communal or public defence system, these examples from Lincolnshire being representative of what was happening across the country. Norman castles conformed to two major designs – the motte, and the ringwork – both of which might have one or more baileys, and it could be argued that the ringwork was basically a standardised version of earlier Anglo-Saxon or Frankish fortifications, but that the motte was a wholly Norman importation. The majority of William's first batch of royal castles tended to be mottes with baileys, as can be seen both at Lincoln and at Stamford. Other castles in the county also conformed to these two models as, for example,

4 CASTLE BYTHAM: a view of the still imposing earthworks of this early twelfth-century ringwork and bailey

at Castle Carlton, Wrangle, Owston, and Swineshead (mottes and baileys); and at Castle Bytham (*4*), Gainsborough, Kingerby and Welbourn (ringworks and baileys). Barrow-upon-Humber started out as a ringwork, possibly in the early 1070s, but was subsequently altered when a motte was raised adjacent to the ringwork, whose earthworks formed one of several baileys.

It must be remembered that castles served a multiplicity of functions. Whilst their military usefulness tends to predominate in the popular imagination, their occupation as residences, and their operation as the administrative centres of estates must be recognised. Alongside these three functions was the often symbolic use of military features in order to make a statement about power and dominance over neighbours and surroundings. Many castles could survive centuries of use without a sword being raised in anger, those forty or so castles built in Lincolnshire during the Middle Ages suffering only a total of sixteen attacks between them, and that total included actions during the Civil War of the seventeenth century as well. However, they fulfilled all their other, more peaceful, everyday functions continuously. Recent research has uncovered a number of examples of towers, sometimes dating from Anglo-Saxon times as at Barton-upon-Humber, which were designed with doorways in their upper storeys and which could only have been for display, either of relics in an ecclesiastical context, or of a ruler in a secular one, much as the balcony of Buckingham Palace functions today. It would appear that the west gate of Lincoln Castle (*5*) may have been adapted some time in the eleventh century, with an open-backed upper floor, and a doorway at that level accessing an external platform.

The Early Medieval Period (c.1000–1300)   27

5 LINCOLN CASTLE: the West Gate showing the blocked upper-level doorway that may have afforded access to an external ceremonial balcony

This suggests a continuance of the idea of the Anglo-Saxon *burh-geat* we have seen previously, which was rooted in the notion of local leaders dispensing justice within an established legal system. The castle provided a fitting setting for such activities, combining the practical and the symbolic, the domestic and the bureaucratic.

The motte and bailey castle consisted of an earth mound, sometimes tall and conical, elsewhere lower, wider and flatter. The raising of the mound, either from scratch, or by scarping an existing hillock, usually created a surrounding ditch, sometimes water-filled. The flat platform on the motte-top often supported a square timber tower of two or three storeys that served as a lookout, or in dire emergencies, a last resort of refuge. Where there was room, the lip of the motte-top would be surrounded by a palisade, often substantial enough to carry a wall-walk and fighting-platform. If the earth was particularly unstable, the tower might be mounted on stout posts that would descend right down through the motte to rest on firmer ground. A timber bridge often connected the motte with a larger enclosure, banked and ditched, and known as the bailey, which contained living accommodation – a communal hall and a private chamber, as well as barns, stables, kitchens, ovens, kilns and storehouses, and possibly a chapel. The bailey was surrounded by palisades, and often entered across a bridge and through a gate-tower. A number of factors such as the availability of construction materials, landscape or fashion determined whether a motte or the alternative ringwork was chosen. The ringwork was a bowl-shaped mound, otherwise serving the same purpose as the motte, and having the same relationship to its bailey(s). Alcock and King have calculated that the ratio of mottes to ringworks in Lincolnshire is 7:3, which can be compared to their national ratio of 7.5:2. It is possible that in the flatter areas of Lincolnshire it was less necessary to build high, since any slight elevation afforded panoramic visibility. A preponderance of low, flat mottes and ring-works of a similar height is therefore to be expected.

THE ANARCHY 1135–54

Lincolnshire had, on the whole, been spared the depredations of the Conquest such as the Harrying of the North, and acted only as a springboard for the campaign in the Fens, but the county was to be the scene of considerable action during the reign of Stephen. The new King had inherited his uncle's officers of state – the bishops Nigel of Ely, Alexander of Lincoln and their uncle Roger of Salisbury – so he engineered an affray involving some of their retainers at the royal court at Oxford in 1139. He was able to dismiss the bishops, confiscating their castles as a pledge of their good behaviour. Despite being called to account for trying this case in a secular court, Stephen talked his way out of immediate trouble, but made many potential enemies in the process. A month later, his cousin Matilda invaded England to claim her inheritance.

Amongst Stephen's new crop of enemies was Ranulf of Chester, some of whose father's estates Stephen had just bestowed on Prince Henry of Scotland. Ranulf determined to seize Prince Henry on his journey back to Scotland. Hearing of the plot, Stephen provided Henry with a strong bodyguard of royal troops, but Ranulf and his half-brother William de Roumare were determined to make a gesture by taking the royal castle of Lincoln (**Fig. 3**). This they achieved, we are told by the chronicler Ordericus Vitalis, by a stratagem. They sent their wives into the castle on a social call, and coming in to collect the ladies some time later, Ranulf and three of his knights, produced weapons, fought off the garrison and admitted de Roumare with more troops, thus seizing the castle. This put Stephen in a quandary, as he was reluctant to take decisive action against the pair, which might force them into Matilda's camp. He therefore feigned friendship and reconciliation, and it was possibly on this occasion that he made de Roumare Earl of Lincoln. On his return to London, word reached Stephen, from the citizens of Lincoln, that he might have an opportunity to catch the half-brothers unawares, an irresistible chance for Stephen to get even with them. He immediately marched his troops to Lincoln, but narrowly missed Ranulf who fled to Chester to raise troops for Matilda in January 1141. The citizens admitted Stephen to the town and he began a siege of the castle, but on 2 February, Ranulf re-appeared at the head of a large army. Stephen was forced to join the battle with little chance of success. He was captured and carried off to imprisonment in Bristol, leaving Ranulf and de Roumare masters of Lincoln once more. Their troops sacked the city as punishment for the aid given to Stephen by the citizens. Bishop Alexander, in the meantime, had already joined Matilda at Winchester, leaving garrisons in his castles of Newark-on-Trent and Sleaford.

Stephen's fortunes were restored in 1142, but other pressing matters kept him from re-taking Lincoln for some time. Not until 1144 could he spare time for an abortive siege, and it was actually the occasion of Ranulf changing sides which was to restore the castle to the king the next year.

Within a year Stephen had contrived another quarrel with Ranulf, depriving him of his lands. Stephen held his Christmas court at Lincoln castle in 1146, and it was about that time that Ranulf attempted to use the former possession of the castle by his mother, the Countess Lucy, to justify his own claim. Ranulf was now back in opposition to Stephen who, in 1149, created Gilbert de Gant Earl of Lincoln, thus dispossessing de Roumare. In order to distract Stephen from his successful southern campaigns, Ranulf once more attacked Lincoln.

By 1150, Matilda's son, the future Henry II, was generally accepted as Stephen's heir. Ranulf had strengthened his position by marrying the daughter of Robert of Gloucester and collaborated with Robert of Leicester in establishing a de-militarized zone in the east midlands, consisting of an area within a roughly 25-mile (40km) radius of Leicester, and operating from 1148–53, with Belvoir Castle (Leicestershire) at its north-eastern corner. Neutral castellans were appointed to key castles – Jordan de Buissi at Lincoln, for instance, and de Roumare, by securing the favour of the Duke Henry, was restored to the earldom of Lincoln. In 1154, Stephen died to be succeeded by Henry. At last the Anarchy was over. The version of the Anglo-Saxon Chronicle written by the monks of Peterborough Abbey described the *'nineteen long winters of Stephen's reign, when Christ and his angels slept'*. Another

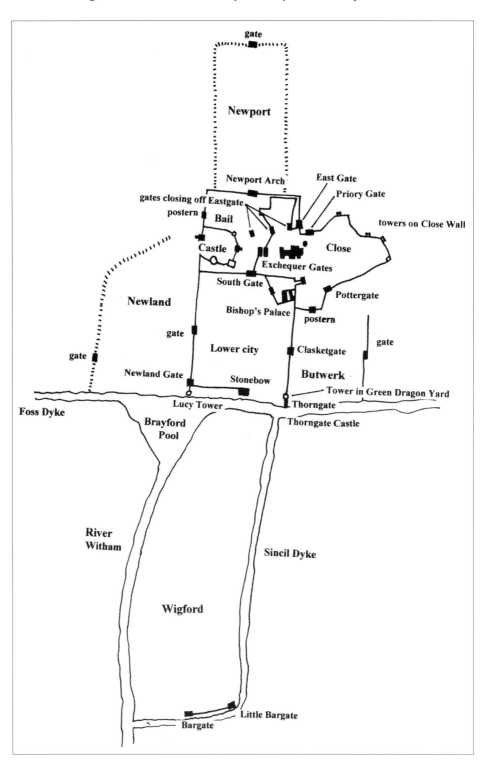

Fig. 3 Map of the medieval defences of Lincoln

contemporary chronicler, Henry of Huntingdon, a canon of Lincoln Cathedral, emphasised Stephen's untrustworthiness. This may have reflected the writer's loyalty to his Bishop Alexander, but he had little good to say of Matilda either. A combination of weak government, lordly ambition, disputed succession, and total contempt for the common people on the part of lords both spiritual and temporal, had combined to create twenty years of mayhem, in which any petty noble could declare war on his neighbours with little fear of retribution.

THE CIRCUMSTANCES OF CASTLE-CONSTRUCTION

Earthwork castles were erected from the Conquest through to the early thirteenth century as centres of royal authority, and by local landowners, both great and small. It has long been accepted that some form of royal licensing was in operation, with much being made of the appearance of illegal or adulterine castles during the time of the Anarchy of Stephen's reign, and of their subsequent demolition once order returned under Henry II. However, whilst the principle of uncontrolled fortress building during this time may hold, the assumption of a tight legal framework is now felt to be a false one, given the few corroborative documented instances. There were, however, times when a particularly sensitive situation demanded some sort of legal recognition, either pseudo or bona fide. When, in 1146, Ranulf, Earl of Chester sought to legitimise his foothold in the (royal) castle of Lincoln, he composed a charter detailing his right to hold a tower there, but hoped to use this occupation as leverage for other ends. He got his permission but did not enjoy it for long. In 1142 the king had specifically granted retrospective permission for William de Roumare, recently created Earl of Lincoln, to hold a castle in Gainsborough, but this was at a time when Stephen had little room for manoeuvre, and may have been attempting damage limitation. Bishop Alexander of Lincoln, in the early 1130s, had previously been allowed to dam the Trent and divert the Great North Road whilst constructing his new castle of Newark, the main condition being that none of these works might impinge on the interests of the royal castles of Nottingham or Lincoln. Such attempts at control might reflect the need to safeguard royal interests in a particular region at a particular moment in time.

Castles were built to provide residential accommodation and as estate offices, to give dignity to members of the land-owning classes, and to control significant points such as bridges, road junctions and markets. Gainsborough, Owston Ferry and Barrow-upon-Humber were located to control crossings of major waterways. Castles also provided refuges in turbulent times, and at such times of conflict, existing castles would have their defences refurbished, and new strongholds – what we would probably now call field-works – would be built. Given the speedy structural deterioration of earth and timber constructions, then only a short life could be expected for many of these forts. One particular class of fort falling into the field-work category is the siege castle, either earthworks or adapted buildings, providing temporary protection for troops besieging a more permanent castle. There were several occasions on which such forts were built during operations against Lincoln Castle. In 1140–1, a St Mary's church was fortified during fighting involving Ranulf and his half-brother de Roumare against Stephen's followers in Lincoln. This church may have been St Mary Crackpole, St Mary le Wigford or even part of the cathedral, itself dedicated to St Mary. In 1144, a square earthwork was raised outside the castle's West Gate, and during its construction, a sally by the defenders reportedly killed eighty workmen. This earthwork, its site now in the grounds of The Lawn, shows up on Victorian maps of the city but has never been properly located. No doubt some of the other short-lived earthwork castles in the county such as Corby Glen, Dalby, Dewy Hill, or Stainby, as well as the re-fortified Roman defences of Caistor and Horncastle may all fall into the category of temporary fortifications.

There was also a fortification in Lincoln itself, known as Thorngate, probably down by the river, and probably short-lived. It was pledged to Stephen before 1141 but then sold on to Bishop Alexander. The motte at Fleet appears to pre-date its neighbouring village by some years, so may have had only a brief independent existence arising from short-term tactical requirements. At Kingerby, the ringwork and bailey appear to have been superimposed on an earlier settlement, displacing a road in the process. Its destruction was ordered in 1218, and the site was subsequently occupied by a stone manor surrounded by a moat. Folkingham was probably established in earthwork form as the centre of Gilbert de Gant's estates, but remained undeveloped until the fourteenth century.

Hough-on-the-Hill and Owston Ferry are intimately connected to village churches; that at Hough, with its imposing Saxon tower, maybe having secular significance. At both these sites, the church stands within the castle bailey. Other relationships between church and castle were possible. At Redbourne, the church lay outside the castle's outer enclosure, and at Bourne, the juxtapositions of castle and abbey within a common enclosure necessitated a change to the line of the Roman road. The demise of the castle at Newhouse was underlined when its site was specifically given by Peter of Goxhill for the foundation, in around 1143, of a Praemonstratensian priory. At some sites, more than just the castle was short-lived. At Castle Carlton, it would seem that a borough enjoying commercial advantages had been established by the middle of the twelfth century, but subsequently failed to thrive.

Given the significance of the castle as an administrative centre, this function usually outweighing the military one in normal times, it is interesting to note the relative densities of castles. Each of Lincolnshire's thirty-seven castles was located in a hinterland averaging 70 square miles (17,500 hectares). Nottinghamshire's twelve castles were each located in very similarly sized catchment areas. This represented a great contrast to counties with vulnerable coastlines such as Kent, with one castle to every 30 square miles (7,500 hectares), or to those shires with even more volatile land frontiers, like Northumberland and Herefordshire, where there was a castle for every 8–9 square miles (2000–2250 hectares).

EARTHWORK CASTLES

Although, as we are about to find out, many earthwork castles were rebuilt in stone, and others became quite sophisticated structures whilst still constructed of timber, some never progressed beyond their first, more basic construction. Dewy Hill, a small motte and bailey on a hill above the later castle of Old Bolingbroke, associated with William de Roumare, was probably in use for only a short while after its construction around the early 1140s. Swineshead, the seat of the de Gresleys, first mentioned in 1186, was a motte with a strong counter-scarp bank, in the fenlands west of Boston. Owston Ferry, also in low-lying land but built to command the River Trent, had a motte with traces of a bailey. Its destruction was ordered in 1176, but four years later a fine was levied as the job was deemed not to have been done properly. North of the town of Gainsborough is the ring-work and bailey built by the Earl of Lincoln sometime just before 1142. It now seems likely that this twelfth-century fortress was a re-fortification of a Danish work, raised around 1012 as a base for King Swein's invading army. Its simple central core, a central raised platform within double banks and ditches, representing this earlier work, may have been refurbished as the ring-work to which were added two baileys by de Roumare in the years after 1140.

Goltho is another good example of an earlier earth and timber work which went through many changes over the years (***Fig. 4***). Here, as we have previously seen, an Anglo-Saxon thegn's house was fortified with a palisade on a bank, within a ditch, some time in the tenth century. This layout was modified during the second half of the eleventh century, or early in the twelfth, to become a more conventional ring-work with bank and ditch covering a wider area in order to accommodate larger residential buildings. Around 1150, a motte was raised in the southeast corner of the enlarged enclosure with, on its summit, a timber tower. This tower was constructed on a cellar, built of stone and tile, embedded within the motte to provide a firm foundation. It has been suggested that, backed by clay, this cellar might have functioned as a water-cistern collecting run-off from the tower itself. The tower, around 20 feet (6m) square at its base, was probably constructed of four high timber posts, cross-braced for strength, and in-filled with cob or clay and wattle. There would have been two or three floors reached by interior ladders, and an open upper platform under a shingled pyramid roof. Parallels have been drawn with detached timber church belfries, and it can be noted that the word 'belfry' originated as a tower serving a military function. The now reduced bailey continued to accommodate an aisled timber hall.

Finally, between 1150 and 1235, the motte and bailey banks were lowered and the earth redistributed to produce a lower, flatter motte, 150ft (45m) long by 130ft (39m) wide, in whose centre stood a much larger aisled hall which reflected an increase in the prosperity of the manor, whose centre then moved to Goltho Manor, a moated site nearby. Another motte, at Hanby Hall, Welton-le-Marsh is almost identical in size and shape to Goltho's final appearance. At Burton Pedwardine there is a moated enclosure which apparently pre-dates the motte which has been superimposed, and

34 Defending Lincolnshire: A Military History from Conquest to Cold War

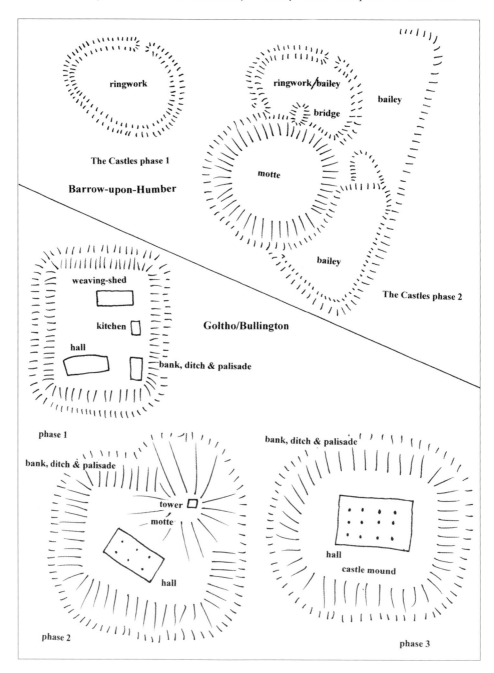

Fig. 4 Plans to show the evolution of two earthwork castles

now forms the platform on which has been built the much later manor-house, itself superceding a possible fourteenth-century re-modelling of the site. Some earthworks, traditionally held to be castles, may have been nothing of the sort. The scarps behind the church at Aslackby are no longer felt to be of any military significance, and the assumed motte at Legsby was more probably a windmill mount.

Some quite important castles never progressed beyond their initial earth and timber construction. Castle Carlton, along with Tothill and Withern, may have been built by Earl Ranulf during the Anarchy, as a link in the chain of castles he intended to build across his entire land-holdings. By 1205 it belonged to Hugh Bardolph, Richard I's justiciar, but its motte and two baileys may never have been walled in stone. Likewise at Wrangle, later to be the site of a monastic grange, or the Gresley's castle at Swineshead, where only pottery, stained glass and roof-tiles have been found, but no masonry. Stone could, of course, have been robbed, as it clearly was from other sites known to have been stone-built, but it seems likely that some medieval castles remained wholly timber structures.

Surviving post-holes at Goltho and elsewhere, showing the scale and grandeur of aisled halls, for instance, underline the indications that lack of masonry in no way detracted from the sophistication of some of these buildings. The series of three timber halls at Goltho, and the later one at Bolingbroke can all stand comparison with, say, those built in stone at Stamford, Goltho's final version, with its two aisles, measuring 64 x 40ft (19.5 x 12.3m) as against Stamford at 50 x 40ft (15 x 12.6m). The hall was considered the heart of the house and in the 1240s we find Bishop Grosseteste of Lincoln advising the Countess of Lincoln to allow no members of her household to eat other than in the hall, in order both to contain waste and to maintain the honour of the lord and lady. It must also be noted that medieval houses were expected to provide pleasant environments for their inhabitants, and therefore gardens and moats – water features as well as fishponds – afforded an aesthetic dimension to medieval lordly lifestyle. The bishop's palace at Stow was especially noted for its surrounding woods and ponds, replete with wildfowl, including swans. This palace, first mentioned in 1170, was surrounded by a 10ft-deep (3m-deep) moat with an inner bank of similar height. Whilst the moat may not have had the primary purpose of defence, it would most certainly have deterred the casual transgressor. A causeway led from the northern entrance, between two dams that kept the ponds filled up, to the main access lane.

STONE CASTLES

Castles of importance, initially constructed of earth and timber, were usually rebuilt in stone quite early on in their lives. Lincoln's early building history is still a subject of great debate. A castle was built in 1068 for the Conqueror, located in The Bail, the Roman upper city and utilising some of the surviving Roman stone defences. This development necessitated the demolition of 166 houses, a very large number, and a reorganisation of the former street plan, and it has been argued that this

6 LINCOLN CASTLE: the twelfth-century shell keep known as the Lucy Tower on what is thought to be the earlier of the two mottes

number of houses (or potentially taxable house-plots) must represent the entire Bail area. A motte was raised in the southwest corner on the lip of the hill on the south side. This was later named for the Countess Lucy who died in 1136. Ultimately there would be two mottes, a most unusual arrangement, and this Lucy Tower is generally thought to be the earlier, originally crowned by a timber palisade enclosing a timber tower.

Continuing the argument for this larger castle, it has been suggested that the west front of the new cathedral, begun by Bishop Remigius soon after 1072, modelled on St Etienne at Caen, and consecrated in 1092, incorporated dominant defensive features, giving it a keep-like aspect. Bishop Gundulf, building at Rochester (Kent) from 1077, had added a freestanding four-storey, apparently defensive tower alongside his cathedral, so other examples are known. Lincoln's second motte, now known as the Observatory Tower from the turret added in the nineteenth century by a prison governor of astronomical bent, is of unusual design in that it contains a stone-built hollow core, apparently of mid-twelfth century date, embedded in the motte as at Ascot Doilly (Oxfordshire) and other examples. This may have been a cellar, forming a solid foundation for another timber tower.

Excavations published in 1975 appear to give credence to the notion that Ranulf of Chester, Lucy's son, built this second motte to defend the approach to the castle from the lower city some time around 1146, when he was seeking to consolidate his weak claim to be the legitimate occupier. The earlier motte (**6**) received a new masonry-built polygonal shell wall later in the twelfth century, with twelve interior faces, fifteen to the outside, and originally of two storeys. Access is now by stone stairs rising from the filled-in ditch, and there would originally have been a timber stairway ascending the motte to the gateway. The Observatory Tower itself consists of an earlier rectangular tower, enlarged in the fourteenth century to a square with sides of 40ft (12m).

Mural chambers connected to the East Gate, and a subterranean passage led off in the other direction. One wall adjacent to the tower contains Roman tiles, re-used in Norman herringbone masonry. The original West Gate of 1068 had stone foundations that probably supported only a timber gateway. When the bailey walls were rebuilt in stone at some time in the twelfth century, a stone gatehouse was built with projecting walls forming a barbican, with an outer arch. At some later date, a stone chamber was added to the barbican's north wall, possibly providing an emplacement for a catapult of some sort. The East Gate (*7*) originated in a similar way, but a radical rebuilding *c*.1220 provided it with a taller inner tower with the twin turrets still to be seen in truncated form, and a stronger barbican whose side walls crossed the ditch to terminate in a pair of drum towers.

If we are to accept the idea that the entire Bail represented the first castle, then it would appear that no new masonry appeared before the mid twelfth century. The enormous earth banks, whenever they were raised, despite containing timber strengthening, recorded in 1836, would have needed time to consolidate before they could take the weight of stone curtain walls. A further suggestion is that the castle, as originally built soon after the Conquest, was triangular, with the Lucy Tower motte at the southern angle, the site of the future Cobb Hall at the northern, and the West Gate as the principal entrance near the western apex. The smaller eastern enclosure with a new motte and a ceremonially significant East Gate was a later addition, possibly for the use of the bishop. The odd arrangement of two mottes may thus be explained by the parallel occupancy of royal and ecclesiastical authorities.

The horse-shoe-shaped tower at the north-east angle of the curtain, known as Cobb Hall (*8*) was built late in the thirteenth century. It retains two of its original three storeys plus a basement, from which lead two sally ports onto the bank on the outside of the walls. There was a well near the Victorian bathhouse on the north curtain. This site is clearly an enigma, and only thorough and extensive excavation can go much further to clarify its development.

The castle of Stamford was another of the Conqueror's strategic foundations, guarding the road north. The site chosen was to the west of the market place and the Viking burh overlooking the River Welland. Several houses were destroyed to create a site for the castle which also overlays the site of an earlier defended house. The castle was built between 1068 and 1071 when the Abbot of Peterborough sought refuge within from Hereward and his Danish allies. A low motte stood on the highest ground whilst the bailey ran down towards the river. At some time, possibly before 1153 when the castle was held for Stephen against Henry of Anjou, the original timber defences may have been rebuilt in stone. Photographs taken during the keep's demolition in 1933 can be interpreted in two ways. Either the motte was revetted by a stone wall, thus producing a shell keep as at Farnham (Surrey),

38 Defending Lincolnshire: A Military History from Conquest to Cold War

7 LINCOLN CASTLE: the East Gate with the twin turrets, now truncated, which along with the barbican were features of its re-building in *c*.1220

8 LINCOLN CASTLE: the horse-shoe-shaped tower known as Cobb Hall, built towards the end of the thirteenth century; originally one storey higher, it had sally-ports out onto the top of the bank

9 STAMFORD CASTLE: the three blocked doorways once leading from the Great Hall into the kitchen, buttery and pantry, possibly re-set into a later building

or a round keep, about 60ft (18m) in diameter was built on top. The bailey was also walled some time in the twelfth century, and stretches of wall survive. A twelfth-century stone hall, repeatedly extended and re-modelled, is represented by only its three service doorways (*9*), possibly re-set, and now incorporated in a much later building. By 1340 the castle was ruinous and serving as a quarry for many of the town's later buildings.

Although thought to have come into the possession of the Wakes from 1166, through a marriage into the de Rulos family, the first specific reference to Bourne Castle is from 1179–81. Its low-lying position suggests that it started life as a motte and bailey fortress with extensive water defences, some of which are still visible as ponds and wet ditches. A number of accounts describe a tower with angle turrets standing on the motte, and excavations carried out in 1861 reported the discovery of the bases of a pair of gatehouse towers with walls 3ft (0.9m) thick and standing 16.5ft (5m) apart. An associated ditch, 44ft (13.5m) wide, was indicated by timbers thought to be part of a bridge. In the 1960s, a trench cut by the Electricity Board found a medieval wall and thirteenth-century pottery. A stone barn contains, in an end-wall, what appears to be a re-used medieval cross-slit (*10*). It would appear that by Leland's visit in the 1530s or 1540s, any stonework had disappeared, leaving only the earthworks and water defences.

A similar scenario can be found at Castle Bytham. Here the earthworks, consisting of a ring-work (but often described as a motte) and at least one bailey, were constructed, possibly around 1086, by modifying the natural contours of the land.

The first actual reference is from 1141 when it was in the possession of the Count of Aumale, who may have introduced masonry structures. However, one of his successors, William de Fortibus, unwisely rebelled against Henry III, and in 1221, after a siege of only two weeks during which the royal forces employed siege machines, the castle was taken, and miners were brought in to carry out demolition work. Its new owner, William de Colevill, re-planned the layout, apparently building two concentric curtains with corner towers. Only slight traces of masonry remain on site, having escaped the wholesale robbing which disposed of the rest.

Bishop Alexander of Lincoln re-modelled an earlier earthwork castle at Newark-on-Trent (Nottinghamshire) around 1133, building a stone gatehouse set in a stone curtain wall. He began Sleaford Castle sometime after 1123, possibly laying out a similar quadrangular moat with masonry defences. He was forced to surrender this castle to Stephen in 1139, but must have regained possession a few years later. It would appear that this castle was enlarged in the thirteenth century, with an outer bailey containing substantial barns. A manorial survey of 1324 describes the castle as a 'grangia', being at the heart of the Bishops' estates, surrounded by mills, and functioning as a fortified storehouse for grain surpluses. The low-lying site lent itself additionally to fishponds and orchards, basically an agricultural establishment underpinning the economic strength of the Lincoln diocese. Only earthworks and a single stone fragment survive on site, but other architectural features are visible incorporated into the Manor House on Northgate.

Traces of stone can also be found at Heydour, where a ring-work, probably of the twelfth century, may have been walled in stone. Two breaks in the rampart, which may have been gateways, appear to be cobbled, but this may represent later use of the site for agriculture. Another ring-work at Welbourn is referred to in a charter of 1158 as having stone defences. The Moulton family's castle is an enigma. An oval earthwork enclosure is all that remains of the castle mentioned in 1217. However, there is a local tradition that the two stone towers planted, as ornaments, in front of the north porch of All Saints church, Holbeach some time in the middle of the sixteenth century, were brought from Moulton Castle, some 5 miles (8km) away. Moated sites will be dealt with in the next chapter, but one deserves a mention here. The Bussy family seat at Hougham consisted of stone domestic buildings within a moat. Architectural fragments, dating from the thirteenth century and earlier, surviving in the present house, were dredged from the moat. Traces of later windows in the perpendicular style may represent the chapel licensed in 1405.

From the later twelfth century onwards, some castles began their life in stone, with no record of earlier earthwork defences, whilst others were to appear as moated sites, with or without stone buildings or defences. Only the site of the castle of Ivo Tailbois in Spalding is known, whose square stone keep is shown on an eighteenth-century map, so it cannot be determined whether this was preceded by earthworks alone. The end of the twelfth century saw two significant buildings of mainly domestic aspect, but nonetheless provided with defensive elements. The first of these is Boothby Pagnell manor (**11**), built in 1200, which consisted of a chamber-block that survives, and a hall, kitchens, stables, barns, etc., which have

10 BOURNE CASTLE: an apparently medieval arrow-loop, set into a later barn on the castle site

11 BOOTHBY PAGNELL: this semi-fortified manor house of AD 1200 has a first-floor entrance into a chamber set over a fireproof undercroft

disappeared. The stone vaults, first-floor entrance and moat all provide defence against fire or intruders. There may have been a bridge across the moat leading to an entrance through a gatehouse. The other is the Bishop's Palace at Lincoln. Although permission was granted by Stephen to annexe a site to the south of the cathedral in 1135–8, it appears that no actual building began for at least another twenty years. The palace site was defined by the Roman wall and ditch to the north, the extension to those defences on the east, and by new walls on the other two sides, forming a trapezoidal enclosure, entered through a gate in the north wall. After a start by Bishop Chesney, a major building programme was initiated by Bishop Hugh, later canonised, who constructed a great hall and kitchen, a chamber-block (usually referred to as the East Hall), and a connecting range, leaving the fourth, south side open. The hall was completed after Hugh's death. Subsequently, further modifications and refinements were carried out, notably by Bishops Hugh of Wells in the thirteenth century, Henry Burghersh in the fourteenth, and William Alnwick in the fifteenth, when he added the gate-tower, a chapel-range, and a bay-window in the hall. Enough of the structure survives to give some idea of the palace's former magnificence, reflecting the usual status of the bishop as one of the kingdom's premier statesmen and prelates.

THE POLYGONAL FORTRESS

We have seen how the keep, either a solid cube or an open circular shell, was often a feature of the Norman castle, but although such structures continued to be built, often for symbolic rather than military purposes, there was a move toward the polygonal fortress consisting of curtain walls connected by strong angle-towers with a powerful gatehouse. The residential and service buildings would be ranged along the inside of the curtains, or freestanding in the bailey.

The county boasts two fine examples of this model, at Bolingbroke (**12**), and at Tattershall. Sadly, neither survives in impressive form, but there is enough to understand the plan and scale. Bolingbroke was built by Randulph de Blundevill, Earl of Chester, and from 1217, Earl of Lincoln as well, about 1220-30, to a roughly hexagonal plan with a D-shaped tower at each of five angles, and a twin-towered gate-house to the north. A great hall backed onto the northeast curtain, and other timber-framed service buildings occupied further stretches of curtain. The courtyard of the castle is basically an artificial platform that would have required undercrofts for any stone buildings inside the walls. The castle had all but disappeared until excavations in 1965 began to reveal some detail. At the end of the thirteenth century the castle passed to Thomas of Lancaster and thence to John of Gaunt, whose son, Henry, later to become Henry IV, was born there in 1367. The castle stayed the centre of the Duchy's Lincolnshire estates. In 1451, the King's Tower, referred to as the New Tower in the accounts, was remodelled in a polygonal shape, probably to accommodate the castle's principal apartments.

12 OLD BOLINGBROOKE: the excavated curtain wall and one of the castle's D-shaped towers, this one part of the gatehouse

The earl built castles at Beeston (Cheshire) and Chartley (Staffordshire) and these fortresses share many characteristics, particularly their gatehouses, and the combination of curtain walls and angle-towers. A little way to the south of the castle is an embanked enclosure known as the 'Rout Yard', latterly a pound for stray animals, but traditionally held to have had some chivalric significance.

The original plan of Robert de Tateshale's castle of *c*.1231 is still visible, but greatly overshadowed by Ralph Cromwell's later tower. The earlier castle was five-sided within a moat, and had maybe as many as seven or eight round towers, parts of three of which have been excavated. There were freestanding buildings in the courtyard, including a great hall (which affected the positioning of the new tower in the 1440s) and a chapel.

The Pipe Rolls record only modest amounts of crown expenditure in Lincolnshire. In the 1190s there are four items totalling just over £120 spent on Lincoln Castle. The largest amount – £82 16s 4d – was expended in 1192–3 on strengthening the bailey, possibly work made necessary after the recent siege by de Longchamp. Another item in the accounts involves the sum of £80 to be spent on the castle at Grimsby in 1199–1200. This work never proceeded, and within a short while the stockpile of materials was being sold off. To put this expenditure into some sort of perspective, Richard I spent £4000 on the Tower of London from 1188–97.

THE BARONS IN REVOLT

Within two generations of the end of the Anarchy, conflict had returned to the county. In the general unrest following the death of Henry II and Richard I's desertion of the country to go on crusade, Lincoln was caught in a power struggle between William de Longchamp, Richard's chancellor, and Gerard de Camville, sheriff of Lincoln, who declared his allegiance to Prince John in 1191. Longchamp marched on Lincoln, successfully besieging the castle and bringing de Camville back onside. Two years later de Camville was not amongst John's rebels. On his return, Richard was less understanding and deposed de Camville as sheriff. In 1199, Richard died of wounds and John succeeded to the throne of England.

At Easter 1214, the barons met at Stamford to organise their resistance to John. One part of their force occupied Lincoln. After the signing of the Magna Carta, Bishop Hugh of Wells brought one of only four surviving copies back to Lincoln, but after the king had had it invalidated by the Pope, the barons invited Louis, the dauphin of France, to become King of England. In 1216 John came to Lincolnshire to impose an enormous fine on his rebellious subjects, receiving it at Stamford, having first taken four burgesses of Lincoln as hostages, and installing a royal garrison in the castle. At about this time, John confirmed the Lady Nicholaa, de Camville's widow, as constable of Lincoln Castle. In May, Gilbert de Gant occupied the city of Lincoln with some French troops, but Lady Nicholaa held out against them in the castle. By September, John was in Lincoln, forcing de Gant to flee, and John then marched his army through Grimsby, Louth and Spalding, sacking towns and villages as he went. The next month he was dead, and de Gant, by now created Earl of Lincoln by Louis, resumed his siege of the castle. Still the constable held out, but the baronial army gathered in Lincoln, to await the castle's capitulation, perceived as imminent. Meanwhile, William the Marshall, and the Earl of Chester, acting for the new King Henry III, marched an army northwards in May 1217. In order to avoid having to fight his way through Wigford and the lower city, he approached the city through Stow, from the west, linking with the garrison and entering the Bail to surprise and defeat the baronial forces.

Amongst the leaders who carried out this coup was the Earl of Chester, great-grandson of the countess Lucy. He was created Earl of Lincoln after the battle. Also leading a section of the royal army was Peter des Roches, Bishop of Winchester. His local knowledge, gained as a former precentor of Lincoln, helped to guarantee victory. A third leader, William Lungespee, later married his son to the Lady Nicholaa's granddaughter, thereby securing the hereditary constableship of the castle. Surprisingly, these men, who appeared to have some affinity with the city, deemed the townsfolk collaborators with the rebels, and allowed their troops to sack the city and to empty the cathedral's treasury, much to the dismay of the current precentor, Geoffrey of Deeping, who lost 11,000 silver marks from his safe-keeping. The poor showing by the baronial troops and their French allies, combined with the vast amount of booty taken from the city, prompted the contemptuous victors to name the battle 'Lincoln Fair'. This marked the end of the barons' rebellion and Louis returned to France, the Lady Nicholaa retaining her role as castellan. In 1216, William de Coleville, lord of Castle Bytham and a member of the barons' party, had his castle confiscated by John, who gave it to William de Forz (Fortibus). After the end of the rebellion, de Coleville had his property returned by Henry III's officers, but de Fortibus defied them, refusing to relinquish the castle, and was deemed to be in revolt. In 1221 a royal force, which included miners, began a two-week-long siege that caused damage sufficient to force the castle's capitulation.

More trouble followed later in Henry's reign when the de Montforts led another baronial rebellion. The governor of Lincoln Castle, Alexander de Montfort, despite his continuing loyalty to the king throughout these troubles, was ordered to deliver up the castle, and the citizens obtained royal letters acknowledging that they were innocent parties caught in the crossfire. In 1265 they renewed this letter of protection, only just in time, as rebels including Baldwin Wake occupied the Isle of Axholme and then went on to sack Lincoln, capturing the castle. The next year Prince Edward led an expedition to expel them. A number of Lincolnshire lords lost their lands as a result of their rebellion and, despite their insurance policy, the citizens of Lincoln still faced another large fine, as it appeared that some had been hedging their bets, or seeking commercial advantage by playing one party off against another. Some of the rebel lords who lost their lands became known as the 'Disinherited' and were virtual pariahs. Over the years, those permitted to buy back their lands, often on an instalment plan, included de Colevill at Castle Bytham, Gilbert de Gant at Folkingham, and Baldwin Wake at Bourne. It has been suggested that Baldwin Wake's rebellion was in part an attempt to emulate his claimed ancestor, Hereward. Such bad behaviour on the part of the nobility, coupled with the cult of violence as applied in tournaments and trial by ordeal, would stimulate the lawlessness which was beginning to appear and which would dominate much of the next two centuries.

DEFENDING HOLY CHURCH

At the time of the Conquest, Crowland was the only monastery recorded in the whole of Lincolnshire, but within a short time, Norman landowners began to endow a variety of religious houses. In addition to these, the Order of Knights Templar was attracted by the richness of the agricultural land and by the lushness of the pasture for sheep-rearing, and invested in a number of sites across the county. By 1200, Templar preceptories had been established at Ashby-de-la-Launde, Aslackby, Eagle, Mere, Raithby-cum-Maltby, South Witham, Temple Bruer and Willoughton. Many preceptories were often no more than large farms with a house accommodating the preceptor and numbers of lay brothers who ran the operations of the farm. There might be a small chapel, some barns and other outbuildings all set within a moat which provided fish for Friday's meals, and stopped the animals straying or being rustled – more for security than defence.

However, at least two of Lincolnshire's preceptories, South Witham and Temple Bruer, were in a different league. South Witham stood near the old course of the River Witham just off the Great North Road a few miles south of Grantham. Excavations in 1966–7 uncovered the complete layout of an extensive manorial complex, established in 1164. Surrounded by a perimeter wall, it was entered through a small gatehouse with the guesthouse alongside. Several large aisled barns, a workshop and a kitchen were ranged around a central court which held the great hall, the chapel (under which were found traces of earlier structures), and most intriguingly, a two-storey stone building with a defensible entrance which the excavator described as a hall-keep. If that interpretation is correct, then it would point to the site paying more than lip-service to defensive measures.

Many of the buildings may have been built of stone, or they may have been timber-framed on dwarf walls. The chapel and hall were isolated in a separate inner enclosure cut off from the rest of the farm, but the supposed hall-keep was adjacent to this group, perhaps acting as a strong-house for treasure and valuables, a not uncommon practice. The monks of Croxton Kerrial (Leicestershire), halfway to Melton Mowbray, for instance, kept a house in Grantham, equipped with a strong-room protected by barred windows, strengthened doors and fireproof stone vaults for the safe-keeping of their valuables, and one of the reasons for the strength of some of the stone houses on Steep Hill, Lincoln was the need to protect valuables and financial records from fire.

It is now thought that the Norman building known as St Mary's Guild in the High Street was built specially for the visit to Lincoln of Henry II for his crown-

13 TEMPLE BRUER: the surviving late-twelfth-century tower, one of a pair that stood at the east end of the round church of this preceptory of the Knights Templar

wearing ceremony at Christmas 1157. It shares many of the characteristics of contemporary town houses, including a strong gate and small windows, and the accommodation is ranged around a courtyard – all measures that can be linked to security consciousness. There was certainly good reason for many of the monastic landowners to look to their security. In 1189, for instance, Crowland Abbey was invaded by land-hungry 'men of Holland' wanting common pasture on marshland around the Abbey.

Another significant Templar preceptory lay just off the Roman road between Lincoln and Sleaford on reclaimed heathland at Temple Bruer. Here the settlement (with its weekly market) was graced by a typical Templar round church, now buried but excavated in 1833 and again in 1908. The circular aisled nave had an apse to the east, whose end was flanked by two square towers, one of which remains (**13**). This is of three storeys over a crypt, with the vaulted ground floor accessed by six steps. The first floor is also vaulted and built of the same fine ashlar masonry as the lower stages. The second floor, under a modern pyramid roof, has ashlar dressings, and all floors have lancets and round-headed windows, pointing, along with other architectural features, to a date at the end of the twelfth century. The outline of a gabled roof on the tower belongs to a later chapel extension. This surviving tower, 54ft (16.5m) in height, has the look of a small keep rather than a church tower, reminiscent of the ambiguous St Leonard's Tower at West Malling (Kent). Perhaps the soldier-monks of the Order felt more comfortable building structures with a military aspect.

By the end of the thirteenth century, kings on both sides of the English Channel were casting envious eyes over the wealth of the Templars, and in 1307, Philip IV of France and Edward I of England suppressed the Order, ultimately with papal approval. Lincoln was selected as one of three centres trying the Templars on trumped-up charges of idolatry, apostasy and gross immorality, and some were imprisoned in the city's Clasket Gate. Most were sentenced to life imprisonment in other religious houses, and what was left of their property was made over to the Knights Hospitaller of St John. South Witham was held by the Hospitallers for a very short while but was abandoned, possibly as early as 1311. Temple Bruer became a commandery of the Knights of St John and continued in use until it was dissolved in 1521. Aslackby's preceptory, founded in 1154, survives as Temple Farm, but the last substantial remnants had disappeared by the end of the nineteenth century. It is thought that here also, as at Temple Bruer, there was a round church with a pair of similar towers. There is now little evidence of the Templars beyond place-names in Lincolnshire, but the Angel and Royal hotel in Grantham – once the property of the Templars, and then of the Hospitallers – still stands as a reminder of their former glory.

TOWN DEFENCES

Lincoln's Roman city walls survived to form the basis for the city's medieval defences, the upper city becoming the outer bailey of the castle, the Bail, with the cathedral precinct straddling its southeast corner, carrying the Close beyond the original walled perimeter. The Roman wall, in fact, provided a solid north–south foundation for the cathedral's extended east end. The Roman south Bail-gate still stood in the thirteenth century. Down the hill to the south, the lower city had stopped short of the river and Brayford Pool, but by the end of the thirteenth century, spur walls were carried down to the waterside. That on the west running from the Newland Gate, built before 1275, terminated in a stout circular tower, known from at least the seventeenth century as the Lucy Tower, not to be confused with the shell-keep in the castle.

On the eastern side the spur ran down to Thorngate, a site temporarily fortified in the twelfth century, terminating in another tower, probably similar in style to that on the west, which stood in the yard of the Green Dragon hotel until 1728. On the eastern walls the Werkdyke ran along the line of the present Broadgate, with an entry through Clasket Gate into the city. The southern entrance was The Stonebow, but not in its present form. Wigford was defended by waterways, but had two gates to control access, one was Bargate on the main road south, and another, Little Bargate, once having twin round towers flanking an archway, on the Canwick road. On the north, the Newport Arch continued in use, and there may have been some defence for the suburb of Newport, possibly a bank and ditch. By the 1300s, the eastern suburb of Butwerk appears to have had a wall, pierced by some form of bar or gate on the line of Bagerholmegate, and running from the river north towards Greetwellgate. On the west a corresponding suburb of Newland was defined by a bank and ditch, with a gate of some sort for Midhergate/Newland Street West to pass through. The medieval city wall proper was 7ft (2m) thick, and its outer ditch was up to 80ft (25m) in width.

We have already seen how Stamford had been fortified by the Danes as one of the Five Boroughs in the ninth century, but that area of their burh was to be proved inadequate as the town grew and the castle was built, displacing at least five houses. The medieval walls contained an area of 75 acres (30 hectares) and were a mile (1.6km) in length. The town received murage grants from Henry III in 1218 and 1226 to pay for timber palings around the town, and from 1261–1350 for the construction, maintenance and repair of stone defences. There were seven gates and a horse-shoe-shaped tower, surviving but much altered (*14*), at one angle at least, and the line of the walls, much rebuilt in the seventeenth century, may still be easily traced.

Grimsby owed its growth in the Middle Ages to the fish trade, which dominated life there by the thirteenth century. Grimsby merchant-ships served on Edward I's expedition to Flanders in 1297. The town was surrounded by the Burdyke, and received a murage grant in 1261, which may not have been taken up. Excavations in the Burdyke uncovered a ditch containing twelfth-century pottery.

The Early Medieval Period (*c*.1000–1300) 51

14 STAMFORD: the north-west angle tower of the town walls built after AD 1261 when the town received its first murage grant for rebuilding its walls in masonry; as it stands now, it is largely a seventeenth-century rebuilding

52 Defending Lincolnshire: A Military History from Conquest to Cold War

KEY: Earthwork Castles   EARTHWORK CASTLES REBUILT IN STONE C11-12
Stone castles and moated sites C12-13   Ecclesiastical fortifications
Castles and moated sites C14   Moated manors, stone or brick towers C15

Fig. 5 Medieval castles in Lincolnshire

Alongside the established towns there were also new planted towns, often intended to secure for the landlord the revenues accruing from a successful market as well as rents for shops and workshops. New Sleaford was started by Bishop Alexander of Lincoln alongside his new castle between 1123–1147, on a site at the junction of the marshland and higher ground to the west of the site of Old Sleaford on the Roman road. Less than 200 years later it was in the top ten of the country's successful planted towns, but its revenue was still only a quarter of Lincoln's. The rise of Boston was more spectacular still. Founded between 1086 and 1113 on former marshland, it was to become one of the country's most important ports. In 1203 it was fourth most successful in the region behind Newcastle-upon-Tyne, Kingston-upon-Hull and Hedon. It is doubtful that Boston was ever strongly fortified. There are no records of murage grants (only one for pavage in 1285), but the Barditch, with inner earth bank, dates from around 1200, and various excavations have uncovered a stretch of 2ft-thick (60cm-thick) wall on stone and brick foundations three times that thickness, as well as evidence of stone revetments to the ditch. Behind the Dominican Friary is a 110ft (34m) length of masonry wall with buttresses, reinforcing the Barditch. The Bargate was a street not a gateway, but it was reached by a bridge over the Barditch, which may have been a useful point for collecting tolls, rather than a defensive feature. Much of the ditch had been bricked over by the mid-1800s, and its circumstances are still obscure.

A number of villages were contained within the outer earthwork enclosures of castles. Castle Carlton was associated with a planned village; Bourne and Castle Bytham both had village enclosures; Barton-upon-Humber's Castledyke appears to be either a defensive or a boundary ditch, possibly dating from the thirteenth century (**Fig. 5**).

three

The Later Medieval and Tudor Period (*c.*1300–1600)

The period covered by this chapter was one of enormous change, both social and political. It encompasses the Black Death, which claimed the lives of possibly as many as two thirds of the population in some places during the major outbreak of the plague in 1349 and in the years following. The effects of this were ultimately to culminate in the Peasants' Revolt of 1381. Along with these upheavals there were other hazards. At the end of the previous century, Lincolnshire had been heavily taxed by Edward I to finance his Welsh and Scottish wars. This taxation was to continue under the two Edwards following. Added to the tax burden was the demand for troops, not only taking workers off the land but emptying the community coffers for their armour and weapons. The wars with France then produced bands of unemployed soldiery that roamed around living off the land. As if all this were not enough for the reduced work force to cope with, the first quarter of the century had seen the start of the Little Ice Age, which was to stunt agricultural production for the next 300 years. A sequence of wet years reduced the amount of arable land available, making sheep farming less economically viable than in previous times, hence reducing income. The unsettling situation countrywide was exacerbated by a number of further local factors. The silting up both of local waterways such as the Fossdyke and the upper reaches of the Witham, and the major port of Boston Haven itself was one of several causes for an enormous decrease in trade in the region. This drop in revenues was made worse in Lincoln by continuous conflict between the Castle, the Bail, the City and the Cathedral, mainly over property rents, market payments and rights, and jurisdictions. In 1334 Boston had been fifth and Lincoln seventh in the league table of absolute wealth of English towns, but those heady days were slipping away. All in all, the fourteenth century was a most uncomfortable and insecure time to be alive.

LICENCES TO CRENELLATE

Whilst there were sound military reasons for taking steps to defend oneself against the threat of violence by fortifying one's home, it would appear that there were also more abstract social ones. It has been suggested by Charles Coulson, amongst others, that a licence to crenellate was as much a badge of social status as a legal permission from the king to fortify one's home. Not all fortified houses or castles were licensed, but this did not necessarily affect their legality. For some, it would appear, royal approval was desirable in order to stay on the right side of some very unpredictable monarchs. It has been argued that the apparently serendipitous nature of grants of licences to crenellate may be explained by interpreting them as a sign that the recipient enjoyed royal favour, an aid to self-preservation he would happily flaunt in front of his friends and foes, his neighbours and his peers. The three Bek brothers were all granted licences to crenellate by Edward I: John Bek, for the family seat at Eresby (Spilsby) in 1276; Bishop Bek of Durham, a career civil servant, at Somerton (**15**) in 1281; and Thomas, the bishop of St Davids, at Pleasley (Derbyshire) in 1285.

Also in 1285, Oliver de Sutton, bishop of Lincoln was licensed to enclose the cathedral precinct with a wall 12ft (3.5m) high, closing off lanes affording access to the cathedral with gates that would be locked and guarded from dusk until sunrise. This was because the cathedral's secular clergy lived in constant fear, both of assault by the townsfolk, and of the 'obscenities and indecencies, horrible to witness and likely to engender scandal', which were otherwise committed nightly in an open precinct.

The bishop received further licences in 1315, 1316 and 1318. The 1316 Parliament was convened in the Dean's house and it was therefore important to present the close as an impressive setting for such a prestigious event, as well as to stress the cathedral's immunity from lay jurisdiction, symbolised by its imposing walls and gates. Bishop Burghersh was well rewarded by Queen Isabella for his service as both Treasurer and Chancellor and, perhaps as part of this approbation, received licence to crenellate his palace in 1329. In 1336, Bishop Henry also received a licence for his palace at Nettleham, on a site dating back to pre-Conquest times, enclosing it within a stone wall. Here, earthworks of the only surviving enclosed medieval garden arrangement in England have been identified. A seventeenth-century survey listed the components of the former palace, which included chambers for accommodating royal visitors, a chapel, a hall and all the usual service buildings. It is possible that views over the walled gardens might have been enjoyed from vantage points within the buildings. The palace complex may have been entered through an imposing gateway flanked by large barns. Much of the stone was taken away to be used in the repair of the palace in Lincoln in the early seventeenth century, and now little may be seen on site, beyond architectural fragments built into the Methodist chapel of 1899. A further dimension to Episcopal building is provided by the allegorical character of such fortified sites, expressed by Robert Grosseteste, bishop of Lincoln, in his poem 'Chateau d'Amour', in which the palace's defensive

15 SOMERTON CASTLE: licensed to Antony Bek, bishop of Durham in 1286; it has the typical plan of its time with a round tower at each corner of a quadrangle with buildings ranged around the central courtyard

16 THORNTON ABBEY: the great gatehouse was licensed in 1382 and 1389 but its apparently defensive features may be no more than window-dressing

components represent ideas concerning defending the true faith, as well as more metaphysical notions of a moat filled by the tears of the Virgin Mary, weeping for her crucified son.

More prosaically, at a time of tension between the Knights Templar and the Crown, licence to crenellate was granted for a great gate at Temple Bruer in 1306. Maybe a secure stable door might have been more appropriate, as their London treasury was seized by Edward I at this time, and they were finally dissolved by the pope a mere six years later. In the context of a long-running dispute with the men of Deeping over grazing rights, the prior of Spalding was granted licence to crenellate his precinct with walls and gates in 1333. It is not known if this work was ever carried out, and if so, whether at the priory itself near the town's market place, or at the residential Monks' House off the road to Bourne. Involved alongside the Abbot of Crowland in armed conflict with Thomas Wake of Liddel, Henry of Edenstowe received a licence, also in 1333. Later in the century, in 1382 and 1389, Thornton Abbey's fortress-like, but ambivalent, great gatehouse was licensed. Nearly half of Lincolnshire's licences were granted to conventual establishments, and to this total must be added the cathedral precinct, and the bishop's palaces of Lincoln, Stow and Nettleham.

In his study of monastic gateways, Roland Morant has defined their functions as regulatory, defensive, symbolic and providing accommodation. A number of Lincolnshire examples include Tupholme, Heynings Priory, Bourne Abbey, Kirkstead Abbey, Thornholme Priory, and the friaries of the Whitefriars and the

Greyfriars in Stamford. Thornton Abbey gatehouse has a strong claim to be the most imposing such structure in Britain (**16**). Standing nearly 70ft (21.5m) high, its façade, 120ft (36.5m) wide, consists of three arches with a wing on each side, these five elements being separated by projecting turrets. The central arch leads into a vaulted gate-hall from which a pedestrian passage leads off to the right through a separate archway in the rear wall. Above the archway is a chamber, 48ft (14.5m) wide by 20ft (7m) deep, with an oriel window on its inner face. There is another chamber above, and it is likely that these two chambers, with their associated garderobes, formed the Abbot's private apartments.

However comfortable and domestic this arrangement may appear, there are nevertheless defensive features. Interspersed between the religious carvings on the façade are a variety of arrow-loops. A portcullis could be operated from the upper chamber, and the gatehouse, with its turrets to front and back, had originally been battlemented. The full-height walls beyond the wings on each side of the gatehouse are unfinished, but the site was surrounded by a wall with turrets, and stood within a moat. The central part of the gatehouse is made of stone, and the wings of brick, rendered in lime mortar. Some time in the early sixteenth century (although Pevsner assigns it to the fifteenth), a barbican was added to the gatehouse. This consists of two parallel brick walls, 120ft (36.5m) long, terminating in round turrets. The walls are 5ft (1.5m) thick, but each contains thirteen deep recesses with arrow-loops rather than gun-ports, and there appears no way of securing the entrance between the turrets. It would appear that the barbican was more ornamental than practical, intended to impress the visitor and to frame the approach to this monumental gatehouse.

THE LATER MEDIEVAL CASTLE

Civil unrest and periods of lawlessness were very different from a state of war, and castle design adapted to prevailing circumstances, offering an element of security and defensibility, but also comfort, and a tangible expression of wealth and power. Many of those castles that were out-and-out fortresses, such as Lincoln and Stamford, were generally allowed to decay with odd buildings retained as prisons. Stamford was reported as ruinous in 1340; Bytham may have existed only as an unfortified dwelling after the siege and demolition of 1221. Lincoln was greatly decayed by 1327 when the cost of repairs was assessed at £1,000, but apparently continued to function effectively only as a court and prison, although work was carried out to enlarge the Observatory Tower during the fourteenth century.

The primary function of other castles was estate centre, as, for instance, at Old Bolingbroke and Sleaford. Where new castles were built, their design tended to be fairly uniform. This was the quadrangle, often moated, with circular or square corner towers, a strong gatehouse, and buildings such as hall, kitchens, chapel, and retainers' lodgings ranged around the walls. Instead of a keep, either the gatehouse or one of the corner towers might be physically distinct from the rest of the castle,

The Later Medieval and Tudor Period (c.1300–1600)   59

17 GRIMSTHORPE CASTLE: King John's tower is the only one remaining of the four that stood at the corners of this quadrangular fortress

18 KYME TOWER: the sole remnant of this mid-fourteenth-century castle that may have been another of the courtyard type, although the previous existence of only a second tower, linked to a hall, is certain providing accommodation for the lord's family by ensuring an element of privacy within an essentially communal dwelling, but also acting as an insurance against the often fickle allegiances of the paid soldiery or household knights. Outer courts containing stables, barns, workshops and kilns were banked and ditched, surrounded by fishponds and orchards. Bishop Bek's castle of Somerton, with its round angle towers, Henry de Beaumont's Folkingham, licensed to 'Bello Monte' in 1312, and the de Gand's Grimsthorpe, slightly earlier than these other examples, with square corner towers, all fit this pattern. One of Grimsthorpe's imposing square towers, King John's Tower (**17**), still stands at the southeast corner of the later mansion. At Folkingham, the importance of the moats puts the castle at a defensive disadvantage, since it is overlooked by higher ground on two sides. This was apparently, for the builder, a risk worth taking in order to enjoy both the practical and the aesthetic benefits of being surrounded by water.

Kyme Castle was built by Sir Gilbert de Umfraville some time in the middle of the fourteenth century. Only a 75ft-high (23m-high) tower remains now (**18**), of four storeys with two-light windows in each face, a south doorway in each of the two lower floors, and a higher stair-turret rising above the battlemented parapet. There was a gabled building, probably a hall attached to the south side of this tower, and apparently another tower, implying the existence of other ranges of buildings within the moat. On an adjacent site is a relic of the Augustinian priory founded before 1169. At Spilsby, the moat of Eresby Castle survives, and excavations in 1968 revealed the footings of a round corner tower and adjoining curtain wall. It is possible that there was also a castle in Grantham at this time, for the house of the Hall family in Castlegate has at its core, part of a hall of *c*.1380 with its screens passage.

Some moated sites defy easy interpretation. At Lea, where a licence to crenellate was granted in 1330 to John de Brehous/Braose, a small moat lies about 300m to the west of a much larger moat with possible traces of building materials, and reports of standing walls into the eighteenth century. The 'Priory' at Goxhill is a medieval house with hall and undercroft, within a moat. Some fortified houses, such as Sir Robert Carr's Old Place in Sleaford, have completely disappeared, original masonry only appearing in later garden walls.

MOATED SITES

For many of the lesser nobility and members of the gentry alike, a moat sufficed to demonstrate the status of the family and to provide a gesture toward defence. Of the hundreds of moats in the country, very few were provided with licences to crenellate. Between 1200 and 1536, only some 460 licences were issued nationally, and there are nearly 300 moats in Lincolnshire alone, where the local landscape often lends itself to the moat, if only as a way of draining a homestead platform. Investigations into the moat at Cherry Holt near Grantham in 1955–6 showed there to be nothing on the moated platform at all. This would suggest that it was sometimes felt worthwhile to provide moats for gardens or orchards, both producing cash crops, and vulnerable to passing ne'r-do-wells. Usually, however, a moat contained something more concrete.

In 1311, Prior Hatfield of Spalding built a moated manor house at Weston (Wykeham), where his chapel survives alongside later buildings. A length of wall with a fourteenth-century window remains at Belleau, a manor of the Welles and Willoughby family. This fragment appears to represent one wall of the hall and chamber block of this house within its moat. An excavated moat at Saxilby revealed that the platform had been occupied by an aisled house measuring about 50ft (15m) by 25ft (7.5m), which had been roofed with stone tiles. Another, at Bassingham's Water Lane, contained an aisled hall measuring 60ft (18m) by 36ft (11m) with an attached garderobe. At Mareham-le-Fen, a Norman corbel was found near the moated Birkwood Hall, possibly from the hall's chapel. At Goxhill, a moat, levelled in 1967, yielded worked stone and brick, tiles, tracery from a window, a pillar and stone quoins. A bank had served as a dam to ensure that the moat was kept full. A licence was granted to Ranulph de Friskney in 1303 for his moated hall. Another large moated house was Cressy Hall near Gosberton. It is worth noting that as late as 1449 the Knights Hospitaller were granted a licence for their preceptory at Eagle, and in 1459, a time of even greater insecurity for many, a licence to crenellate was granted to Thomas Fitzwilliam of Mablethorpe, possibly for the moat which can still be traced at Mablethorpe Hall. Some moats have particular associations attached, as at Countess Close, Alkborough, a moat from which dressed stones have been retrieved, reputedly one of the manors of the Countess Lucy.

Katherine Swynford was a lady-in-waiting to John of Gaunt's first wife, who married one of his household knights, Sir Hugh Swynford. When she was widowed, she became mistress, and later wife to John of Gaunt, her Swynford son becoming the most loyal companion to the future Henry IV, now his stepbrother. She found the Swynford's moated house at Kettlethorpe in a derelict state and spent much time and money during the 1370s restoring and developing it, extending the nucleus of the manor by absorbing much of the village to create a deer park. Kettlethorpe has been in the news again recently for reasons connected to the maintenance of its moat. Only fragments of the stone manor house survive inside the present house, and although the present 'medieval' gatehouse appears to be a Victorian reconstruction using fourteenth-century materials, there would originally have been an imposing entrance reflecting the lady's status.

The other local Swynford manor was Coleby, south of Lincoln, where the manor house, dating from the twelfth century, was on a site now occupied by a seventeenth-century house. Coleby too was in a run-down state, so Katherine spent much time in alternative accommodation. For long periods of her life she lived in Lincoln cathedral precinct, first of all in the Chancery, and later on, after she was widowed, in the house now known as the Priory. The Chancery was a house with stone solar block, chapel and service-block. From the kitchen the screens passage gave access into a timber-framed hall, measuring 40ft (12m) long by 28ft (8.5m) wide, built by Chancellor Bek in 1321, and demolished in 1714. There was also a gatehouse.

John of Gaunt's London palace had been burnt to the ground in the Peasants' Revolt, and Katherine herself was harassed by townsfolk in Lincoln in 1384, so some measure of security would have been necessary. Bishop Russell rebuilt the front part of the Chancery in brick in the 1480s. The Priory was all of stone and again consisted of a hall, a solar block with private chambers, a chapel and a parlour, measuring 28ft (8.5m) long by 21ft (6.5m) wide. The hall, very similar in size to that in the Chancery, was of stone with walls 2–3ft (0.6–0.9m) thick. The major difference between the two houses is the fact that the Priory had a three-storey strong-tower built as an integral part of the precinct wall after 1316. The tower had a spiral staircase, two comfortable rooms with fireplaces, an octagonal chimney and possibly garderobes as well. It may have served a variety of purposes, but it may simply have represented a convenient and secure bolt-hole for an often-troubled lady in troubling times. St Mary's Guild in the High Street was once known as John of Gaunt's Stables, since the house opposite was thought to be his palace. However, it would appear that the house in question, whose oriel window now graces the inside face of the castle's East Gate, was built by the de Sutton family who, as tenants of the duke, incorporated his coat-of-arms in their Lincoln town house, possibly as a token of their loyalty.

An element of caution must be exercised when moated sites are being assessed for, as well as homestead moats, there were a number which were dug for quite other and specific purposes. These include Bardney Abbey's bleeding house, monastic granges at Collow and Burton Pedwardine, and a hermitage at Tealby. Beyond the medieval period, moats continued to be dug well into the seventeenth century, both for drainage and as garden features, as, for instance, at Goltho Manor.

LINCOLN CATHEDRAL PRECINCT

The cathedral precinct at Lincoln purported to be dedicated to the prevention of crime, but the walls, gates and towers – built as a result of the grant of licences to crenellate (much of whose fabric remains) – clearly met the needs of an altogether different agenda. The physical isolation of the cathedral community behind these defences emphasised its independence from the lay authorities of the civil city. The defences were also designed to enhance the importance of the bishop as a man of power and influence in the land in secular as well as ecclesiastical matters. The most imposing gateway, the ornate Exchequer Gate (**19**) faced the castle's East Gate, and consisted of three archways with a lodging over the deep gate-passages, and two turrets. It originally had an outer gate, of similar size and style, which was demolished before 1816.

The next access point running clockwise round the circuit, was at the west end of Eastgate, where the Bail Gate, at the northwest corner of the White Hart, and an inner Close Gate stood. Each consisted of a single archway set in a gatehouse with a room above. The lane, known as East Bight, must have originated as the Roman *pomerium* for moving troops around inside the walls, and the precinct wall runs

19 LINCOLN CATHEDRAL PRECINCT: the Exchequer Gate was originally the inner part of a double gate, built in the early fourteenth century following the grant of several licences to crenellate

inside this, parallel to the Roman wall, with a northern Close Gate, in the same style as the previous two, providing an exit onto the northern part of East Bight.

The appearance of all these three gates was recorded in Peter de Wint's drawings prior to their demolition. Another Close Gate stood north of the Old Deanery, just inside the Roman East Gate. The precinct wall then ran almost to the cathedral chapter house before turning east to the Priory Gate across Minster Yard. The present insubstantial arch is a replacement of 1816, built a year after the original gate (taking a similar form to the Exchequer Gate) had been demolished. The last major gateway into the close is Pottergate (*20*), restored in the late nineteenth century. It consists of a tower with a single archway, with a portcullis chamber above, and a polygonal stair-turret on one corner. It has been suggested that there was a barbican in advance of the main gateway. The southern section of walls was pierced by two posterns, one, much rebuilt, on Greestone Stairs, the steep path down the hill, and the other providing access to the bishop's palace. Much of the wall remains, but only a few of the towers. Two can be found on Winnowsty Lane and are visible from the Chancery garden (*21*), and a third forms the northwest corner of 2 Minster Yard, known as the Priory. All these defences of the cathedral precinct were built in the first half of the fourteenth century, legitimised by the grant of several licences to crenellate.

The Later Medieval and Tudor Period (c.1300–1600)   65

20 LINCOLN CATHEDRAL PRECINCT: Pottergate is the southernmost gate into the precinct, and may have originally been reinforced by a barbican

21 LINCOLN CATHEDRAL PRECINCT: one of three towers remaining on the precinct wall, standing in Winnowsty Lane

TOWNS IN THE LATER MEDIEVAL PERIOD

Lawlessness and poverty appeared to pervade all facets of life in the fourteenth century, continuing into the fifteenth. Throughout the first half of the fourteenth century, royal pressure was exerted to maintain Lincoln's city walls. A murage grant was made in 1322 followed by a commission to survey the walls, and to comment on the various encroachments that reduced their strength, such as the practice of building houses on the city wall. This concern re-appeared in 1338 when war with France had again raised the matter of national security. It would appear that money raised for maintaining the walls or paving the streets was not always spent as it should have been, not so much because of corruption, but more because of differing perceptions of priorities.

This was to prove only the start of continuing economic problems caused by the French wars. Within a hundred years, the economic state of Lincoln had sunk so low, owing particularly to changes in the volume and patterns of trade, that exemption from taxation was granted to the city seven times between 1445 and 1472. The volume of fishing enjoyed by such ports as Grimsby, Saltfleet, Wrangle and Wainfleet prior to the Black Death was also diminishing, and it may have been seen as beneficial to the town that Grimsby was required to contribute ships to the military expeditions of the French wars. Some towns never made it at all. The Prior of St John of Jerusalem had founded a new town near his preceptory of Eagle in 1345. New Eagle stood astride the Fosse Way near what is now the Half-way House Inn on Swinderby Moor. There was a chapel dedicated to the Holy Trinity, houses and building plots, a weekly market and two annual fairs, but after the Black Death it never really took off, and the charter was cancelled.

General lawlessness moreover affected all sections of society. Lincoln's representative at the Westminster Parliament, Hugh de Garwell, was pardoned for whatever part he might have played in the disturbances, only so long as he had not been one of those who actually murdered Simon of Sudbury, Archbishop of Canterbury, or any of the other officers of state who were victims of the mob. Apparently simple disputes could escalate into localised warfare. William de Roos, a keeper of the king's peace in Lincolnshire, and Robert Tyrwhit, a justice of the court of the King's bench, were in dispute over grazing rights near Brigg. When summoned to appear before the Chief Justice, Tyrwhit set out with 500 armed retainers in order to ambush de Roos on the road. De Roos was not pleased, and demanded an apology and restitution through Parliament. These little local disagreements, however, paled into insignificance against what was happening on the national stage.

RICHARD II AND BOLINGBROKE

In 1386, Richard II had visited Lincoln to canvass the city's support in his struggle with the Lancastrians, John of Gaunt and his son Henry Bolingbroke, who were perceived – probably incorrectly – as having designs on the throne. Only after the death of his father, and his own perpetual banishment and the confiscation of all his lands, did Bolingbroke decide that it was time to end the tyranny of the king.

Born at Old Bolingbroke in 1367, Henry was deeply embedded in Lincolnshire. His father had held Lincoln Castle for the king, his step-mother lived at Kettlethorpe and in the cathedral close, all three of them had been admitted to the con-fraternity of the cathedral, and Repingdon, his confessor, was shortly to become Bishop of Lincoln and later accompanied Henry in visiting the relics at Bardney Abbey. It was unsurprising then, that when, in 1399, Henry landed at Ravenspur at the mouth of the Humber, he was accompanied by those close Lincolnshire supporters, Roos, Darcy, Beaumont, Lovell and Willoughby, amongst others. Support for the unpopular Richard quickly melted away and he was captured and imprisoned at the Lancastrian stronghold of Pontefract (Yorkshire), in the care of Sir Thomas Swynford, where he died, officially as a result of a hunger strike. Bolingbroke then proclaimed himself king as Henry IV, rewarding his supporters with high office, with William Lord Roos, for instance, being appointed as Treasurer.

Another prominent office-holder was Sir Thomas Dymoke of Scrivelsby, Champion of England, who exercised his right to ride fully armed into Westminster Abbey during the coronation in 1399, and to challenge to a duel anyone doubting the king's right to the throne. Whilst this invitation brought forth no takers at the time, there was nevertheless active opposition to the new king. Sir John Bussy, lord of Folkingham and sheriff of Lincolnshire, had been one of Richard's ministers, had resisted Henry's usurpation of the throne, and had paid with his life. Others had kept a lower profile, biding their time. The Cistercian abbot of Revesby Abbey, next door to Old Bolingbroke, preached a sermon in June 1404 claiming that Richard II still lived, and that there were 10,000 men in England who believed so, thereby encouraging the idea of rebellion. One such rebellion that really hurt Henry was that of his childhood companion, Shakespeare's 'Hotspur', Percy, Earl of Northumberland, and the Battle of Shrewsbury in which Hotspur was killed has been claimed as effectively marking the beginning of the Wars of the Roses. One prominent Lincolnshire noble who had backed the wrong side against Henry was the Lord Bardolf, of Castle Carlton, who died of wounds received at the Battle of Bramham Moor in 1408. His dismembered corpse was distributed around the land as an example, and unusually for the times, all the bits arrived back home for burial within a mere couple of months.

The failure of Percy's rebellion was to have serious consequences for another Lincolnshire family. Some of Percy's confiscated lands went via Lord Cromwell's heiress, Maud Stanhope, to the hated Neville family through her marriage at Tattershall Castle in 1453 to Sir Thomas Neville. A skirmish involving the Percys and the wedding party was to lead ultimately to the first Battle of St Albans in 1455.

RALPH LORD CROMWELL AND TATTERSHALL

If the burghers of Lincoln were suffering from a downturn in fortune in the middle years of the fifteenth century, some of their neighbours were flourishing. Ralph Cromwell, Lord High Treasurer to Henry VI from 1433 to 1443, may have eased the pain of Lincoln's taxpayers, but it was at no expense to his own deep pockets, which paid for Tattershall Castle, his lasting legacy. Born in 1394, he had inherited the old castle in 1419, part of a property portfolio which had been assembled over the years by a series of judicious marriages. Further additions would come via the benefits of public office, for Cromwell received two of the Percy manors confiscated after the Battle of Shrewsbury, including Burwell in Lincolnshire. His career, however, would keep him away for nearly twenty-five years.

As a member of Henry V's retinue in France he served his political apprenticeship hammering out treaties and marriage agreements with the French, and was also present at the Battle of Agincourt in 1415. All this experience led him into government posts in England prior to his elevation to the office of Chamberlain and then to the Treasury. At Tattershall, he found a decayed, outmoded fortress lacking in comfort, style and particularly the grandeur befitting his status and wealth, and determined to create a monument which more fittingly might reflect his own worth. Cromwell's experience also recognised the uncertainty of the times. During Henry VI's minority he had lost his post as Chamberlain for no apparent reason beyond the whim of the Regent Bedford. As a new man, a professional administrator from the gentry rather than the nobility, he remained subject to both the patronage of the ruling class, and to its withholding of favour. Another important factor to be taken into account in turbulent times was the ease with which the administrators of the kingdom would be scape-goated and thrown to the wolves if things went wrong. In 1381, the Chancellor, Simon of Sudbury, Archbishop of Canterbury, along with Lord Treasurer Hales was murdered by a mob. In the absence of the network of family and household knights enjoyed by the nobility, the bureaucrats were forced to find their own salvation. Despite the decline of the castle as pure fortress, prudence alone demanded that some attempt be made by those in the public eye to build secure bases. The Fiennes family, for example, built at Herstmonceux (East Sussex), Lord Hastings at Ashby-de-la-Zouch and Kirby Muxloe (both Leicestershire), Cromwell's friend Sir John Falstolf at Caister (Norfolk), and Cromwell himself at Tattershall and at South Wingfield (Derbyshire). Some of these men had made their money from public office or by being in the right place at the right time. Sir Roger Fiennes had fought at Agincourt and was Treasurer to the household of Henry VI. Hastings was Chamberlain and Master of the Mint under Edward IV. Falstolf's windfall wealth reputedly came from French ransoms after Agincourt.

Sometimes these grand architectural statements were their builders' undoing. Periodically, insecure kings attempted to outlaw the keeping of private armies by enacting statutes of livery and maintenance, as did the council of regency in the name of Henry VI in 1450, a year of turmoil with Cade's Rebellion, the murder of the Duke of Suffolk, and the impeachment and subsequent death in prison of

22 TATTERSHALL CASTLE: Ralph Cromwell's Great Tower of the 1440s with its ostentatious display of medieval defensive features

the Duke of Gloucester. Cromwell himself, as a member of the Council of State, was caught up in these events along with other Lincolnshire neighbours, particularly Lord Beaumont of Folkingham and William Tailboys of Kyme. Both the latter outlived Cromwell, but died violent deaths ten years later. Also in 1450, Bishops Ayscough and Moleyns, and Sir James Fiennes, Lord Saye and Sele, the new Treasurer and Suffolk's son-in-law, would all be assassinated. Lord Hastings was executed in 1483, partly for his opposition to Richard III, leaving his great brick pseudo-fortress of Kirby Muxloe unfinished. Even as late as 1521, Henry VII executed Stafford, Earl of Buckingham for building Thornbury Castle (Gloucestershire) as a virtual barracks for his private army. The fifteenth century also saw roving gangs of bandits attacking travellers, kidnapping widows and heiresses, and extorting, stealing and murdering to order. In many cases these thugs were well enough connected to avoid justice. This was the backdrop against which Cromwell adopted the risky, but nevertheless necessary, strategy of developing Tattershall as a secure and palatial home base.

Tattershall, begun in 1433 and completed in 1448, is a mix of contradictions and ambiguities. Ostensibly it is a fortress, dominating the surrounding fenland and visible from miles away (**22**). It is furnished with crenellations, turrets and machicolations, but its very height renders it vulnerable to the fast-developing use of gunpowder artillery, and it has no provision for defensive use of hand-guns or cannon, although gun-loops had been common in fortifications for the previous fifty years. Cromwell would have seen cannon in action in France, and Froissart records a breach being made by cannon in the walls of Ardres as early as 1377. Tattershall, however, remained a gunpowder-free zone.

It would appear that it was more important to Cromwell that his castle might more closely resemble a fortress, echoing the dominance of the Norman keeps and the chivalric tradition, than actually be truly defensible with the consequent sacrifice of convenience and comfort that an authentic work of fortification would have entailed. There was a general feeling at the time that wealth should be flaunted. Amongst the nobility, conspicuous consumption was a norm, and the new men were no different in pursuing material goals and in not being frightened to display their wealth. Cromwell's arms include purses, representing his time as Treasurer, and this motif figures prominently in the decoration of his Great Tower. Like the Herberts' Yellow Tower of Gwent at Raglan (Monmouthshire) and the Great Tower of Lord Hastings at Ashby, this tower of Cromwell's at Tattershall, along with his Strong Tower at South Wingfield, was built to broadcast a message about power, arrival and permanence. Although brick, in low profile and backed by thick earthen banks (the favoured building material for fortifications in the next century), might seem an odd choice for Cromwell, but he would have justified his choice with a number of practical, aesthetic and symbolic considerations. Particularly in the eastern counties, brick was in the process of becoming a popular material. Whilst there are stories of bricks being used as ballast in the wool-ships returning empty from northern Europe, there were also local clay-pits and a brick-making industry.

At Edlington Moor, 4 miles (6km) to the north of Tattershall, Cromwell established extensive brick-pits, run by a Dutchman, who produced a million bricks there in the 1434/5 season. Cromwell also owned pits in Boston, from which he supplied large quantities of bricks to Bardney Abbey as part of a commercial operation. There was also a growing pool of craftsmen who could challenge the skills of the stone-masons, foremost amongst them being John Cowper who worked for William Waynflete, bishop of Winchester who built brick palaces with Great Towers at Esher and Farnham (Surrey). Waynflete, a local boy, and Cromwell's friend and executor of his will, also built the grammar school in his native town. Apart from John Southell, the clerk of works, John Cowper's is one of the few names recorded in Tattershall's building accounts, the builders generally being referred to as 'breke-masons' of mainly Flemish or north German origin. To set off the brickwork, the local Ancaster stone is used only for quoins, stringcourses and fireplaces. The tower is 110ft (33.5m) high, with sides of 87ft (26.5m) by 67ft (20.5m).

If Tattershall fails to meet the strictest criteria of a castle, then it must be described as a palace. Despite the constraints of pre-existing structures, Cromwell's builder managed to insert the monumental great tower between two earlier towers and the hall in the courtyard, but still maintain its dominant aspect. The east front we see today would have been largely obscured by the complex of buildings that included the hall through which the tower was accessed at two levels. So the show front would have been that on the west. The inspiration for the tower is thought by Lord Curzon to have come from some of the chateaux Cromwell would have seen in France, and in particular, Vez (Oise), with its tall square donjon and corner turrets. At Tattershall, the vaulted basement, with walls 20ft (6m) thick, contained a well and storage space. The ground floor room has been interpreted as a mess hall for the immediate household servants, and both basement and ground floor were disconnected from the rest of the tower for security reasons. Contemporary accounts by Falstolf's secretary speak of Cromwell having over one hundred liveried retainers living at Tattershall, in addition to his household servants. When he rode to London prior to being invested with the office of Treasurer, he was accompanied by 120 armed and liveried horsemen. It was often prudent to hold such retainers at arm's length, so the tower was a private retreat for Cromwell and his immediate suite of family and servants. The upper three floors were connected by spiral staircases in the southeast corner turret, but the first floor room was entered from the adjoining hall complex. This arrangement made for a much more imposing entrance into the Lord's private domain, but also allowed for more control over who actually made it that far. The second and third floors contained an audience chamber and a private chamber. The decoration is sumptuous and the workmanship remarkable. Decorative brickwork, mouldings, rib-vaults, panelling, carving and traceried windows all contribute to a feeling that provincial life could not get much better than this. Above these was the open roof level, now much restored, giving access to the machicolation gallery and the four octagonal corner turrets. Although there are several dozen rooms in the tower, there are no services, as there was never any intention that the tower should be self-sufficient. The communal activities of the castle took place in the attached hall and chapel, serviced by their adjacent kitchens, whose foundations survive to the south of the tower.

An eighteenth-century engraving by Buck shows the hall with a double-height bay window, similar to that in the bishop's palace at Lincoln. The inner bailey, basically the original thirteenth-century castle, thus accommodated the nucleus of Cromwell's palace. An outer bailey, surrounded by a moat fed by the River Bain, contained the rest of the buildings necessary for a grand household of at least two hundred souls. The gabled building known as the Guardhouse (now serving as the National Trust shop) probably represents one end of a range of lodgings for the liveried retainers whose stables still occupy the northern part of the outer bailey. The rest of the bailey was taken up by stores, brew-houses, smithies and all the other services necessary for the smooth running of a fifteenth-century palace.

In 1458, a Dutchman named Peter Lyndon is recorded as being paid to build a tower on the northeast of the College site. Tattershall castle was only one component in Cromwell's grand design. The adjacent rebuilt church, the College and the row of almshouses completed the complex. Having been appointed to further, more local, office as Constable of Nottingham Castle and Warden of Sherwood Forest, Cromwell died in 1456, unable to see his project finished, but Bishop Waynflete saw it through to completion. Whether Cromwell was satisfied with the balance he achieved, we will never know. The tensions between creating a fortress and palace, comfortable and ostentatious on the one hand, and not quite becoming the over-mighty subject on the other, not to mention overawing the local peasantry whilst not provoking royal disapproval, must all have contributed to a feeling of being on the knife-edge. Cromwell must have thought it worthwhile.

TOWER-HOUSES IN BRICK

Such was the impact of Tattershall that it spawned a whole clutch of imitations. In fact Cromwell seemed so pleased with his tower that he built it twice. The Tower on the Moor at Woodhall Spa is only 4 miles (6km) from Tattershall on the Cromwell manor of Whitehall, and has been described as a hunting lodge. Only an octagonal corner turret of 60ft (18m) remains, although there was more than this once, but it is impossible to know just how much was completed. By 1472, just sixteen years after Cromwell's death, bricks were being removed to complete work at Tattershall itself.

A more obvious copy is Buckden Towers (Cambridgeshire), the palace built between 1472 and 1496, by two bishops of Lincoln Rotherham, and Russell who also built in brick at the Chancery in the cathedral close. The similarities are so striking that Buckden has been described as a two-thirds scale replica of Tattershall. Many shared characteristics include: the tower itself with basement, four upper storeys and octagonal corner turrets; the brickwork with diapering; quoins and stringcourses in stone; the gabled gatehouses and their connecting ranges. The one striking difference is that any pretence at a serious defensive capability is undermined by the fact that the great tower is overshadowed by the adjacent pre-existing church tower. A survey of 1647 referred to the great tower at Buckden as 'the king's lodgings', which would suggest that the purpose of the building was to offer suitably grand surroundings for the bishops' most important patron, the one to whom they owed their status and style. It must be remembered that Buckden was not only on the Great North Road, but deep in the heart of the diocese of Lincoln, right up until a re-organisation of boundaries in 1836, which took it into Ely.

Nearer to Tattershall geographically, but later in date, are two square, brick towers on the outskirts of Boston. Rochford Tower in Skirbeck/Fishtoft has a vaulted basement with three floors above, reached by a spiral staircase. Each corner has a corbelled-out octagonal turret, that at the southeast angle containing the stairs being higher than the others. There are some details in stone mainly around the windows. Peter Lyndon, who worked at Tattershall, has been linked to Rochford as well. This makes Pevsner's building date of *c.*1450–60 more likely than Wight's *c.*1510. Rochford also displays signs of comfortable living, with traces of religious mural paintings remaining in the first-floor chamber. Nearer to the centre of Boston is the slightly shorter Hussey Tower (*23*), of two storeys over a vaulted ground floor, and with similarly corbelled-out angle turrets. At the northeast angle, an octagonal turret projects through its whole height, and contains the spiral staircase. The tower has stone detail in the two-light windows, and surviving door openings and a roof scar show that a hall and a chamber-block abutted the tower on its east side, giving spacious accommodation. The tower was long known as Benyngton's Tower and it may be inferred that it was built around 1460 by John Benyngton, Boston's collector of customs, and as a JP, an associate of Ralph Cromwell. John, Lord Hussey was attainted after the 1536 Pilgrimage of Grace, and the tower was being dismantled by 1565.

It appears fairly certain that both Rochford and Hussey Towers were built around 1460 from bricks made at Cromwell's Boston brick-works. A number of quite specific details, most tellingly the construction of the stairs, link them both to the Tower on the Moor, itself a spin-off from Tattershall. That leaves the question of defence. As at Tattershall, there are enough gestures to suggest that defence was a consideration, if not the over-arching one. The final putative member of the Tattershall school is less obvious and may not be a candidate at all. Ayscoughfee Hall in Spalding is an agglomeration of several periods and styles. It would appear that a simple rectangular tenement built at right-angles to the river possibly sometime around 1420, soon after had a tower-like feature, with two floors over a semi-basement, added to its north side. This exhibits similar features to the towers we have been examining, except that all the detailing was in cut or moulded brick. A nineteenth-century makeover heightened the tower and added stone details in an attempt at Tattershallisation. All these subsequent enlargements and modifications have obscured the origins of this house, which is often described as a Tudor H-plan house. However, there is ample evidence that a much earlier house had a brick strong-tower, in many ways similar to others of the period in the county.

The Later Medieval and Tudor Period (c.1300–1600)   75

23 ROCHFORD TOWER: near Boston, this is one of a series of local brick tower-houses that appear to be influenced by Tattershall Castle

THE WARS OF THE ROSES IN LINCOLNSHIRE

Here is not the place to attempt even a summary of the ramifications of the Wars of the Roses, but there were events which either took place in Lincolnshire, or intimately involved Lincolnshire's inhabitants. Following the comprehensive Yorkist defeat at Wakefield in 1460, the victorious Lancastrian army set out on its journey south intent on ravaging the Yorkists' properties on the way. As rumours of this approaching 'plague of locusts … the whirlwind from the north' filtered through, those with property and treasure to protect took precautions. Abbot John of Crowland blocked the causeways and staked the waterways leading to the abbey, hiding away the abbey's treasures, fearing something 'worse than Attila's Huns'. He need not have worried, as the rampaging troops kept to the Great North Road, pausing only to sack the Yorkist towns of Grantham, Stamford, Peterborough and Huntingdon as they passed through. Within a short while however, Henry VI had been deposed and the Yorkist Edward IV was on the throne. Other fallout from this turnaround meant that prominent Lancastrians paid the ultimate price. Examples amongst the Lincolnshire lords include William Lord Tailboys of Kyme who was beheaded in 1461, and Thomas de Roos likewise three years later having been on the losing side at the Battle of Hexham.

Before long, Edward, in turn, was threatened by a cabal of nobles, including the earl of Warwick who had been plotting with his brother Clarence and the exiled Queen Margaret. In 1470, they latched onto the wholly disproportionate escalation of what appears to have been a private quarrel between Sir Thomas Burgh of Gainsborough, a staunch Yorkist who had rescued the king from captivity, and Richard Lord Willoughby, now Lord Welles, of an opposite persuasion. Having damaged de Burgh's manor house, Welles raised the men of Lincolnshire in rebellion against Edward who, having realised that Warwick's offer of help in putting down the rebellion was false, set off with his army to intercept the rebels before they could meet up with Warwick and Clarence's army at Leicester. The ensuing battle outside Stamford was a disaster for the Lincolnshire rebels. Having located their position, Edward drew up his army to the north, cutting off their retreat, and executed the older Welles in full view of both armies. Thus demoralised it took only a volley of cannon fire to disperse them. So panic-stricken were the fleeing soldiers that in their haste to get away and to dissociate themselves from Warwick, they threw away their livery as they ran, hence the popular name for the battle of 'Lo(o)secoat Field', although there are more prosaic explanations involving pig-sties. Many of the fleeing rebels were cut down, and local woodland is still known as 'Bloody Oaks'. The inevitable round of summary executions that quickly followed included the younger Welles, his brother-in-law, Sir Thomas Dymoke of Scrivelsby, and Richard Warren, commander of the rebel infantry. Incidentally, the Dymokes' challenging behaviour at coronations continued up to that of George IV's, where it was felt that the unseemly rowdiness was inappropriate to such a solemn occasion, and the practice was discontinued.

There are a number of further fifteenth-century sites which, though not strictly fortifications, display defensive features and warrant examination. It has often been

The Later Medieval and Tudor Period (c.1300–1600) 77

24 GAINSBOROUGH OLD HALL: the strong tower of the de Burgh's manor that was repeatedly damaged during the fifteenth century

25 SCRIVELSBY: within this later building is the timber-framed gatehouse range, all that survives of the home of the Dymokes, hereditary Champions of England

assumed that Sir Thomas Burgh's house at Gainsborough (*24*) was completely destroyed by the Lancastrians under Lord Welles in 1470, but given that much work of the first half of the fifteenth century remains, and that the house had been completely repaired prior to a visit by Richard III in 1484, it is likely that time has over-estimated the damage. It might also have been in Burgh's interest at the time to over-inflate his claim for political mileage. Burgh's house was probably a quadrangle, although there is no evidence of its fourth (south) side, but there is every likelihood that there was a curtain wall with a gatehouse thus enclosing a courtyard. The timber-framed hall is from the original build, and materials used in the kitchen point to a similar date. It has been suggested that the two-storey oriel window inserted into the fabric of the hall might have been imported. The octagonal strong-tower on the northeast corner dates from the third quarter of the fifteenth century, the time of rebuilding after the misunderstanding with Lord Welles. The tower is an irregular octagon in shape, of two storeys, and is built in brick with a half-hexagonal projection to the east, and a higher hexagonal stair-turret to the south. It is embattled, but its faux machicolations would deceive few attackers. A number of brick details are very similar to features at Tattershall. Successive re-modellings, particularly Hickman's around 1600, have drastically altered the building's general appearance, but the tower is still impressive and represents Burgh's quest for domestic security.

Little remains of the Dymokes' house at Scrivelsby (*25*) beyond a late fourteenth-century timber-framed gatehouse range, later encased in brick. It would have formed one side of a quadrangle within a moat. Halstead Hall, near Stixwould on the doorstep of Edlington Moor brick-works, stands in a moat, dated by excavation to the late thirteenth century, dug around a pre-existing timber aisled hall on a stone foundation. Subsequently a brick house was built whose gatehouse remains, now converted to use as a barn and usually dated to the early fifteenth century. It has been argued that it could be earlier, and might have been the home of Baldwin the Dutchman, whose bricks were used to build Tattershall, and who was known to have a farm in the Edlington neighbourhood. Another Tudor house built as a quadrangle was South Kelsey Hall. Here, one of the octagonal, brick corner towers survives attached to the farmhouse that now occupies the site.

LOVELL'S REBELLION AND THE LINCOLNSHIRE RISING

Though these events were some forty years apart, they are linked together by some of the personalities involved. Even after the apparent conclusion of the Wars of the Roses and the firm hand with which Henry VII governed, troubles continued. Sir William Lovell had come ashore with Henry Bolingbroke and accompanied Henry V to France in 1430, but after his death fighting on the Lancastrian side, his son, Sir Francis was brought up as a Yorkist. He was with Richard III in Lincoln when news of Buckingham's revolt came through in October 1483. Richard ennobled him and they fought side-by-side at Bosworth Field, after which Lovell was declared a traitor. In 1486 he was one of the leaders of a rebellion against Henry VII that was quickly crushed. Amongst those local notables fighting on Henry's behalf on this occasion was Lord John Hussey, son of Sir William, who had served as Edward IV's Lord Chief Justice. The young Hussey's efforts brought him to royal attention and he was given diplomatic assignments abroad. In 1529, as Baron Hussey of Sleaford, he was a signatory to Henry VIII's petition to the Pope for divorce, but his next post as chamberlain to the Princess Mary exposed him to the intrigues surrounding the king's actions, particularly those deemed to be anti-catholic. He was involved in the movement, centred on the north of England, to depose Henry, substitute Mary as a catholic monarch, and to reverse the dissolution of the monasteries. This came to a head in Lincolnshire in October 1536, beginning as a riot in Louth when Nicholas Melton, a shoemaker calling himself Captain Cobbler, occupied the parish church along with fellow concerned parishioners, to protest about growing government control and interference in religious affairs, as personified in Thomas Cromwell, Henry VIII's minister.

It so happened that the visits of commissioners for tax assessment, for the suppression of the monasteries, and for the visitation of the clergy, had all coincidentally fetched up together around Louth, Caistor and Horncastle. Many of the local gentry were coerced into joining in the disturbances, and their apparent support was misconstrued as leadership by many of the locals. Similar riots occurred in Gainsborough where the Old Hall was burned (again), in Alford, and in Market Rasen. Arrangements were made to muster men from all over Lindsey, under their own elected captains, in Lincoln. Meanwhile at Horncastle, the bishop's chancellor, Dr Raynes, was murdered, and a servant of Lord Cromwell, unfortunately named Thomas Wolsey, was hanged. The host then marched toward Lincoln gathering numbers as it progressed. The bishop's palace at Nettleham was sacked, suffering damage but remaining habitable, and the host camped outside the city. The city authorities were advised by Lord Hussey to secure the city against the host, but unable to persuade his own tenants to march against the rebels, he laid himself open to accusations of taking their side. The king mustered troops at Nottingham under the earl of Shrewsbury, and at Huntingdon and waited for ordnance to arrive from the Tower of London. The rebels, with cannon of their own from Grimsby, next marched on Sleaford and Lincoln.

All this time, the gentry were trying to dissociate themselves from the Rising, and waiting for the host's enthusiasm to abate, and the money to run out. Always maintaining their loyalty to the king, the rebel army was in a cleft stick. By continuing their violent protest they were committing treason. The Duke of Suffolk had arrived at his wife's house, Grimsthorpe Castle, with several thousand troops, and the Rising was rapidly running out of steam. Orders were given that arms should be abandoned in Lincoln market place, that folk should return home, and that Henry, their king for nearly thirty years, would be merciful, despite great provocation, and would issue conditional pardons. However, the collapse of the Rising brought swift retribution. Two dozen ringleaders were executed, many of them priests, including the abbots of Kirkstead and Barlings. Lord Hussey of Sleaford was accused of not taking prompt action against the rebels, and despite his defence that he could not have mustered troops locally as no one would have borne arms against his neighbour, he was found guilty of lack of moral fibre and beheaded. There appears to be an element of sour grapes behind the accusation by Robert Carre of Sleaford, that Hussey could find manpower easily enough when he wanted to show off his pomp and importance at the assize, but failed to gather support in what might have become a national emergency. Hussey must certainly have been in sympathy with the aims of the rebels, but seems to have paid a heavy price for trying to sit on the fence. One leader, Robert Aske, fled north to take part in what became known as the Pilgrimage of Grace, for which this Lincolnshire venture had but raised the curtain.

ALARMS AND EXCURSIONS

A number of events in Elizabeth's reign necessitated raising troops, ensuring that powder and shot had been obtained, and that the organisation to mobilise troops was in place. Parades were held in 1569 when measures were taken to counter the revolt of the northern earls. Again in 1588, the year of the Armada, and 1595, when invasion was anticipated with an English force securing Brest on behalf of the future Henry IV against a Spanish attack, the county's military resources were inspected and assessed. In 1599, some 300 men, including twenty-seven lances and thirty-nine light horse, were raised in Lincolnshire to fight against the Irish rebels under Tyrone. The army was under the command of the Earl of Essex, and Sir Edward Dymoke, by virtue of his post as Champion of England, sought to command the Lincolnshire contingent, given that Sir John Bolles, possibly a more competent commander, was already serving in Ireland.

four

The Stuart and Georgian Periods (*c.*1600–1815)

THE CIVIL WARS

During the Civil Wars, Lincolnshire occupied a strategically uncomfortable, constantly contested, and largely uncommitted position between the firmly held territories of the protagonists. To the south, the River Welland effectively marked the northern border of the parliamentarian heartlands of East Anglia. To the north, the River Humber formed a barrier to the southward expansion of royalist Yorkshire, and occupation of its south bank was to play a part in the siege of parliamentarian Hull. On the west, control of the Trent crossings was to become a key factor in the operations around the great fortress of Newark-upon-Trent, whose retention by the royalists was crucial to keeping open their lines of communication between Oxford and the north. On the east, the coastal havens provided inviting opportunities to land reinforcements, arms and equipment for the waiting militias. Support for both sides was therefore always patchy.

The king visited Lincoln to rally support in July 1642, and must have been disappointed by the lukewarm response, with fewer than 200 horses and men promised. However there were royalist supporters who did a little more to help. Stephen Anderson of Manby Hall, for instance, sold the village and attached lands of Appleby, to raise money for the king. An attempt to land arms from a royalist ship at Skegness was unsuccessful, but the armoury of the Lincolnshire trained bands was seized for the king in August. A group of officers with experience in the continental wars, landed near Boston intending to join the royalist army, but were seized by local troops and sent under escort to London. Appointed Lord Lieutenant of Lincolnshire by the king, Lord Willoughby d'Eresby, created Earl of Lindsey in

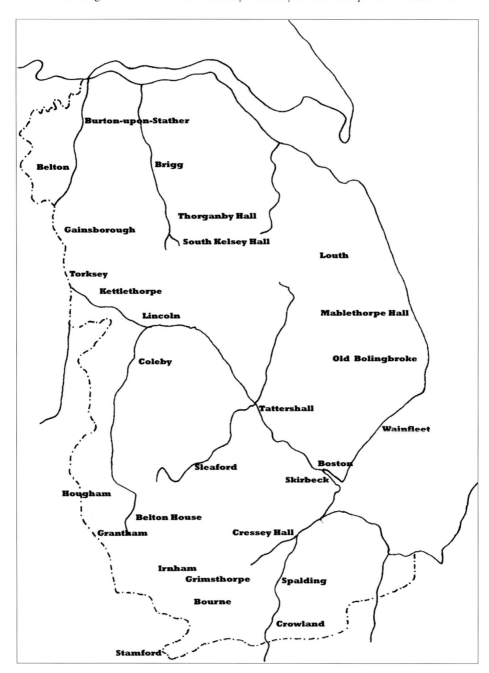

Fig. 6 Civil War sites mentioned in the text

1627, began to raise troops, assisted by Sir Charles Bolle and Sir William Pelham, who had already denied the parliamentarians access to the Lincoln magazine. Parliament, however, regarding the county as within its own sphere of influence, appointed Lord Willoughby of Parham as its commissioner, and invoked the Militia Act to declare delinquent any men of Lincolnshire promoting the king's recruitment campaign or failing to enrol for Parliament. This confused situation set the tone for the up and down campaigns of the four years ahead, played out within a context where neutrality was the preferred option for many wishing to avoid social upheaval (**Fig. 6**).

ACTION ON THE HUMBER AND IN NORTH LINCOLNSHIRE

The first siege of parliamentarian Hull in July 1642 demonstrated the importance of the Lincolnshire bank of the Humber. As part of the blockade, 200 royalist horse were sent to take Barton-upon-Humber to prevent reinforcements being shipped across the river. The parliamentarian navy was instrumental in breaking the blockade, running past the ineffectual royalist batteries established on both sides of the river.

A second siege in the autumn of 1643, involving a much closer investment of the town, resulted in the evacuation of the parliamentarian horse and up to twenty troops of cavalry under Sir Thomas Fairfax by boat across the river into Lincolnshire – there were neither sufficient fresh water nor grazing for the horses within the tight defended perimeter. Royalist batteries were set up east of Hull on the north bank at Paull, and to the west at Whitgift on the south bank, but it was still impossible to prevent ships, such as those that landed 500 men under Sir John Meldrum in October, getting through. Once again, the siege was lifted, partly because there was insufficient royalist support in Lincolnshire to make the blockade conclusive, especially after Winceby (see below). Not only did the royalists fail to capture Hull, but the siege also tied up a large army that could have been better employed in the south, threatening London.

One function of the garrison throughout the war, was to carry out raids on royalist centres in north Lincolnshire, such as Thorganby Hall near Caistor. Having changed hands, the hall was again sacked, this time by rebel royalists in 1648, to which year evidence of re-building may still be dated. Brigg had been established as a parliamentarian garrison by mid-1643, and earthwork defences were dug around the town in 1644. Burton upon Stather marked the most northerly crossing of the Trent before it joined the Humber, and this key point with its ferry changed hands several times before parliamentarian troops, brought by boat from Hull, secured it in late 1643, raising earthwork defences on both sides of the river.

NEWARK AND THE GREAT NORTH ROAD

Whilst royalist armies attempted to take Hull, parliamentarian ones in February 1643 commenced an almost continuous siege of Newark-upon-Trent, lasting until its final fall in May 1646. Despite occasional hard-fought onslaughts – such as that of Major-General Ballard leading Lincolnshire men in February 1643, and almost penetrating the defences – most of the time was spent in watchful idleness. It could be argued that most of the action was going on in the detached royalist garrisons and in the corresponding parliamentarian outposts that had been established in an attempt to prevent relief from reaching Newark itself. It was this proliferation of garrisons and all the raiding that went with them that caused so much trouble to the people of Lincolnshire for the duration of the war. By 1644, Lincolnshire was described as:

> A ruinated country [where] noe mann hath anny thing to call his owne or asur himself a quiett nights slep they are so surrounded with garrisons both of the king's and the parliaments what the one leaves the other takes.

Within a short time of the king raising his standard at Nottingham, Coleby Hall was raided by royalists led by the sheriff, Sir Edward Heron, with sixty troopers, attempting to assert the king's influence around Lincoln by arresting known parliamentarians.

So right from the beginning of the war, nobility and gentry alike began to fortify their houses. In 1642, South Kelsey Hall, the moated manor house of the parliamentarian Sir Edward Ayscough, was targeted by local royalists seeking to pre-empt a parliamentarian takeover of the county by seizing arms. An earthwork consisting of a three-sided, open-backed, banked and ditched enclosure lies to the south of the moat, commanding much of the approach road, from some height. Behind it is a raised bank, and in front, and slightly lower, was a scarped platform overlaying earlier features. It is possible that this represents a battery, equipped with cannon, and raised by Sir Edward to defend his house against an expected attack.

Cressey Hall near Gosberton, the residence of sheriff Heron was garrisoned and fortified in order to receive the arms thus confiscated. As royalist troops returned with the arms taken from South Kelsey, they were attacked. Heron and his men sallied forth from Cressey Hall to aid this detachment, but were routed and captured. The hall was then garrisoned for a while by a parliamentarian detachment. One of the problems facing both sides was establishing a balance between placing troops in static garrisons and in maintaining effective field armies, capable of movement and forcing issues.

By 1645, half the royalist strength was deployed in garrisons, and therefore unavailable for the big set-piece battles that would ultimately decide the outcome of the war. Early in the war, royalist interests on the Great North Road and the River Trent were secured by a ring of strongholds that included Belton House, Grantham, Stamford and Gainsborough. Grantham was taken by Parliament but was always vulnerable to attack from Newark, and the town was stormed and its fortifications destroyed in spring 1643. Although the royalists never left a permanent garrison, the town continued to be disputed for the rest of the year. Around the same time, on 13 May, Belton, held for the king by the Brownlows, was the scene of a significant skirmish when a royalist force of twenty troops of horse was scattered by a smaller body of cavalry under Cromwell and Willoughby. This was one of the first tests for Cromwell's newly trained Ironsides and the action is notable for the tactics employed. Cavendish drew up his cavalry three deep in the Swedish manner, offering a longer front to the enemy, but Lord Willoughby and Cromwell preferred the Dutch deployment of cavalry five deep, giving a smaller target. When the parliamentarian cavalry charged, they were ordered to hold their fire until within half a pistol shot of the royalists. Their volley was devastating, and the more so as royalist cavalry wore no back armour, so were cut down as they fled, with some sixty being killed and forty-five being taken prisoner, along with six colours. A lane on the south side of Syston Park is still known as Dead Mans Lane, and has yielded skeletons, possibly those of fleeing royalists. Cavendish was killed two months later trying to retake Gainsborough.

Stamford was held for Parliament and its medieval defences were put into a state of repair, but it fell to royalist raiding parties in April 1643 and again the next year, although the raiders moved on each time. The burghers of Stamford must eventually have indulged in a collective sigh of relief in 1646 when engineers from both sides surveyed the place and found it indefensible, and unsuitable for military purposes, despite its position astride the Great North Road. Kettlethorpe Hall was held by the parliamentarian Hall family, who may have been involved in the skirmishing that went on around the Trent crossings in 1644–5. A roughly square banked and ditched enclosure overlies earlier features, and dominates falling ground to the north. On one side was a small, two-celled building. This could represent a battery with magazine or powder store. Other adjacent earthworks may indicate outworks.

There were many limited engagements, of which one at Hougham was fairly typical. Hougham House (**26**), guarding an important crossing of the river Witham near Grantham, was a medieval fortified manor house, the hunting-lodge of the Brudenell family. It had a strong gatehouse, 4ft-thick (1.5m-thick) walls and a moat, which remains near the present house. It was taken by surprise by a royalist raiding party from Newark in the early hours of 10 June 1645, when they found the gate left ajar. Colonel Rossiter attempted to recapture it later the same day and seized the gatehouse. He then sent for reinforcements, possibly because he needed musketeers to take the inner house to which the royalists had retired. On 12 June the house fell to Rossiter and Colonel Grey's infantry, storming across the moat, waist-deep in places, and scaling a 10ft-high (3m-high) wall. Some sixty prisoners were taken, for the loss of half-a-dozen parliamentarian soldiers, and around twenty wounded.

The strategically placed town of Gainsborough, controlling an important crossing of the Trent, was attacked by Willoughby's parliamentarians. Robert, earl of Kingstown, the royalist commander, was caught unawares, but retreated to the strongest house in town. He was forced to surrender on 20 July 1643, when the

26 HOUGHAM MANOR: the moated platform of the medieval house is visible here, occupied by both the Georgian rebuilding of the 1620 house, and remnants of the medieval one; the house was a royalist outpost until taken by surprise in June 1645

27 TORKSEY MANOR: occupying an important location at the junction of the Fossdyke and the Trent, this unfortified Tudor house changed hands several times during the War; it was finally retaken by surprise by royalist troops from Newark who fired it before withdrawing with 140 prisoners

building was fired, but was then unfortunately killed by friendly fire. Within a short ten days, the town was attacked by Newcastle, who began a bombardment. The terrifying and unpredictable plunging fire from a mortar caused the townsfolk to riot, insisting that Willoughby should surrender the town. A few months later, on 20 December 1643, the town was retaken by Meldrum's parliamentarians. The undefended Tudor brick manor house of Torksey Castle (**27**), with its four octagonal towers, which commanded the junction of the Fossdyke and the Trent, also changed hands several times. The castle was in temporary occupation by royalist troops from Newark in October 1644. In August of the next year, now occupied by parliamentarian troops, a force from Newark returned and stormed the house using scaling ladders, taking the garrison by surprise whilst their commander was away. Taking 140 prisoners, they fired the house and retired before parliamentarian reinforcements could arrive. The gaunt ruins still stand by the river. Even Woolsthorpe church, held as an outpost of royalist Belvoir, was wrecked by cannon fire in early 1646, prior to the taking of Belvoir itself by Rossiter, and thereafter abandoned for a chapel situated conveniently nearer to the village. Another version has the church set on fire by negligent parliamentarian troopers who were camped out in it.

CIVIL WAR FORTIFICATIONS

The actual fortifications themselves were not of anything like the sophistication found on the continent of Europe, where the miseries of the Thirty Years War were coming to an end. While many soldiers and engineers had gained experience on one or both sides in that protracted ordeal, there was neither the time nor the resources to replicate the complex defences constructed around most continental cities, or added to many of the castles in the disputed areas. The fighting in the Civil Wars was often so fluid, so fragmented and so localised that such efforts were usually unwarranted anyway, even had they been practicable. Any stone building with a moat and a stout door could be adapted as a temporary strongpoint. As soon as the artillery arrived, then that was the time to surrender, but nine times out of ten, this point would never be reached as cannon tended to be held in a siege train and deployed only for the most important campaigns. It was usually enough to knock a few loopholes for muskets in stone or brick walls, to throw up banks and ditches, and to place obstacles across approach roads. If the odd light artillery piece was available, then an earthwork sconce with arrowhead bastions might be constructed. Banks were topped by palisades, and sharpened storm-poles were embedded at an angle of forty-five degrees to make it difficult for the enemy assault. Pits were dug with sharpened stakes in the bottom, and camouflaged with branches, and treetrunks with sharp branches, or with iron spikes knocked through them; *abbatis* and *chexaux-de-frises* were laid as further obstacles.

Many of these devices had been employed since ancient times, and would be used again in the Vietnam War. Towns with existing medieval defences piled earth up against the inner face of town walls to absorb the shock and penetration of cannon balls and to provide a stable platform for the defenders' guns. Earth bastions were sometimes added to particularly vulnerable points, such as gates or angles. Inside each gate was a fall-back position, or *retrenchment*, constructed of wagons, timber, wool-sacks or whatever was available, providing a second line of defence. Despite the professionalism and experience of many of the leaders and specialists, we must remember that the majority of participants on both sides were largely untrained, unwilling, and inexperienced. As the war progressed, many formations had become well drilled and had proved their competence, with a consequent gain in both confidence and morale. But there was nevertheless a strong element of amateurism and incompetence on both sides throughout the conflict.

CROWLAND AND SOUTH LINCOLNSHIRE

From the outbreak of war, the south of the county saw constant skirmishing between the parliamentarians based along the line of the Nene and the Welland, and isolated pockets of royalist resistance such as Crowland, fortified by royalists in March 1643. This action was notable for its use by the defenders of a human shield. On word getting abroad that Captain Welbie was planning to declare Crowland for the king, a Spalding minister, one Mr Ram, wrote to the Crowland folk, seeking to dissuade them from this course. Mr Ram and three elderly colleagues were then abducted from Spalding, and taken forcibly to Crowland. When the parliamentarian assault under Colonels Hobart and Irby began, these four were tied to stakes on the rampart, and only by chance were they not hit. When the attackers realised their identity, they broke off the assault and withdrew.

In the meantime, artillery had arrived and a bombardment began which lasted three days. The story goes that the defenders of Crowland became a little complacent after their first repulse of the parliamentarian assault, and were taken by surprise when the assault was renewed from three directions. Even then, the hostages were once again exposed to the attackers' fire before the town fell on 28 April. However, the conditions of such skirmishing meant that each side had to be prepared to relinquish gains, only to retake them at a later date as the balance of power, and the two sides' relative priorities, oscillated.

Twice evacuated by Parliament during 1644, Crowland was again garrisoned by royalists in October. It was besieged by Fairfax and Rossiter, but the flooded fen conditions hindered an assault and surrender came at the end of 1644 through starvation. The defences must have been makeshift but effective, consisting of strong banks and wet ditches linking the various surviving elements of the abbey ruins themselves and the town's defences. One aisle of the old abbey church now forms the parish church, but the rest was already ruinous at that time. During October, the defenders had attempted a breakout from Crowland, hoping to link up with a relief expedition from Belvoir and Newark. Following up a royalist raid on Burghley House to obtain livestock, the parliamentarian troops occupied Bourne, possibly re-fortifying the castle there, to prevent a royalist move on Crowland. However,

28 GRIMSTHORPE CASTLE: the medieval castle had been transformed in Tudor times and was the home of Montagu Bertie, Earl of Lindsey, whose father, the royalist commander, had died at Edgehill; it was held as a royalist garrison before being taken by parliamentarian troops in April 1644

they were then fortunate to intercept a royalist messenger and realised that the main royalist relief force was moving down from Belvoir. Arrangements were made for the Derby, Nottingham and Leicestershire army to send a force to rendezvous at Woolsthorpe. The force from Bourne arrived first and began to skirmish in a bid to delay action until the other force arrived. They were eventually forced into engaging the royalists just as, as if right on cue, the second parliamentarian force arrived to take them in the flank. The result was a royalist rout with some sixty dead, many by drowning in the millpond, and some 300 prisoners taken.

To protect the borders of the Eastern Association, there were parliamentarian redoubts in the fens immediately south of Crowland, at Clough's Cross, Dowesdale, and Guyhirn (whose exact locations are unknown), as well as stronger defences at Wisbech, Leverington and Stanground near Peterborough. The Earl of Lindsey's castle of Grimsthorpe (**28**) was garrisoned in 1643, only falling to the Earl of Manchester's troops in April 1644. Irnham House, a little to the north of Grimsthorpe, was garrisoned in July 1644 by royalists from Newark, possibly to fill the vacuum caused by the fall of Grimsthorpe. Burghley House, just to the south of Stamford, but now in Cambridgeshire, represents another disputed pile. A royalist force took possession of the late-Tudor mansion in July 1643, but Colonel Cromwell, the local parliamentarian commander, moved swiftly to counter this threat to the Eastern Association border, and after a short, preliminary bombardment – whose effects can still be seen in the fabric of the house – prepared to storm.

There were very clear conventions governing the conduct of conflict at this time, and they were well understood. One such convention held that defenders, having been given the opportunity to surrender, but choosing to fight on, thus forcing their assailants to storm the place and to incur what they saw as unnecessary casualties, automatically forfeited any right to quarter, and could be slaughtered out of hand quite legitimately. The royalist surrender was immediate, and half-a-dozen officers and several hundred troops were captured.

Sleaford was another of those towns that regularly changed hands. Although it was a parliamentarian base for much of the war, it suffered constantly from royalist raids throughout 1643 and twice, in 1644, it actually fell to Rupert, but was quickly regained each time. A difficult place to defend with its decayed castle, its garrison was centred on the Old Place, a fortified house of the Carre family, 800 yards from the town centre on the Boston road.

LINCOLN IN THE WARS

The city of Lincoln played less of a decisive part in the wars than might have been expected, partly because of its vulnerability to raids from royalist Newark on one hand, and to its isolation in a ring of parliamentarian centres on the other. In spite of this, or more probably because of this, it changed hands several times. Early in the war it was held by Parliament but by July 1643 had been occupied by the Earl of Newcastle in an attempt to stem the advance of Cromwell and Willoughby, who had enjoyed a string of successes. Newcastle's initiative stopped the parliamentarian advance in its tracks, and as well as Lincoln, he garrisoned the castles of Bolingbroke and Tattershall, the moated Mablethorpe Hall and the town of Wainfleet. Tattershall was held throughout the war by Theophilus, third Earl of Lincolnshire, who had served as a colonel of a regiment in the service of Elizabeth of Bohemia in the 1620s. As a protestant peer, he declared for Parliament in 1642, and was named joint lord lieutenant with Willoughby of Parham, only relinquishing his hold on the castle for the duration of this brief royalist occupation in the summer of 1643.

At Wainfleet, the royalists attempted to fortify the bridge with earthwork defences in August 1643, in an attempt to isolate Boston, for a few months Parliament's last remaining stronghold in the county, and the base for any counter-attack. The parliamentarian response began by chasing the royalists out of Wainfleet, and laying siege to Bolingbroke Castle. In an attempt to raise this siege and to strengthen his hold on Lincoln, Newcastle sent a force that ran into Manchester's army outside Horncastle. Manchester, accompanied by Cromwell, had also been joined by Sir Thomas Fairfax and his cavalry, who had crossed the Humber from the besieged town of Hull. The resulting Battle of Winceby, on 11 October 1643, was a disaster for the royalists, losing 800 prisoners and having twenty-six colours captured. Under the pressure of successive cavalry charges, first by Cromwell, and then by Fairfax, the royalist foot were broken, and their cavalry fled the field, some being caught and cut down in a dead-end still known locally as 'Slash Hollow'. Two pieces of armour have been

The Stuart and Georgian Periods (c.1600-1815)   91

29 LINCOLN CASTLE: the second motte bearing the Observatory Tower, up whose slippery slopes parliamentarian troops swarmed to storm the castle in May 1644, retaining it for the duration

excavated in nearby Scrafield. By their late sixteenth-century style it would appear that they had been taken down off someone's wall, and brought back into service by some local gentleman fighting for his monarch.

Manchester's troops went on to mop up the remnants, and to retake a number of royalist garrisons such as Mablethorpe Hall and Brigg. In the middle of November, Bolingbroke surrendered to Willoughby, who slighted its defences. Lincoln had been retaken ten days after the battle, and a garrison under Sir John Gell was installed. These parliamentarian successes were followed by the re-capture of Gainsborough in December, and a resumption of the siege of Newark. In March 1644, Gell's troops were amongst those under Meldrum defeated by Prince Rupert outside Newark, and Lincoln was once again occupied by a royalist garrison of 2,000 men under Sir Francis Fane. With Rupert's main force back in Oxford, this garrison was left in a vulnerable position and Manchester took full advantage of the situation, investing the city in May with an army of 6,000 men.

The Roman and medieval defences of the castle, city, and cathedral close were all patched up by the defenders, and there is a contemporary reference to a sconce straddling one of the main roads into the city. A number of houses that had encroached onto the walls, as well as two churches, St Nicholas, Newport, and St Peter, Eastgate, were torn down. Following this controlled demolition, other houses were destroyed in an accidental fire, along with St Swithun's church. The defences at the top of the hill were now considered to be impregnable, added to which, on the next day (4 May), heavy rain rendered the slopes of the hill so slippery that an assault was

30 LINCOLN BISHOP'S PALACE: defended by Captain Bee and thirty men against 600 royalists in June 1648 during the Second Civil War; the palace, whose gatehouse, shown here, was built by Bishop Alnwick around 1440, was the smallest defensible space in the city available for the tiny garrison who were soon overwhelmed

impossible. Cromwell was despatched with the parliamentarian cavalry to intercept a relief force, and the foot began their attack at 3am on 6 May. Swarming up the hill with scaling ladders, they quickly reached the walls (**29**). The defenders hurled rocks down on them, but were soon overrun and begging for quarter. Some fifty royalists were killed, and the governor and 650 men captured, along with 2,000 muskets, while parliamentarian casualties were light. Manchester's troops were allowed to pillage the upper city.

The city, as a whole, suffered a great deal of damage in the fighting. An exploding gunpowder barrel demolished a church – probably St Michael-on-the-Mount. Four further churches were badly damaged in the fighting, one, St Botolphs, collapsing some time later, weakened by damage caused during the assault. After its capture, the city was garrisoned by parliamentarian troops under Thomas Hatcher, of Boston. After the Battle of Marston Moor, Manchester returned to Lincoln, but later in 1644, his army moved south, leaving the coast clear again for royalist adventures into Lincolnshire. Lincoln, along with Caistor, was only briefly occupied.

However, Lincoln's tribulations were not yet over. In June 1648, in the second Civil War, a force of rebel royalists, some 600 strong, crossed the Trent at Gainsborough and marched on Lincoln, which was defended only by Captain Bee with thirty men. Vastly outnumbered, Bee was forced to fall back into the Bishop's Palace (**30**), the only defensible structure small enough for his force to defend. The royalists under Sir Philip Monckton stormed the palace, setting fire to it, emptying the gaol of its occupants, looting the houses of known parliamentarians, and laying waste the city. Bee had managed to surrender on terms, but Monckton reneged on the agreement, taking Bee, his men and the city's mayor and aldermen away as prisoners, and heading back to Gainsborough. The royalists were soon overtaken and defeated near Nottingham by a strong force under Rossiter, and the prisoners were released. At last the city would have a chance to recover from the traumas of the war years.

BOSTON AND HOLLAND

Boston remained in parliamentarian hands for the entire war, and was one of the reasons why royalist gains could never be consolidated effectively. Newcastle failed to press home his advantage in 1643 because of this parliamentarian presence in his rear, and this ultimately led to the royalist defeat at Winceby. The town, strangely enough, despite its prominence in medieval times, had no significant fortifications, and this caused great anxiety to its defenders. After the dismissal of its governor, his successor Thomas Hatcher ensured that the town was surrounded by entrenchments that were anchored on the dykes and waterways around the town. Three brass sakers, two of them from Kings Lynn, were purchased for its defence during 1643, and mounted on the main roads into town.

A moated site in Skirbeck Quarter (TF321429) has been attributed to the Civil War period, and may represent an outer defence on the vulnerable southwestern approach. The estates of local royalists were sequestered to pay for the garrison troops and the fortifications, but few records of such expenditure survive. The Corporation may have thriftily put work out to contract, for Sir Samuel Luke, governor of Newport Pagnell (Buckinghamshire), having trouble getting his own fortifications built, wanted to know how Boston had saved two shillings in the pound. He found out when the rampart, built by an officer loaned to him from Boston, collapsed. Hatcher was replaced by Colonel Edward King of Ashby de la Launde, who became governor of Boston and Holland, building a power-base from which he might challenge Willoughby of Parham. He must have made enemies though, for it was Hatcher who headed the county's parliamentary committee in 1646. In 1649, Parliament rewarded the town's constancy by re-establishing a magazine there, and there was talk of a citadel. The town provided a regiment of foot to the army, which fought the final action of the war at Worcester in 1651, and no more was heard of the fort.

OTHER SIGNIFICANT ACTIONS

Apart from Winceby, there were only three other actions approaching the status of set-piece battles. The first was at Ancaster Heath, where the royalist army under Cavendish defeated a parliamentarian force led by Lord Willoughby on 11 April 1643, prior to advancing in the direction of Boston. Willoughby had sought to disrupt a royalist assembly in Grantham aimed at indicting parliamentarian supporters, but he was forced to retire and his cavalry put to flight. The second was at Gainsborough in July 1643 when Cromwell and Willoughby led their cavalry to the relief of the town. Having scattered the royalist cavalry they learned that a body of foot with two guns was a short distance away. Borrowing some infantry from the Gainsborough garrison, they advanced on the enemy, only to come up against the whole of Newcastle's army. A fighting withdrawal was hurriedly made. The third was at Riby Gap near Grimsby, where a parliamentarian force under Colonel Harrison was bested by royalists led by Colonel Foster, on 18 June 1645. Harrison, along with nine of his troopers, was killed, and was buried in Stallingborough church.

Along with all the other stories of the civil wars, a number relate to manor houses, one such local story being that Girsby Manor, a medieval house near Burgh-on-Bain, was destroyed by military action. In the ubiquitous 'Mary Queen of Scots slept here' tradition, Saltfleet Manor is claimed as Cromwell's lodging the night before Winceby, but this would seem rather too far distant if Cromwell played the part in the battle with which he is plausibly credited.

THE INVOLVEMENT OF THE LOCAL PEOPLE IN THE WARS

Lincolnshire people involved in the wars suffered mixed fortunes. Having commanded the royalist forces at the siege of Hull from April to August 1642, Robert Bertie, Earl of Lindsey led his Lincolnshire men to join the king's army at Edgehill.

The sixty-year-old Lindsey had wide and varied experience of war on the Continent, commanding Danish and Dutch troops. He had also served as Admiral, and as governor of Berwick. This experience, and his rank of Lieutenant General, gave him command of the royalist army. Having the wisdom to recognise that his Dutch methods of deployment would be easier for his inexperienced officers to apply, he advocated such an appropriate deployment of the army. Prince Rupert, however, was an exponent of the Swedish method of which he had successful experience, and so prevailed on the king to exempt him from accepting orders from anyone else. Charles I who had no experience of war at all chose to indulge the arrogance of his twenty-two-year-old nephew. In disgust, Lindsey stormed off to lead his own men into battle, resigning the post of commander-in-chief. In the ensuing fighting he was grievously wounded, and despite the attempts of his son Montagu to get treatment for him, he died of his wounds on 24 October 1642. His surviving son, Montagu Bertie, now the second Earl of Lindsey, was exchanged for a parliamentarian prisoner. He later fought at Newbury, was wounded at Naseby, and became Lord Chamberlain to Charles II at the Restoration.

Another royalist colonel at Edgehill was Sir John Bolles of Scampton. He survived Edgehill, but at the head of his regiment he was surprised by a strong parliamentarian force at Alton (Hampshire) on 13 December 1642. While the royalist cavalry escaped to Winchester, Bolles' men attempted to resist Waller's assault, first from positions in the churchyard, and then in the parish church itself. Tradition has it that after eighty of his men had been killed, Bolles was killed in the pulpit. The family continued to be represented in the royalist foot as both Colonel Bolles, an officer with previous experience, and Richard Bolles were signatories of the May 1643 'Humble Desires', a petition to Charles I to provide what we would now call logistical support, i.e. medical attention on the battlefield, recruiting and drafts into battle-weary regiments, pay, provisions and clothing. This Colonel Bolles may have been Sir John's brother, Sir George, killed at Winceby. Sir Charles Bolle, who was instrumental in raising royalist troops in 1642, raided Louth in 1644.

Happier was the case of Sir Gervase Scrope of Cockerington, one of those pledging support to the king at Lincoln, and another Lincolnshire gentleman fighting at Edgehill. Having received some sixteen wounds, he was stripped and left for dead on the battlefield, where he lay for two whole days. His son too was looking out for his father's interest, and having located him, revived him and got him to the safety of Oxford. Here, he made a full and miraculous recovery, and, one hopes, took no further part in the conflict, although after the war he was in great financial distress.

Just as the Earl of Lindsey and Sir John Bolles raised royalist regiments in Lincolnshire for service where they were needed, so did the parliamentarian army. In 1645, Colonel Rossiter raised a regiment composed of Lincolnshire men, which went on to fight on the right flank at Naseby. Interestingly, it had been intended as a force for use only in local operations. Sir Edward Ayscough, whom we met earlier, fortifying his house at South Kelsey against the local royalists, fought alongside Cromwell as a Captain of Horse at Gainsborough, and is one of the signatories of a letter in which the battle is described in some detail. He seems to have been part of Whalley's troop, and since Whalley had regimental responsibilities, perhaps Ayscough deputised for him. Colonel Edward King, as Manchester's proxy, having thoroughly undermined Willoughby's authority, sabotaged some of his plans, and broadcast his incompetence and lack of military success at every opportunity, assumed responsibility for leading the parliamentarian forces in Lincolnshire. In this he was aided by Cromwell, who regarded Willoughby as not entirely committed to the parliamentarian cause. In fact, in 1648, Willoughby was moved to join the royalist court in exile, but whether this reflects his leanings all along, or his disappointment at his treatment by supposed comrades, is impossible to say.

Whether under Colonel King or Willoughby of Parham, there seem to have been few attempts to achieve any wider co-ordination of local efforts in order to support regional initiatives, let alone national priorities. As did Grey in Leicestershire, King appears to have confined his activities to the insularity of his home county. No real sense of all for one, then. It is surely of significance that, no less than the royalists, the parliamentarian leadership were all inter-connected by a web of kinship and marriage. Within this network could be traced Ayscough, King, Wray, Irby, Whichcote and Hatcher, with a further connection by marriage to the Earl of Manchester. Many were offended when, in January 1644, Lincolnshire was absorbed into the Eastern Association, feeling that their local identity and freedom of action had been compromised. It can also be argued that little support was forthcoming from London. On 1 August 1643, Willoughby, apologising for being 'two teadious', had written to the speaker of the House of Lords, pointing out that his hold on Lincoln was tenuous, since 'these people are so coued that they will not defend the place'. He goes on to explain that Lincolnshire:

> hath neather reaceaved mony nor armes from the Parliament since I came into it, and if you expect any service from them, or that you hould it of any consequence, it must be supplied with both, and with that speed, or else it will be too late.

Such appeals may well have gone some way to diluting Parliament's confidence in their man in Lincolnshire. Confirming the ambivalence, alienation and reluctance of many of Lincolnshire's inhabitants' involvement in the wars, it comes as no surprise that many exploited the confused and fast-changing nature of the conflict to settle old scores, to secure personal fortunes, and to accrue political influence. Grantham was particularly bi-partisan, with the town councillors divided 50:50 in their allegiance, and the town assessed for taxation by both sides. Two of the royalist supporters, Robert Calcroft and George Lloyd, went off to serve in the royalist army. Along with several others, they were dismissed from their offices in 1647.

Those who stayed in the countryside for the duration will have had it no easier. The old order was eroded as the traditional leaders were replaced by less aristocratic pillars of society, and even the parish priest was quite likely to go off to fight for one side or the other, leaving his parishioners with nobody to 'officiate the cure'. Like many other isolated parts of the country, there was little real interest in what was happening on the national stage. In 1642, the inhabitants of the

Isle of Axholme opened the newly-built sluice-gates to flood their land, as a protest against the royal commission which had brought Cornelius Vermuyden, the Huguenot drainage engineer, to prepare the area for enclosure and development as arable land. Charles I had initiated this enterprise as a way of raising money independent of Parliament. The politics of this were no concern of the fen-dwellers, who merely resisted the threatened loss of their livelihood by attacking the drainage engineers who were forced to fortify their settlement at Belton – possibly known as 'Fort Dunkirk' – with timber palisades and ditches, traces of which were found during excavations in 2002. Many of the Huguenots were driven away to resettle in Thorney near Peterborough.

After the war was over, in 1649–50, the Levellers sought to hijack this revolutionary potential on the Isle of Axholme. They quickly found that neither king nor parliament figured in the argument. The locals were simply interested in seeking to safeguard their own future on a strictly parochial level. What was essentially a local affair petered out as the fen-men successfully sabotaged all the new works, resisted attempts to collect drainage tax by rioting, and were soon able to resume their normal lifestyle.

THE DUTCH WARS

Towards the end of the seventeenth century, Britain's rivalry with the Dutch over their respective spheres of influence in international trade had brought the two nations into a state of intermittent war. Although the recent experience of the civil wars and a distrust of soldiery in general aroused strongly held feelings in the general population, the government still felt the need to maintain garrisons around the country. This was basically as a precaution against the Dutch landing troops in an extended raid.

Hull was the local garrison, and a detachment of troops from Hull under an Ensign Elvidge was stationed in Lincoln in 1673 during the Third Dutch War. In an attempt to put a positive spin on the presence of troops belonging to a standing army, soldiers were allowed to perform useful acts for the community, or at least influential sections of that community. For example, in 1676 a file of musketeers formed an escort for a convoy of merchants' wagons travelling from Gainsborough down to London. Although the defences of Hull were kept up and armed with cannon, and a new Citadel was begun in 1681, there was no attempt at this time to place batteries on the Lincolnshire bank of the Humber, as had happened previously during the first civil war.

In 1660, Colonel Rossiter's Regiment had been re-constituted as the Lincolnshire trained band, which was re-branded in 1663 as the Militia. The 1696 Militia Returns list three companies of foot and a troop of horse under the Earl of Lindsey in Kesteven, and four companies of foot and a troop of horse in Holland. Doubts were expressed about the status of the militia on the Lindsey Coast, as there had been no muster in the previous six years. However, reasonable numbers were confidently recorded: eight companies of foot under Colonel Charles Dymocke (still the champion of England), and two troops of foot under Sir Edward Ayscough and Captain Matthew Lister. All these totalled almost 1,500 foot, and 333 horse.

Other upheavals in national affairs appear to have impacted little on the lives of Lincolnshire folk. A few indiscreet gentlemen were suspected of supporting the duke of Monmouth's claims to the throne, but no local action seems to have resulted. Despite reports of horsemen gathering at night near Tattershall, and the undoubted allegiance of some Lincolnshire gentry to the Jacobite cause, the county experienced little effect from the Glorious Revolution of 1688. Lord Willoughby of Eresby, both Lord Lieutenant and Earl of Lindsey following his father's death in 1701, was a supporter of William of Orange, and this generally set the tone for the county.

THE WARS WITH FRANCE

In contrast to the previous century, with the possible exception of contact with the odd privateer, the east coast had a relatively peaceful eighteenth century. The Enclosure Acts of the 1760s provoked some civil disorder in the fenlands, which could have got out of hand. The presence of four troops of the Royal North British Dragoons (later the Scots Greys) in Boston prevented the town being fired by rioters. By 1774 the common rights had been abolished in Holland, and the protesters had been beaten.

There was a scare in 1779 when a combined French and Spanish fleet sailed into the English Channel, raising the possibility of invasion. This was doubly disturbing, as the British warships stayed in harbour, and much of the army – including the locally raised Tenth Foot and 17th Light Dragoons – was away fighting in the American colonies. The response to this fright was the construction of batteries at Paull Cliff and on the opposite side of the river at Skitter Point. The operations and subsequent defeat of the American privateer John Paul Jones also spurred the Admiralty into stationing more powerful warships in the Humber estuary on a permanent basis. Some were there to support the convoy system, and some to be moored as floating batteries to protect the docks. Ships of the Royal Navy were based on many east coast ports to protect merchant shipping and the fishing fleet. The two-gun sloop, HMS *Woolf*, for instance, was based at Grimsby and intervened to capture a French privateer attacking English ships in the Humber estuary.

SAFEGUARDING THE COAST

As the international situation deteriorated further, so the need for stronger defences was recognised. The Humber was seen as a possible destination for a French invasion force from Holland, and so new batteries were built, one at Paull Point, another across the river at Stallingborough, and a further battery on the

Lincolnshire bank at Goxhill Ferry or White Booth Road. Later on in the war in 1811, the batteries at Skitter Point and Stallingborough were up-gunned with five and four twenty-four-pounders respectively. These batteries probably mounted their guns on stable platforms of granite setts or flagstones, firing either *en barbette* over a low parapet of stone, planks or earth-filled barrels, or else protruding through embrasures fashioned from *gabions*, wicker baskets filled with rubble. They may have been surrounded by ditches and earth banks as a precaution against landing parties. Larger warships made their appearance with the arrival of the sixty-four-gun HMS *Standard* and HMS *Lion* on station to intercept enemy raiders, and guard-ships such as HMS *Nonsuch* and HMS *Redoubt* giving close cover to ships moving within the estuary.

In spite of efforts to protect the interests of the local ship-owners going about their legitimate business, often strenuous efforts were made to recruit their seamen into the navy, particularly at a time of tension and consequent naval expansion. Returning whalers were fair game, as was any boat's crew being paid off after a voyage. Grimsby fishermen returning from lengthy trips to the Dogger Bank were often pressed. Although the navy clearly preferred trained sailors, landlubbers were also targeted by the pressgang. In 1793 the Golden Fleece in Gainsborough was a *Rendezvous*, the euphemism of the time for a recruiting office for the Navy's Impress Service. An advertisement in the Lincoln, Rutland and Stamford Mercury of December 1796, one of many such current at the time, lights on the men of Middle Raisin (sic), Tealby, Croxby and Usselby as being the potential recipients of £40 bounties for joining the navy.

At any time of threatened invasion along a vulnerable coast, one of the problems for the defenders is obtaining accurate information upon which decisions about the deployment of troops and the level of response to reports of a landing might be based. From the days of the Armada and the Dutch wars, beacons and bonfires had been used, but a more technical system was needed. The Admiralty had already established a workable network of signal stations on the south coast in 1794, and now a similar system was therefore to be extended to the east coast. Admiralty signals were passed along a chain of inter-visible signal-stations using a combination of red and blue flags and pennants, and four black signal balls. The position of the pennant immediately flagged up the type of message being sent and, depending on their position, the black balls represented either a numerical value, or a number-based code that could be converted to letters of the alphabet.

A pre-determined, but limited, system of codes enabled simple messages to be sent quickly along the coast and then inland. The early signal-stations consisted of a 30ft-high (9m-high) mast with a 30ft-long (9m-long) yardarm, from which were suspended the balls, and to which were attached yards for flying the flags and pennants. Alongside the mast there was a white-painted timber hut, later given a tarred finish. This provided limited accommodation for the signallers. Crews, drawn from the navy, and sometimes designated as Sea Fencibles, were commanded by a lieutenant, often on half-pay, assisted by either a petty officer or a midshipman and two ratings. They all drew pay from the Admiralty, but the officer, in addition, was paid a subsistence allowance. It was the officer's task to use a telescope to ensure that signals were received correctly for onward transmission. Captain Lloyd, of the Lincolnshire Sea Fencibles, was moved to express to Messrs Dolland his thoughts regarding the inadequacy of their issue telescope. The Dollands' reply was to the effect that others too shared his dissatisfaction, and that the purchase of a stronger model was advised. Procurement problems clearly go back a long way.

The Lincolnshire signal-stations formed a chain which extended from Holkham in Norfolk, crossing the Wash to Skegness, then up to Sutton-on-Sea, to Saltfleet, to Cleaness (Cleethorpes) and thence across the Humber estuary to Spurn Point, and to Dimlington (Holderness), where there was a strong military encampment against an invasion. In the long-established tradition of the belt-and-braces approach to emergency planning, beacons were also reinstated along the coast.

THE ARMY AND THE MILITIA

After the navy, the gun batteries and the signal-stations, the next line of defence against foreign invasion was the army. Given the country's burgeoning overseas commitments and the general aversion of the British public to the presence of a standing army, there were few regular troops in Britain. In 1685, the Tenth Foot, later to become the Lincolnshire Regiment had been raised, and in 1763, the 17th Lancers, with their death's head badge, were raised locally by the Marquis of Granby. One of the solutions to the problem of the lack of regular troops had long been the existence of the Constitutional Force, better known as the Militia. In 1757, Pitt had introduced legislation designed to revitalise the force and to eradicate some of the abuses surrounding it. Stronger links were forged with the regular army, all-year-round training was instituted, and stricter forfeits for non-attendance and other offences were to be enforced. The establishment for the county of Lincolnshire, recruited by ballot and organised by the lord lieutenant, was to be 1,200 men, one of the three highest totals in the country.

There were still problems over the use of substitutes by those who preferred to stay out of the military, and the poaching by the regular army of many of the more suitable militiamen. Further legislation served only to cloud the issue further by encouraging the establishment of volunteer units, specifically for home defence. Membership of such units exempted the volunteer from service in the Militia, thus undermining its efficiency still further. However, the Militia was all there was, so attempts were made to increase its effectiveness. In 1779, Parliament sanctioned the raising of Militia coast defence companies, each of three officers and fifty men, which would be added to the existing establishment with the specific role of manning the guns in the new batteries. This provision extended to Military District 1, which comprised Lincolnshire and East Anglia. Lincolnshire had two regiments of Militia, the 8th North Lincolnshire Regiment recruiting from Lindsey and based in Lincoln, and the 29th South Lincolnshire Regiment recruiting from Kesteven and Holland, and based in New Sleaford. The Militia, as a complementary force to the regular army, was subject to any home posting, but the North Lincolnshire had only a short distance to travel when they formed part of the Hull Citadel garrison from 1803–7, and again in 1813.

A depot was established in Carholme Road, Lincoln, to store weapons, munitions and equipment for the Militia, but not considered large enough to warrant the appointment of a full-time Board of Ordnance Storekeeper, as was the case in other towns such as Derby or Great Yarmouth. However, when the site was taken over by Dawber's Brewery, the central armoury building, with its heavy pediment, was incorporated into the brewery and, from photographs taken around 1900, appears to have been built to Wyatt's standard design, like those erected across the country from Hyde Park to Brecon, all around 1806–7.

Traditionally, the Militia's officers came from the landowning families of the county, and a few had served in the fashionable regular regiments such as the Guards or the cavalry. In 1798 the earl of Brownlow had commanded two companies of volunteers at Belton and Hough, known as the Loyal Lincoln Villagers. As Lord Lieutenant of Lincolnshire from 1809, he became colonel of the local supplementary militia, which assembled at Stamford. In 1811, he then became Colonel of the South Lincolnshire Militia, an essentially honorary appointment, and was still in post in 1850. The regiment was actually run on a day-to-day basis by the Lt. Colonel. The Colonel of the North Lincolnshire Militia was Lord Portmore, son-in-law to the duke of Ancaster, himself a former Lord Lieutenant. Both regiments volunteered for service in Ireland at various times during the wars, in order to release the regular garrison troops for foreign service.

VOLUNTEER FORCES

In order to increase the number of troops available for the defence of the country against invasion, much effort was put into recruiting volunteer units. This process began in 1794 when Lords Lieutenant were instructed to raise local units of volunteer horse and foot in their respective counties. In a mainly rural county like Lincolnshire, it was inevitable that units of horsed Yeomanry would attract recruits initially. There was social cachet to be gained by membership, since it was the gentry who provided the officers, and mainly yeoman farmers the troopers. It was all a bit like hunting, but in even more impressive costume.

Troops were quickly formed at Bourne, Market Deeping and Folkingham. The splendid uniforms deserved to be seen at their best, so fundraising events took the form of balls and concerts. The Spalding Troop of the Gentlemen Yeomenry (sic) Cavalry, for instance, offered a dramatic programme in the theatre in July 1796, accompanied by the Spalding Cavalry Band, which would play select pieces of martial music, with everyone joining in 'Rule Britannia' and 'God Save the King'. In Bourne, it was Sir Gilbert Heathcote who took the lead, but a local wool-stapler called Thomas Rawnsley was also prominent. He had business premises in South Street and re-named his house on the Peterborough road 'Cavalry House' (*31*).

31 BOURNE: Cavalry House, the home of Thomas Rawnsley, a wool-stapler who was involved in raising a troop of volunteer horse in the Napoleonic Wars

Sir John Trollope and Sir Thomas Whichcote formed the Market Deeping troop, and there were also the Spalding and Long Sutton troops which, somewhat ironically, were mobilised against anti-Militia riots in 1796. The Grantham Cavalry, sixty troopers under three officers, had been formed in 1794, and the next year saw the formation of the Grantham Volunteer Infantry, with two companies, each a hundred strong.

Not all towns were as quick off the mark, and it was generally a heightened fear of invasion in 1797–8 which was to accelerate the growth of volunteer infantry units in the towns, but in March 1801 the Peace of Amiens removed the need for all these military distractions, and most units disbanded. This period of peace, however, was short-lived, and hostilities resumed in May 1803, prompting a renewal of military fervour. In Lindsey, Lord Yarborough put up a thousand guineas to fund a volunteer force based on his Brocklesby estates and the towns of Brigg and Caistor. The Yeomanry cavalry exercised in the park with its temples and grottoes, and had use of the stables, while the officers might dine at the earl's table in the big house.

Legislation had required all those farmers owning ten or more horses to contribute a fully horsed and equipped Yeomanry trooper. Troops of horse were raised after 1803, in Market Rasen, Louth, Spalding, Folkingham and Bourne, Loveden, Grantham, Boston, Ness, and the city of Lincoln. Meanwhile the Horncastle and North Reston Battalion of Volunteer Infantry drilled under the command of Major Simpson, and honed their musketry skills in an old pit near The Garth on the Lincoln road.

In March 1804, the totals of volunteers for Lincolnshire, recorded in a letter from the Duke of York, as Commander-in-Chief, to General Officers commanding military districts, stood at 6,720 infantry and 661 cavalry. They were part of the Yorkshire Military District, and their assembly point was Wakefield. As well as those two arms of horse and foot, there were a handful of specialist units. The Grimsby Artillery Volunteer Corps was formed in 1805 to man the local coast defence guns, and remained in being until the end of the war in 1815. Even though after Trafalgar in 1805 there was no longer a realistic possibility of invasion, the majority of the volunteer infantry units continued in being at least until 1813, when they were disbanded. The troops of Yeomanry cavalry were retained, not as a defence against external threats, but rather to be used to control civil unrest at home, there being an assumption in the minds of the governing classes that those who joined the Yeomanry were more likely to be sympathetic to the wishes of the landowners than to those of either the urban labouring classes or the rural poor.

five

The Victorian Period (*c*.1815–1914)

The hundred years between the end of the Napoleonic wars and the beginning of the First World War saw enormous changes in the state of the nation's armed forces. As well as both radical organisational and technological change, there were also changes in the way the nation regarded its navy, and especially its army. The navy, as an institution, had always enjoyed the regard of the public, but now sailors themselves began to be seen in a better light. Until the recent successes, the army was still seen as being composed of incompetent officers who had bought their advancement at the expense of less wealthy or less well-connected colleagues, and soldiers who were the scum of the earth. These perceptions were to change, but only slowly, as it was to be another sixty years or so before the reforms of Cardwell and others abolished many of the abuses in the system, and re-organised the regiments to give them local identities. However, as happens after most enervating wars, there was a period of contraction, particularly in the voluntary sector (**Fig. 7**).

ORGANISING THE COUNTY'S FORCES: THE MILITIA

We have already seen how the majority of the volunteers had been disbanded: the infantry by 1813, and the artillery in 1815. Where a military presence was required, it was provided by the regulars. A small detachment of troops serving in Brigg in 1826/7 consisted of forty-six men of the 56th Foot (later the Essex Regiment) from the Hull garrison. Units of the Yeomanry cavalry hung on for a while, but they too went in 1827. Four years later, rural unrest characterised by rick burning – a protest against the loss of labour expected in the wake of mechanisation – was just what many of the farmers thought the Yeomanry was there to deal with. There were two responses to this trouble. In 1831, Lord Yarborough's North Lincoln Regiment of Yeomanry Cavalry was formed in Lindsey, and its Gainsborough troop was called out in June 1837 to control a crowd unhappy about the new Poor Law arrangements.

The Victorian Period (c.1815–1914)

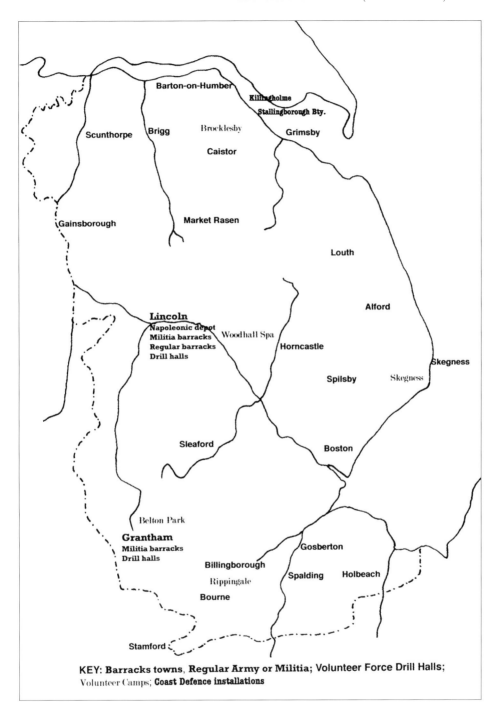

Fig. 7 Military installations 1815–1914

A temporary volunteer corps had to be re-formed by the farmers in the heathlands of Kesteven. Even the Militia was allowed to stagnate, with no mobilisation from 1831 until 1853, and Lord Yarborough's force had disappeared by 1846. The peak year for incendiarism was 1831, when thirty-six cases were reported, with repeat outbreaks in 1834 and 1850, recording twenty-one and twenty cases respectively.

It was another foreign policy crisis that precipitated the recall of the Militia. A new Militia Act of 1852 re-established the Constitutional Force, but on more of a voluntary basis than was possible through the ballot with its in-built abuses of substitution, the Act only requiring its application 'if necessary'. Subsequent Circulars defined Great Britain and Ireland as the Militia's theatre of operation, and allowed a fixed percentage to be recruited to the regular army. However, it was soon seen how disruptive this practice of transfer had become, and this was spelt out in 1860:

> It is important for the Militia as a reserve Force upon which dependence can be placed in case of National danger that it should be raised from among men of settled habits and fixed residence within the County to which the Regiment belongs.

Therefore the militiaman who subsequently joined up as a regular soldier without his commanding officer's permission was to be treated as a deserter. It was also recognised that there should be incentives too, and a bounty system was set up allowing for re-enlistment for further service, and also with opportunities to volunteer for service outside the home area.

Lincolnshire retained its two regiments under the new order: the 8th Regiment in the north still based in Lincoln, and the 29th in the south, based for a short while longer in New Sleaford, but soon to move to Grantham. Both regiments had been created 'Royal' in 1760. The 8th were commanded by Lt. Colonel Tomline of Reby (Riby), and formerly of the 1st Life Guards. Their Honorary Colonel was The Viscount Alford and their Major Ellison was from Boultham Hall, Lincoln. The Commanding Officer of the 29th was Lt. Colonel Sibthorp, assisted by Major Welby, and their Honorary Colonel of forty years remained Lord Brownlow.

One key aspect of the move to give Militia units some degree of stability and professionalism was the simple notion of providing them with a permanent depot. Barracks, permanently dedicated to the accommodation of soldiers, were quite a new idea in the regular army, and some of the earliest, erected in the first quarter of the nineteenth century in areas of industrial unrest, had been made defensible by the inclusion of musketry loops in external walls. It was but a short step to adopting the entire vocabulary of medieval warfare to produce battlemented castles for the Militia. These depots were officially described as 'storehouses', since they housed the arms and equipment of the Militia, administered by a small permanent staff, resident on site. Militiamen would arrive periodically for their compulsory periods of training, and to be kitted out for mobilisation when embodied for service. Both regiments were among the fifty Militia units nationally which volunteered for foreign-service during the Crimean War, and among the ten actually posted to Mediterranean stations, Malta, Gibraltar, Rhodes and Corfu, serving from 1854 through to mid-1856 to release regular garrison troops for the Crimean War. Lincolnshire's two regiments together totalled 1,200 effectives, and around 500 served overseas. Both regiments are credited with Crimean War battle honours in a survey of such units in 1905.

THE NEW MILITIA BARRACKS

Although the style of architecture seems to have been agreed, the actual Militia storehouses across the country are all quite different. However, Lincolnshire's two are almost identical. It may be that counties that had two regiments of Militia commissioned two storehouses from the same architect; this is certainly true of Staffordshire's two at Stafford and Newcastle-under-Lyme. The most obvious difference is that Lincoln is built of brick, while Grantham is finished in stone. In 1854 the Lord Lieutenant, the Marquess of Granby, working through the County Gaol Committee, instructed the County Surveyor to organise the construction of the Lincoln Militia storehouse. A green-field site of 3 acres (1.2 hectares) on Burton Road just outside the city's built-up area was chosen. The new building, opened in May 1857, consisted of a two-storey secure storehouse with central gatehouse, holding arms and equipment for 1,000 men, fronting onto Burton Road. Two single-storey ranges enclosed a parade ground, and the fourth side was closed by a blank wall. There were loop-holed bastions at each corner serving both symbolic and functional purposes. The two single-storey ranges originally provided accommodation for permanent staff, both NCOs and their families, and an officer, perhaps the adjutant, Captain Kennedy, a veteran of the Peninsular War. There was also room on one side for a drill-shed. The architect, Henry Goddard, was well known locally for his public buildings and private houses. As a result of his highly regarded work, he had been appointed County and Diocesan Surveyor. In the 1860s, further permanent accommodation was built for the adjutant, quartermaster, sergeants and drummers. These comprise a large villa on Burton Road for the adjutant, and two terraces of two-storey housing on Mill Road, backing onto the west wall of the depot. Incorporated in these terraces are three houses, Elm House at the south end, and one labelled 'DRUMMERS' in the middle. There may have been a hospital where the cart hovel now stands north of the northwest turret.

The main depot building is now home to the Museum of Lincolnshire Life. Goddard's Grantham building in the angle of Sandon Road and Beacon Lane, opened in 1858 (*32*), has slightly more elaborate ranges than at Lincoln. Behind the east wall is a close of terraced cottages, added by 1872, at a similar time to those at Lincoln. The close is entered through gate pillars on whose east side is a two-storey stone-built house, corresponding to Elm House in Lincoln. At the end of the close facing the entrance is a substantial, brick-built two-storey house of three bays, perhaps for the adjutant. In 1913, when the Territorial Force (TF) took over both depots, a more substantial new drill shed was built on the back wall of each, the west wall at Lincoln and the east at Grantham. That at Lincoln is now the Transport Gallery

108 Defending Lincolnshire: A Military History from Conquest to Cold War

32 GRANTHAM: the barracks opened in 1858 to house the Royal South Lincolnshire Militia; it is identical in plan to its counterpart in Lincoln but built in stone rather than brick

33 GRANTHAM: the drill hall added to the Militia barracks in 1913, to accommodate a company of the 4th Volunteer Battalion of the Lincolnshire Regiment, Territorial Force

of the museum, whilst that at Grantham (*33*), once having served as a girls' school gymnasium, is now an auction house. The rest of the ranges at Grantham are used as offices, and the cottages and houses at both locations are now in private ownership.

THE VOLUNTEER FORCE

Yet another perceived threat of invasion from across the Channel in 1859 brought a number of responses. That of the government was to convene a Royal Commission to examine the state of Britain's defences, particularly around its naval bases. This Commission was eventually to recommend massive casemated fortresses, which would in time be recognised as the white elephants known as Palmerston's Follies. The populist response was very different. One lesson from the recent fighting in the Crimea and in India was the need for trained riflemen, so just as medieval folk had practised their archery skills at the local butts, then the same principles could be applied to rifle-shooting. A civilian National Rifle Association was formed in November 1859 with a rally on Wimbledon Common, at which Queen Victoria pulled the first trigger. But this did not satisfy those of the urban middle-classes who felt that they too, like their country cousins in the Yeomanry, should have the opportunity to contribute meaningfully to the defence of their country.

Memories of the volunteers of earlier in the century survived, but now within the minds of a wholly different section of society with a very different perception of themselves. Many of those previous volunteers had been sucked into the Militia, a fate that these respectable tradespeople and artisans refused to countenance. Bowing to popular pressure, the Secretary of State for War authorised Lords Lieutenant to form volunteer rifle corps, and to commission the appropriate officers to lead them. By the end of 1860, over 120,000 men had joined such corps, capitalising on their own enthusiasm, civic pride and private resources, but more often those of their officers, for uniform and equipment. It was soon realised that some central control and co-ordination was needed for this runaway organisation. If the War Office wanted a role then it had to put something in the kitty. Inspection of corps by the War Office was accepted on the basis that the corps would be paid a per capita sum for each man deemed to be competent. In order to avoid too much unhelpful individualism, and to support commanding officers' efforts, neighbouring corps were soon grouped into Administrative Battalions.

The first Rifle Volunteer Corps to be formed in Lincolnshire was on 26 October 1859 in Lincoln, shortly followed by the 2nd Corps the next month in Louth. February 1860 saw the 3rd Corps at Grantham, the 4th Corps at Boston, the 5th at Stamford, the 8th at Sleaford, the 11th at Alford, and the 13th Corps at Spalding. Over the next five months, ten more corps were formed. These eighteen corps were divided between three Administrative Battalions centred on Lincoln, Grantham and Boston, but the 3rd Admin. Bn. was broken up in 1862, and its five constituent corps transferred to the 2nd Admin. Bn. The 14th Corps, which had been formed at Swineshead in March 1860, lasted no longer than a year. Some counties had retained Yeomanry units right through the century but, possibly to compensate for the fact that Lincolnshire was not one of them, Lord Yarborough formed a volunteer cavalry unit, the Lincolnshire Light Horse, centred on Brocklesby once more. Operating from 1867 to 1887, it was the longest-lived of such units apart from the Fife and Forfar Light Horse in Scotland, which survived beyond the end of the Second World War as an armoured regiment.

Based on Brocklesby Park, the Lincolnshire Light Horse soon became known by its patron's name as the Earl of Yarborough's Light Horse, and were kitted out by him in the finery of the regular Hussar regiments. It must also be remembered that there was no abatement of the navy's recruitment programme, and in 1859 Boston's Angel Inn was a rendezvous for potential sailors.

While the Yeomanry had been able to enjoy the facilities of a conveniently located stately home for their musters, this facility being extended to the Light Horse, the town-dwellers of the Rifle Volunteer corps were thrown on their own resources. The actual requirements in terms of accommodation were modest. In order to meet the War Office conditions for being eligible for the payment of a grant, each corps needed a secure armoury for storing weapons and ammunition, an office, or orderly-room for the administration of the corps, an open space for drilling and an indoor space for lectures, and a range, either indoor or out, for shooting practice. Once it became usual to have a regular NCO seconded as drill-sergeant, a house was also needed. The CO was often a doctor or solicitor who could find space for the orderly-room at his professional premises or his home; a house could also be rented for the drill-sergeant. Any reasonably level field was adequate for drill, a strong-room in the local town hall was ideal as an armoury, and a strip of land up the side of a field could serve as a range. This, however, left the problem of the indoor space.

At Alford, Boston and Grimsby, use was made of the Corn Exchanges. At Louth, the Town Hall, opened in 1853, became the depot for the Rifle Volunteers. At Horncastle, the British School built on The Wong in 1813 was taken over for use as a drill hall in 1867; it is now an antiques centre. There was a drill hall in Wharf Road, Grantham, around this time, which looks to have been built onto the side of part of the Brownlow Carriage Works. At Spilsby, the old village lock-up became a freestanding Armoury and still survives, in use as an office. In these early days, the only purpose-built drill halls were those of the Lincolnshire Volunteer Artillery in Boston and Louth. Opened in 1869, that at Boston in Main Ridge, now a snooker club, has a large hall with a Dutch-gabled roof, and a long, tall gun-store along one side. The hall in Louth was in Charles Street (formerly Eve Street). The artillery needed space to deploy their guns and practise their gun drill, since speed as well as accuracy was the essence of good gunnery. The Grimsby Volunteer Artillery would have practised their skills on guns emplaced in the actual batteries it was their duty to man in wartime. Next to the Baptist Chapel in West Street, Bourne is a former recruiting office for the volunteers. Part of the original inscription survives: '2nd BATT. LINCS. V rifles', perhaps suggesting a date prior to 1908, when this unit became the 5th Battalion of the Lincolnshire Regiment.

THE ROYAL COMMISSION'S FORTIFICATIONS

The Royal Commission's remit included the defence of the Humber estuary and the mercantile ports of Hull and Grimsby. Already under construction as the Commission was deliberating, was a new battery at Stallingborough. This consisted of earthworks that protected the open pivots for RML guns, which were to fire *en barbette* over the parapet. This found little favour and more powerful works were put in hand across the river at Paull Point. It is possible that the Stallingborough battery was never armed, as there were no guns there in 1885 when the Stanhope Committee reported. A Brennan Torpedo station, for launching wire-guided torpedoes at enemy ships as they passed upstream, was suggested for Stallingborough, but never implemented. It was also decided at this time that defence works around Grimsby could be only partially effective, so the Royal Navy should have the responsibility for the defence of the port.

THE CARDWELL REFORMS OF THE REGULAR ARMY AND THE VOLUNTEERS

Despite the long-term reluctance of the authorities to provide proper barracks for the regular army, this was about to change. While regiments might have traditionally recruited in particular localities, this was as much down to recruits wishing to follow fathers and brothers into a familiar unit as to any official policy. The Tenth Foot, formed in 1685, and the 17th Light Dragoons (later Lancers), raised in 1760, drew many of their recruits from parts of Lincolnshire, but only as a result of custom and geographical accident respectively. During the 1870s, a number of reforms, carried out by Edward (later Viscount) Cardwell, Gladstone's Secretary of State for War, included a localization programme for the regulars. Under this scheme, a Regimental District became the organisation for a county regiment of two battalions, each alternating between home and foreign service postings, with one or two battalions of Militia as a reserve. The administrative battalions of the Rifle Volunteers then became additional volunteer battalions of this county regiment, whose depot was generally in their county town. This particular re-grouping sought to give the regulars a local identity, the local population a focus for their support, and the reserves and volunteers both a sense of personal involvement in a greater enterprise and a pride in their professional affiliations. If the public's changing perception of the army, and the rush to the colours in 1914, are any measure of outcome, then the new policy may be regarded as having achieved some success.

The regimental depot of the Lincolnshire Regiment, Sobraon Barracks (*34*), opened in 1878 on Burton Road in Lincoln, was fairly typical of such establishments around the country. A central suite of designs had been developed by the design office at the War Office under the direction of Major Seddon of the Royal Engineers. This included designs for a standard barrack-block, an officers' mess, and an armoury, the whole contained along with guardroom/gatehouse, drill shed, stables, stores, hospital and workshops within a loop-holed wall with corner bastions.

The engineer officer in each regimental district could draw on these plans to produce a design to meet local needs.

The armoury at Lincoln (*35*) is a three-storey, medieval-style tower keep with two higher towers carrying faux machicolations and stone battlemented parapets. In order to ensure that the floors were strong enough to support large amounts of boxed munitions, each floor rests on a grid of rolled wrought-iron I-beams carried on cast-iron columns, and supporting un-reinforced mass-concrete slabs each measuring 7 x 14ft (2 x 4m). The barrack-blocks, now all demolished, were of two storeys with projections housing stairs, NCOs' quarters and ablutions. On each floor were sufficient dormitories, each containing twenty-four beds, for a company. Thus each block held two companies, and four blocks accommodated a whole battalion. At first, meals were collected from the cookhouse and eaten in the dormitories, but eventually a canteen was built for the men, while the officers and senior NCOs continued to eat in their own messes. Separate blocks of married quarters were also built. At Lincoln, only the armoury/keep parts of the boundary walls and gatehouse survive of the original barracks. Extensions have been added over the years for the current TA use, but most of the site has now been given over for modern housing.

In 1880, the Tenth Military Regimental District centred on Lincoln thus consisted of the 1st and 2nd Battalions of regular infantry, the 3rd and 4th Militia Battalions, and the 1st and 2nd Lincolnshire Rifle Volunteer Corps of the Lincolnshire Regiment, three years later becoming respectively the 1st and 2nd Volunteer Battalions of the Lincolnshire Regiment, the 1st Bn. based on Lincoln (with three companies there and a further eight scattered across Lindsey), and the 2nd with HQ in Grantham (with two companies based there and the other six distributed across Kesteven and Holland). This re-organisation marked a further step in the professionalisation of the volunteers, and it was generally felt that these units deserved better dedicated premises.

Still funded by a variety of sources – the deep pockets of their officers, annual subscriptions, philanthropic benefactors, War Office grants, fund-raising activities and public donations – the volunteers struggled to maintain standards of efficiency, public show and enthusiasm, but it was clear that new premises would be good for morale. Between 1883 and 1900, many of the volunteer units managed to build themselves new drill halls. In Lincoln, the local employer and engineer Joseph Ruston funded the construction of a splendid drill hall in Broadgate (*36*). It is of red brick with stone dressings, castellated with arrow-loops, and carries the royal crest, an 'X' for the Tenth Foot, and one of their battle honours, 'Egypt'. Over a grand entrance arch surmounted by a three-storey tower with turrets is the oriel window of the officers' mess. Behind is a capacious hall, large enough to accommodate the three companies of volunteers based there. Behind all that is a yard with more buildings and the guardroom. The architect was probably William Watkins. Ruston always justified the not inconsiderable profits of his business by pleading that he was entitled to a bit of bread and cheese, so the volunteers' new home became 'Bread and Cheese Hall'. At the time he was seeking election as the city's Liberal MP, but that, of course, can have had no influence on the grandeur of his gesture. The

The Victorian Period (c.1815–1914)   113

34 LINCOLN: the badge of the Lincolnshire Regiment at the gates of their new regimental depot opened in 1878

35 LINCOLN: Sobraon Barracks on Burton Road with its medieval-inspired 'Keep/Armoury', still a TA Centre

114 Defending Lincolnshire: A Military History from Conquest to Cold War

36 LINCOLN: the Broadgate drill hall commissioned by the local industrialist Joseph Ruston as HQ for the 1st Volunteer Battalion the Lincolnshire Regiment in 1891. It has recently been splendidly refurbished as a performance and exhibition centre

37 GRIMSBY: the drill hall in Victoria Street North opened in 1891 for the volunteer coast gunners of the 1st Lincolnshire Royal Garrison Artillery

building has recently been completely re-furbished and provides event, conference, performance and exhibition spaces. In Gainsborough, the Public or Temperance Hall in Spital Street was in volunteer use by 1892.

Louth had gained a new drill hall by this time for D Coy. of the 1st Volunteer Bn. in Northgate, while F Coy. of the 2nd Volunteer Bn. had a new drill hall in Spalding's Sheepmarket. This had a three-storey front block containing the armoury, orderly-room and messes, with a hall behind measuring 75 x 45ft (23 x 14m). It became a garage in 1909 and was demolished in 1927. The Grimsby Volunteer Artillery of the 1st Lincolnshire Royal Garrison Artillery got a new drill hall in Victoria Street North in 1891 (**37**). A two-storey front block with oriel, tower, castellation and turret housed the offices and mess. Behind was a large hall in which was mounted an enormous 7" rifled muzzle-loader, weighing seven tons, on which crews could practise their gun drill indoors on cold winter evenings. This building is now a printing works. Boston's volunteer artillery retained their original hall, but may have fired their 15-pounder guns on a range on the coast, perhaps at Battery Farm on the Haven.

In Billingborough the volunteers continued to make use of the public hall. In Skegness, the drill hall was in the Sea View Hotel, which had opened in 1862. By the turn of the century, many long-standing arrangements were judged unsatisfactory, and Alford, Horncastle and Spilsby all gained new purpose-built drill halls. All three are similar in design with a large gabled hall to the street frontage. Alford and Horncastle have a 25-yard indoor range alongside, and Alford and Spilsby a staff house to one side. Alford has an orderly-room block across the back. Both Horncastle and Spilsby now serve as town halls, whilst Alford houses bric-a-brac.

Regular training was carried out locally, there being 800-yard rifle ranges off the Boston road in Horncastle for instance, and at Slippery Gowt marsh on the south bank of the Haven at Boston. Prior to 1908, 'H' company of the 2nd Volunteer Bn. was based at Billingborough, and a range was built in the old cellar of Ringston Hall. Camps were held in Rippingale and, along with other companies, in Belton Park. Woodhall Spa provided a venue for G Coy. of the 1st Volunteer Bn. from 24 June to 1 July 1893, with their tents being set up in the Spa grounds. Summer camps, however, where the whole battalion got together for a week, were often a little further afield. The Lincolnshire coast offered plenty of suitably empty terrain for shooting and for training manoeuvres, which was also attractive to neighbouring counties. For several seasons between 1883 and 1898, the Robin Hood Rifles, Nottinghamshire's volunteer rifle corps, came to Gibraltar Point in August Bank Holiday week for their summer camps, either arriving by train, or one year, by bicycle. A map of Skegness in 1905 shows a 'drill field' and several 'camp grounds' just to the south of the railway station.

Lincolnshire was not one of those counties that had retained its Yeomanry throughout the century, hence the earl of Yarborough's excursion into the Light Horse. It was not until the end of the century and the start of the South African wars that a crisis in the army led to the creation of the Imperial Yeomanry. A succession of disastrous defeats for the British fighting the Boer Commandos resulted in an appeal for volunteers to form new mounted infantry units. Once legislation had been passed, enabling them to serve abroad, the existing yeomanry volunteers, men who could both ride and shoot like the Boers, would form the nucleus of the Imperial Yeomanry. A new Lincolnshire Yeomanry unit was raised in May 1901, mainly from the members of the Brocklesby and neighbouring hunts, and the Militia or Old Barracks was leased for twenty-one years as its base. It was equipped as a lancer regiment, and was the only lancer regiment in the British Army, regular or volunteer, to wear green. Their full-dress uniform included the lancer cap, those of the officers carrying black ostrich feathers, and a silver plastron.

THE TERRITORIAL FORCE

Just as previous conflicts had thrown up questions about the relative roles of the various components of the army, this last war was no different. The Militia and the Yeomanry had both fought abroad, and the volunteers had presented themselves as competent and professional soldiers. The key question related to the role and status of the Volunteer Force. Despite opposition from many who believed that any attempt to bring the volunteers into the official fold would merely undercut the regular army and promote amateurism, Richard (later Lord) Haldane, the Secretary of State for War in the new Liberal government of 1906, prepared plans for a government-sponsored Territorial Force. This new national volunteer force of fourteen divisions, self-sufficient in artillery, engineering, transport and medical corps, would be centrally funded but organised on a local basis by County Territorial Associations. The Militia, too, would be absorbed into a new integrated structure. Lincolnshire now became part of the North Midland Division. The Yeomanry was brigaded with those of Staffordshire and Leicestershire as the North Midland Mounted Brigade. The local volunteer artillery were re-organised as the 1st North Midland Brigade, Royal Field Artillery based at Grimsby and Louth, losing their heavy guns to the East Riding RGA at Hull, alongside the engineers and signals. The two existing regular battalions of the Lincolnshire Regiment continued as before, the two Militia battalions combined as a 3rd Special Reserve Bn. and the two Volunteer Battalions became the 4th and 5th Bns., each of eight companies with their HQs in Lincoln and Grimsby respectively. The HQ of the Lincoln and Leicester Infantry Brigade, consisting of four battalions, was at Grantham; the HQ of the 4th Northern General Hospital RAMC was in Lincoln, with offices in Guildhall Street. Other service units were scattered across the divisional area, with one section of the Nottinghamshire and Derbyshire Mounted Brigade's field ambulance based in Lincoln.

The County Territorial Association thus administered seven distinct units. Many of these were in out-dated premises and new ones had to be found or built from scratch over the next few years as this new army found its feet. As we have seen, drill-sheds for the use of the volunteers were added to the two militia barracks in Grantham and Lincoln in 1913. The local architects Scorer and Gamble were commissioned to design a new drill hall in Main Ridge, Boston, opened by General

The Victorian Period (c.1815–1914)

38 SCUNTHORPE: the drill hall opened in Cole Street just prior to the outbreak of the First World War for the local yeomanry and infantry units of the Territorial Force, and almost identical in design to contemporary drill halls opened in 1913 in Boston and Spalding

Bethune in 1913. It has a two-storey front-block containing armoury, orderly-room, sergeants' and officers' messes, with a hall behind and a 25-yard indoor rifle range along one side. A mirror image, but otherwise identical building, was opened in Haverfield Road, Spalding at the same time, and there is a very similar drill hall in Cole Street, Scunthorpe (*38*). All three buildings are in a neo-Georgian style with a pediment, a long way from some of the utilitarian structures that appeared elsewhere in the country at this time. The fairly recently built drill halls at Alford, Lincoln, Louth, Spilsby, and Horncastle were deemed more than adequate for twentieth-century use, as were the existing arrangements at Gainsborough, Grantham and Barton-upon-Humber. It was clear that new drill halls were necessary at Stamford and Grimsby. That in Stamford, with its stone front-block onto St Peters Street replaced an armoury in the High Street. In Grimsby, the artillery facility had been supplemented (by 1907) by a new infantry drill hall in Doughty Road, which replaced the Armoury in the Bull Ring and the use of the Corn Exchange, providing a new base for the 5th Volunteer Bn. of the Lincolnshire Regiment.

A SCHEME OF COAST DEFENCE

Over this period, little had been done to the fixed defences of the south bank of the Humber. In 1894, coast defence searchlights, Defence Electric Lights (DELs) had been installed at Paull Point, and the Owen Committee, reporting in 1905, found that for a Class C port, the level of protection afforded by the 6" guns at Paull Point was perfectly adequate. The provision may have stood still, but the need to protect potential targets had suddenly become more acute. After five years in the building, the new deep-water Immingham Docks opened in 1912, along with important Admiralty fuel tanks at Killingholme. In 1907, the Admiralty's Wireless Station at Cleethorpes (Waltham), the first in the country to be equipped with a high-powered transmitter, had opened with a 450ft-high (140m-high) wooden tower topped by aerials, intended to carry all naval signals traffic in the North Sea, and powered by the Corporation Eletricity works in Grimsby. The Royal Navy decided to maintain a permanent presence with an East Coast Command and, before long, numbers of submarines began to use the port of Immingham on a regular basis.

In 1907, the Admiralty had established HMS *Pekin* as a shore base in Grimsby for the boats of the Auxiliary Patrol. These boats, usually converted fishing vessels and steam yachts, were used to escort coastal shipping and to service other naval installations, and were used as minesweepers. All this activity warranted increased protection, and it was decided to install a pair of 6" batteries, one either side of the river, at Sunk Island on the north, and at Stallingborough on the south. The initial plans for both batteries in 1911 were for two concrete gun positions with a Battery Observation Post (BOP) to be built on a 30ft-high (9m-high) earth rampart with concrete magazines buried beneath, all contained within a hexagonal fort with a ditch covered by flanking caponiers containing *Maxim* guns. Within the defended space were to be barracks, workshops and stores. In actuality, these plans were overtaken by events, and the final construction substituted a pair of concrete towers, 12ft (3.5m) in diameter, and 100ft (30m) apart, for the grassy mound. These towers were topped by platforms that were spacious enough for the operation of 6" BL guns. All the other battery buildings were contained within a fortified enclosure with blockhouses at the angles.

Stallingborough Battery eventually entered service early in 1915, and Sunk Island a few months later. While all this construction was about to commence, the 1913 Defence Plan for Fortress Humber, the third in a sequence covering east coast ports, identified the defence priorities. Areas of strategic importance listed included: the south bank of the river between Thrunscoe, south of Cleethorpes, and Grimsby Docks; the W/T station; Immingham and Grimsby Docks; and the Killingholme fuel depot. These plans had been finalised just in time for the outbreak of the First World War.

six

The First World War (1914–18)

DEPLOYMENT OF LOCALLY BASED UNITS, 1914–18

At the outbreak of war in August 1914, there were few troops in the county. The two regular battalions of the Lincolnshire Regiment were away, the 1st Bn. in Portsmouth, and the 2nd on foreign service in Bermuda. Both these units were hurriedly despatched straight to the Western Front. The Territorials of the 4th and 5th Bns. were immediately called up as part of the 46th (North Midland) Division TF, brigaded with the corresponding battalions of the Leicestershire Regiment, alongside brigades of the Nottinghamshire and Derbyshire Regiment (Sherwood Foresters), and the North and South Staffordshire Regiments. The division assembled in Luton, moved onto training areas in Essex, then left for France in April 1915, the very first division of the TF to be sent there. The 2/4th and 2/5th Bns. formed part of the similarly constituted 59th (2nd North Midland) Division, assembling in Hertfordshire, moving to Essex and thence to France in March 1917. Both these divisions spent the rest of the war there. The 1/1st Lincolnshire Yeomanry, part of the North Midland Mounted Brigade, assembled in East Anglia, prior to a move to Egypt in October 1915 with the 1st Mounted Division. They fought in the desert campaigns as cavalry, but lost their horses early in 1918, when they were joined with the East Riding Yeomanry and converted to machine-gun troops, becoming 'D' Bn. of the Machine Gun Corps and landing at Marseilles in June 1918. Re-numbered as 102nd (Lincolnshire and East Riding Yeomanry) Bn. MGC, one of four such battalions formed from dismounted Yeomanry regiments, they served with 1st Army on the Western Front. The 2/1st Lincolnshire Yeomanry was posted as a cyclist unit on anti-invasion duties in first Norfolk, and then Kent, whilst the 3/1st, formed in 1915, were absorbed into the 1st Reserve Cavalry Bde. at the Curragh in Dublin.

As each new wave of recruitment to Kitchener's New Armies (K1, K2, K3, etc.) got under way, new battalions of the Lincolnshire Regiment were formed. The 6th

Service Bn. (K1) went to Gallipoli, then to France. The 7th Service Bn. (K2) was sent straight to France, as were the 8th Service Bn. (K3), the 10th Service Bn. and the 12th Labour Bn. The 10th Service Bn. was raised in Grimsby, when old boys and staff of the Municipal College (later Winteringham Grammar School) OTC attempted to enlist in the TF battalion *en masse*. That unit already had its full complement of twenty-four officers and 780 other ranks, so with the support of the Mayor, a local battalion, known as the Grimsby Chums, was raised, meeting for drill on the Clee Fields with an orderly-room in the pavilion. They then assembled in a hutted camp in Brocklesby Park for seven months of basic training, after which they went to the camp at Ripon for their final preparation before going to France. In the battle of the Somme in July 1916, the Chums lost half their number, killed, wounded or missing. Twice more they sustained losses at a similar level, clearly demonstrating the downside of pals and chums units, with communities being devastated by the loss of entire cohorts of their young men.

Along with the fact that not all of the newly forming units were suitable for service in France, there were other needs for these troops to fulfil. The 9th Reserve Bn., raised as a Service Bn. (K4) along with the 11th Reserve Bn. became a training unit for the local infantry regiments, at the vast camp at Cannock Chase in Staffordshire. The 13th Bn. was a home service battalion composed of soldiers unsuitable for active service and carried out anti-invasion duties in Suffolk. The 1st Garrison Bn. was sent to India to release regular troops for other duties. Others of the Regiment's battalions had very local postings. The 3rd (Reserve) Bn. spent the whole war until early 1918 on garrison duty in Grimsby, and the 2nd (Home Service) Garrison Bn. was stationed at North Coates initially, then at Grimsby. The twelve third line territorial battalions of the North Midland Reserve Division, assembling at Grantham in September 1915, were all dispersed to defensive positions on the Lincolnshire coast. The 3/4th and 3/5th Bns. of the Lincolnshire Regiment were at Saltfleet; stationed at Louth and North Coates were the 3/4th and 3/5th Bns. Leicestershire Regiment; the 3/5th and 3/6th Bns of the South Staffordshires were at Mablethorpe and Sutton-on-Sea; the 3/5th and 3/6th Bns. North Staffordshires were stationed at Lincoln and Mablethorpe; and the 3/5th, 3/6th, 3/7th, and 3/8th Bns. of the Sherwood Foresters served at Louth and Saltfleet. A general lack of manpower and constant drafts to other units serving abroad meant that most of these units were gradually amalgamated in pairs to produce six full-strength battalions.

ANTI-INVASION DEFENCES ON THE LINCOLNSHIRE COAST

Although the Humber estuary had always had fixed defences against seaborne raiders, the notion of invasion across the North Sea was relatively novel. Only in the decade leading up to the outbreak of the Second World War was Germany seen as a major threat, prompting a re-orientation of the country's defences. Throughout the war, this threat of invasion was never seen to be diminishing; in fact, it was thought in the latter stages of the war that an invasion might become more likely, launched in a bid to break the stalemate of the Western Front. Plans were drawn up to evacuate the civilian population, to ensure that munitions, transport, food reserves and livestock were denied the enemy, and that dedicated lines of communication were kept clear to enable a defensive response, in the event of an invasion on this vulnerable coast. This concern led to large numbers of troops being retained for home defence throughout the war. A gesture to mobility was made by employing first cavalry, and then cyclist units in this role, some of which were un-horsed Yeomanry cavalry, expecting them to respond to alarms more quickly than might infantry.

The Highland Mounted Brigade was based at Skegness and Alford for nine months from November 1914, the Lovat's Scouts arriving with 3,000 horses. The Scottish Horse Mounted Brigade was based in the county from July 1916 to the end of 1917, and the 19th Mounted Brigade, later re-designated the 12th Cyclist Brigade, from January to May 1918. The 10th Cyclist Brigade, composed of second-line Yeomanry units from the northwest was based at Skegness, Alford, Spilsby and Burgh-le-Marsh. As well as these, specialist Territorial cyclist units from the East Yorkshire and Suffolk Regiments, and also the Northern and Huntingdonshire Cyclist Battalions were based at Louth, Sutton-le-Marsh, Alford, Chapel-St-Leonards, Grimsby and Skegness throughout the war. The 62nd (2nd West Riding) Division, part of the Northern Army along with the 58th and 64th Divisions, was based in Lincolnshire until finally posted to France in February 1917. These formations accounted for enormous numbers (each infantry division numbered over 18,000 men), and although much of their time was notionally spent preparing for the fighting in France, it nevertheless represented a disproportionate commitment of non-renewable manpower when that resource was growing scarcer with every offensive.

The fixed defences of the Humber were mainly located on the north bank, but there were batteries at Killingholme and Stallingborough on the south bank. Virtually all of the up-to-date batteries were completed once the war had started, Stallingborough's two 6" guns on concrete towers opening early in 1915. The same solution to the problem of firing over high flood-defence embankments was applied at Killingholme. Here, twin octagonal concrete towers mounting 12-pounder QF guns were built side-by-side on a plinth, and were also completed in 1915. Following the first German bombardments of east coast ports late in 1914, a War Emergency Programme of building fixed defences was implemented. As well as new batteries on Spurn Head and up the Holderness coast, this plan provided for two sea-forts in the estuary. Bull Sand Fort was nearer to Spurn Head, but Haile Sand Fort was located just off Humberston Fitties. The first piles were sunk in April 1915, and within two years, two 4" QF guns had been installed on the gun-deck, with searchlights in sponsons on the first floor. Its purpose was to prevent enemy torpedo boats from sneaking through the shallow channel close to the Lincolnshire coast. Basically, it was a circular tower constructed from a hollow double-skin of steel plating filled with concrete, sitting on a concrete raft bedded onto steel piles driven deep into the sea-bed. On the roof behind the two gun-positions was a steel tower containing the Battery Observation Post with a Barr and Stroud range finder, and a director station for the searchlights. A boom ran across the estuary, with gaps controlled by boom-defence vessels, and covered by the forts' guns, to allow legitimate traffic through to the ports. The two 4" guns installed in the fort were naval guns which only came into use in 1914. They were designed to be dual-use, with an AA capability, being able to reach a ceiling of 28,000ft (8,550m), but a design fault which made it difficult to load at elevations over 20 degrees meant that its rate of fire was much reduced. Only this pair on Haile Sand Fort, on special coast-defence mountings, remained in army use.

An element of mobile defence was added to the area when a 9.2" howitzer on a railway mounting was allocated on the line between Grimsby and Cleethorpes. Its range of nearly 6 miles (9km) gave it coverage of around 15 square miles (4,000 hectares) of the estuary. Its mounting, which sat on a railway well-wagon, allowed it to traverse through 360 degrees, although it was often ill-advisable to shoot at right-angles to the line, as the recoil could topple the whole equipment off the narrow track. This problem was usually solved by curving the track so that the gun was always firing within a few degrees of straight, and using stabilisers in the same way as do modern cranes. Later models of this 9.2" howitzer had a range of up to 15 miles (24km).

In addition to these defences around the estuary, the whole Lincolnshire coast was defended by pillboxes and barbed wire obstacles. Although dugouts had become common as refuges in the trenches, and concrete shelters were provided for machine-gunners, the actual pillbox, a structure to be defended by its garrison firing weapons through loopholes, was a latecomer, only appearing in numbers in 1918. Still mindful of the dangers of a German sea-borne invasion, pillboxes were built along the Lincolnshire coast. A number of types were built, mainly hexagonal, circular or trapezoidal. These were designed as machine-gun posts for the defence of beaches particularly vulnerable to attack by infantry being ferried ashore by landing-barge. There were no specialist flat-bottomed landing craft at this time, but barges could be carried by larger ships and lowered into the water from davits in the same way as were lifeboats, filled with troops.

A number of First World War pillboxes survive on the Lincolnshire coast, often in conjunction with examples from the Second World War (*39*). They usually have sides 15–18in (0.38–0.46m) in thickness, made of concrete blocks or poured concrete using timber shuttering. There will usually be a concrete roof, four or five loopholes, sometimes with steel shutters, and a low doorway, often protected by a steel door. They were often the most visible element in a defensive scheme using mines, wire, and trenches. Although there were no coast batteries as such on the coast, field guns and heavier artillery were often dug in and camouflaged, or emplaced in fieldworks made of logs and concrete blocks with their roofs turfed over. Many of the guns emplaced in these works would have been old 15-pounder Ehrhardt guns that had been replaced after 1903 by British-designed models, and then passed down to the TF. There was also a coast-watching operation in place. Until 1923, the coastguard service was part of the Royal Navy and was controlled by the Admiralty. Coastguards were members of the RNR, so were automatically mobilised for service at sea, many of them serving in the *Agincourt* class of cruiser, three of which were sunk by *U9* in the North Sea in September 1914, with enor-

39 THEDDLETHORPE-St-HELEN (TF445958): a First World War pillbox built to enfilade the beach with machine-gun fire, with a Second World War pillbox built in front

mous loss of life. Coastguard stations such as that at Barrow-upon-Humber, for instance, also acted as naval recruiting offices. Since so many coastguards had been called up for service afloat, their places were taken by groups of Boy Scouts who were proficient in semaphore signalling.

As well as all the troops in full-time occupation guarding the coast, there was a First World War version of the Home Guard. Known as the Volunteer Training Corps, it was meant to fulfil a dual role. As a means of mobilising those who were in reserved occupations, it provided a part-time defence force for guarding vulnerable points such as railways or munitions factories, and also provided youngsters with an opportunity to gain some military training prior to their official call-up. Units were set up all over the country, staffed by superannuated NCOs, some of whom will have fought in the Crimea. Their GR armbands were unkindly, interpreted as standing for 'Grandad's Relics'. In Bourne, for example, members used an indoor miniature rifle range in the basement of the Institute in West Street, and drilled on the nearby open spaces of the castle meadows.

THE ROYAL NAVY IN LINCOLNSHIRE IN THE FIRST WORLD WAR

In June 1907, elements of the Channel Fleet paid an official visit to Grimsby, and this was the start of a more formal relationship with the navy. From 1907, HMS *Pekin* was the shore base of the Auxiliary Patrol Service, and after the opening of the port of Immingham in 1912, the Admiralty made it the centre of its newly established Eastern Command. Operational forces were expanded to include the Seventh Destroyer Flotilla, along with the 'C' Class submarines that had made use of the facilities here for some time. The trawlers *St George* and *Wallington* (aka *Sheraton* and *Oriflamme*) were hired as depot ship and boom defence vessel respectively. An old gunboat, *Hebe*, became the submarine depot ship, and the obsolete cruiser *Wallaroo* served as overflow accommodation for the base, and as a tender for *Hebe*. In order to ensure that the best use was made of the escort ships available to protect coastal merchant shipping, a Port Convoy Office was set up. All these developments created a sudden need for clerks, secretaries, and telephone-operators and, as male writers were needed at sea, local women were recruited for these jobs, becoming the first members of the WRNS. Their role was later extended into manual and technical tasks such as servicing mines and depth charges, and maintaining A/S nets. Towards the end of the war, all these shore facilities were put together as HMS *Pembroke VII* and *VIII*. Completing the complex of naval installations were the W/T station at Waltham, and the Immingham oil depot at Killingholme Haven. The W/T station would handle the naval signals during the Battle of Jutland, along with all the routine traffic generated by the Command.

With the commissioning of the two sea-forts in the Humber estuary, civilian vessels of the WD fleet were based in Grimsby to service them. From 1917, the *Lord Wolseley* (built 1912) was fitted with water tanks to carry fresh water out to the gunners. The *Sir Herbert Miles* (built 1912) was used as a target-tower and as a general tender for the forts. Grimsby was the base for all WD vessels operating in the northeast.

THE ROYAL NAVAL AIR SERVICE (RNAS)

Early in the war, the RNAS was assigned the task of defending sea- and land-based targets against attack by both aircraft and submarines. A suitable site next to the oil depot was identified as a base for aircraft, kite balloons and floatplanes. Two-seater Sopwith *Scouts* carried out the first anti-*Zeppelin* patrols, armed only with a rifle. Soon these were supplemented by Sopwith *Schneiders* armed with a Lewis gun firing incendiary bullets. It was also intended that these sea-planes would patrol the convoy routes, as well as being used to intercept *Zeppelins* as they crossed the coast on their way to bomb industrial targets. A new plan for combating the *Zeppelins* involved taking the aircraft out to sea by boat. The aptly named GNR paddle steamer *Killingholme*, built in 1912 as a ferry across the Humber, was requisitioned for this purpose. Its sister-ship *Brocklesby* went to the RNAS base at Great Yarmouth (Norfolk) to fulfil the same role there. It could ferry three or four *Schneider* floatplanes out to their patrol areas, lowering them into the sea by derricks, so they could take off and seek out the airships. This was a way of conserving their fuel and giving them a longer time in the air in the likely target area. However, this was not a success as the paddle steamers were neither sufficiently robust for the task, nor able to defend themselves against enemy attack, so the *Schneiders* reverted to conventional methods.

Stored in large aeroplane sheds, they were towed down the slipways, and launched into the water for take-off. In 1914, a timber slipway 700ft (215m) long and 60ft (18m) wide was constructed, and two years later, two more, 850ft (260m) long and 35ft (11m) wide, were added. The aircraft were originally stored in canvas *Bessoneau* hangars, but these were replaced by four timber Dutch-barn-type sheds in the technical area, and then four very much larger hangars were added, including one measuring 800ft (245m) wide by 220ft (70m) deep to accommodate the larger sea-planes such as the *Felixstowe*. The officers' mess was in the Old Vicarage. In July 1918, the station was handed over to the US Navy who flew *Curtiss* flying boats on North Sea patrols until the end of the war. The station closed in 1920. The one remaining slipway was surveyed in 2007 prior to its demolition on safety grounds.

Throughout the war, landplanes continued to operate from Killingholme alongside seaplanes and kite balloons. Kite balloons were towed on wires from destroyers, and were intended to provide elevated platforms for observers to spot U-boats that would shadow convoys awaiting the opportunity to strike. Anti-submarine escorts could then be directed on to the target. On occasions, the combination of destroyer and kite balloon completed the job themselves. An odd assortment of gunboats and steamers served as depot ships for Number 8 Kite Balloon Base, located in Immingham Dock, adjacent to land temporarily requisitioned from the Grand Central Railway, now within the Container Port. After the failure of the *Schneider* ferrying operation, *Killingholme* stayed on to become the depot ship for barrage balloons in the next war. Non-rigid airships known as 'Submarine Scouts' also carried out patrols with the fuselage of a *BE2c* aircraft slung beneath to carry the observers. Soon there was a need for a slightly larger non-rigid airship, still for coastal patrolling but carrying a bigger bomb-load. The *Coast Patrol* class was just under 200ft (60m) long, and used a four/five-seater *Avro* fuselage as a gondola.

In 1914, the Admiralty acquired a site at Cranwell to set up a training airfield for pilots of kite balloons, non-rigid and dirigible airships and aeroplanes. In December 1915 work started on what would become HMS *Daedalus*, the Navy's first stone frigate, with a detached bombing and gunnery range on the salt marshes at Freiston. Seaplane pilots would train at Killingholme. By the end of the war, by which time the RNAS had joined the RFC to form the RAF, there were two airfields at Cranwell holding three training depot stations, a W/T school, and a Lighter-than-Air training section. This extensive aerodrome was the largest in the British Isles and had its own branch railway line from Sleaford, the old railway station now serving as the College guardroom. On what was to become the North Airfield, an enormous hangar, 700ft (215m) long by 150ft (45m) wide, and 100ft (30m) high, for rigid airships was built. From opposite corners, wind-screens, each as long as the hangar and 70ft (20m) high, prevented airships, emerging from the hangar, from being blown away by sudden gusts of wind. Two smaller sheds, both equipped with wind-screens held *Submarine Scout* (SS) and *Coast Patrol* (CP) non-rigid airships, kite balloons and spherical coal-gas balloons. Grouped around the hangars were the hydrogen gas plant, cylindrical gasholders and workshops. A little way away were the other buildings of the camp, including a solitary survivor, currently in use as an Italian restaurant. In 1917, the South Airfield was developed to accommodate the seven flights of the aeroplane section which instructed pilots, who had completed their standardised preliminary training at other RNAS stations, in the advanced skills of cross-country navigation, wireless, aerial photography, bombing and aerial gunnery.

THE ROYAL FLYING CORPS (RFC) AND AIR DEFENCE

As soon as war broke out, troops were despatched to Burgh Road, Skegness to establish an airfield for a squadron of RNAS aircraft from Eastchurch (Kent). The aircraft were to carry out patrols along the coast, on the lookout for *Zeppelins*. Within a few days, the detachment was sent to Ostend, and their duties were taken over by the Killingholme units. By early 1916, *Zeppelin* attacks were becoming more frequent. Bombs were dropped on Scunthorpe, Humberston and Cleethorpes. On 31 March, Cleethorpes was bombed, and thirty-one soldiers sleeping in a chapel were killed. The response was to establish RFC Home Defence squadrons of fighters to intercept and destroy the intruders. No. 33 Squadron, flying mainly *Bristol Fighters*, with its HQ at 'The Lawns' on Summerhill Road, Gainsborough, maintained flights of eight aircraft each at Elsham, Kirton in Lindsey (Manton), and Scampton (Brattleby). Another Home Defence squadron, No. 38, used Leadenham, Buckminster and Melton Mowbray (Leicestershire). Tydd St Mary, right on the county boundary, was one of the three airfields of 51 Squadron for a while, with most of the unit operating from Norfolk.

These airfields had only rudimentary buildings to begin with, with perhaps a couple of *Bessoneau* hangars, and wooden huts for accommodation, offices, garages and workshops. Gradually these airfields acquired permanent hangars, usually with brick walls and bowstring roofs supported on timber trusses. The officer of the watch occupied a small brick or timber building, hence the term 'Watch Office'. A brick watch office in a very ruinous condition barely survives at Tydd. In order to keep aircraft in the air for as long as possible, a network of a dozen or so landing grounds was established by paying farmers to keep fields clear for casual daytime landings. More important were the similar number of night landing-grounds. Here a small permanent staff would maintain a field, and stand by to light fires or launch flares. Small sheds were supplied for fuel and other stores, and sometimes a living-hut or tents for the ground staff. Emergency Landing Grounds included Braceby, Moorby, Gosberton, and Kelstern, and examples of Night Landing Grounds are Anwick, Cockthorne, Greenland Top, Market Deeping, North Coates and Blyborough. Operating these night landing-grounds could be a dangerous business, as the flare that helped friendly aircraft to land could also attract unwelcome attention. One night in September 1917, a *Zeppelin* dropped its bombs on Cuxwold.

40 SCOPWICK/DIGBY: the Officers' Mess at this RFC airfield is still in use as an inter-Service training centre for communications specialists

The high casualty rate amongst fliers on the Western Front, and the vast expansion of the RFC with ever more roles to carry out, necessitated an extensive training organisation. Spitalgate, Waddington, South Carlton, and Harlaxton were all established for training, and finished the war as Training Depot Stations (TDS), Nos 39, 48, 46 and 40 respectively. Some former operational stations also fulfilled this function, No. 34 TDS at Scampton, No. 59 at Scopwick/Digby, and 199 and 200 Night Training squadrons at Harpswell. The TDS was built to a standard layout with six large General Service (GS) hangars, with their distinctive bowstring roofs with timber trusses, often referred to as 'Belfast Truss' hangars, and a single, smaller, Aircraft Repair Shed (ARS). The remains of a similar set-up to this can still be seen at Bracebridge Heath (see below).

Flying control often consisted of a cabin, high up on the corner of one of the hangars, with a view over the airfield. Most of the other buildings of the TDS were single-storey huts. Some may still be seen at Spitalgate and at Digby (**40**). Many of these huts were quite substantial and have had quite long lives, but not necessarily on their original sites. Much of the original officers' mess from Scampton, for instance, was moved to Werrington, outside Peterborough (Cambridgeshire) serving as private homes into the new Millennium, and only then being demolished as they occupied valuable building plots. A number of hangars extended their useful lives by becoming bus garages or workshops on new sites. Towards the end of the war, coastal shipping losses to U-boats continued to escalate, so a regular sequence of coastal shipping patrols was implemented using aircraft based at Greenland Top and

North Coates, both airfields already established as night landing-grounds. By the end of the war there were thirty-four operational/training airfields in the county, and a stores distribution centre at Longdales Road, Lincoln that supplied spare parts to the operational stations.

AIRCRAFT CONSTRUCTION IN LINCOLNSHIRE

Not only were aircraft flown from Lincolnshire, but they were also built in very large numbers by Lincolnshire factories. Although there were no dedicated aircraft manufacturing companies in Lincoln, the skills base in the well-established local engineering industry provided the perfect conditions for meeting the need to expand the national capacity for aircraft production. The process was begun by Ruston, Proctor & Co. Ltd, whose works on Spike Island, and at Boultham, both sides of the Witham west of High Street, had produced 2,000 aircraft, 3,000 aircraft-engines, and many more spares by the end of the war, with 3,000 men and women in just the firm's aviation workforce. Many men had volunteered for the services so women, known as 'munitionettes', were recruited, having to learn new skills. They were also required to help implement new methods of mass-production. Amongst Ruston's output were *BE2c* two-seater biplanes, later followed by *BE2d*s and *BE2e*s, Sopwith 1½ *Strutter* scouts, *Camel* and *Snipe* fighters. Rustons became the largest manufacturer of aircraft engines nationally, including types designed by Rolls Royce, Bentley and Clerget. Some parts were sub-contracted, such as the propellers, cut and shaped at the Kerr Pattern Co. in Rosemary Lane. A Ruston-built Sopwith *Camel 2F1* (No. F4043), responsible for shooting down the last *Zeppelin* of the war, is on show at the Imperial War Museum in London. This model was designed for naval use, being launched from ships, and in this particular case, from a lighter.

Another Lincoln firm pressed into building aircraft was Clayton & Shuttleworth at their Stamp End and Titanic works east of the railway and south of the Witham. Starting with the construction of Submarine Scout non-rigid airships, they graduated to building Sopwith *Triplanes* for the Admiralty, Sopwith *Camels* and *Snipes*, and then the enormous Handley-Page *0/400* bomber, for which operation the Abbey and Tower works were built. This building work was carried out by prisoners-of-war accommodated in the adjacent camp. Their final order for 150 Vickers *Vimy* bombers was cancelled as the war was over, and only three were built. Two *Camels* built by Clayton & Shuttleworth survive, one (No. B7280) in the Polish Aviation Museum in Kracow, and another (No. B5747) in the Brussels Air Museum.

Robey & Co. Ltd first built the Sopwith *806 Gunbus* at their Globe works south of Pelham Bridge (*41*), and in two new shops put up in Coultham Street. This was followed by the *Short 184* seaplane, which went to RNAS Killingholme. Next were orders for Maurice Farman *Longhorn* trainers. Alongside this contract work, Robey's was the only Lincoln firm to design new models of their own. One of these projects was a three-seater, heavily armed Robey *Fighting Machine*, designed by J. A. Peters. This carried two 7ft-long (2.15m-long) recoil-less 2-pounder Davis guns and a

41 LINCOLN: the offices of Robey's 'Globe' works, south of Pelham Bridge, where aircraft including the Sopwith *Gunbus* were produced

130 Defending Lincolnshire: A Military History from Conquest to Cold War

42 LINCOLN WEST COMMON: the RFC crest over a fireplace in the Grandstand that served as the officers' mess of No. 4 Aircraft Acceptance Park during the Second World War

43 LINCOLN WEST COMMON: now used as the Bowls Clubhouse, this building, formerly standing adjacent to the main hangars of the Acceptance Park, may have served as flight offices

The First World War (1914–18) 131

44 BRACEBRIDGE HEATH: the Aircraft Repair Shed of No. 4 Aircraft Acceptance Park after its move here from West Common

45 BRACEBRIDGE HEATH: residential bungalows on the west side of Sleaford Road, fashioned from the workshops of the Acceptance Park; the clerestory roof has been removed and new gable ends inserted

conventional Lewis machine gun. Sadly its test flight ended in disaster on the roof of the County Lunatic Asylum at Bracebridge, and a second aircraft enjoyed no better fortune, crashing nearby. Despite being in the process of developing a seaplane, Peters left the firm in 1917.

As well as these three Lincoln companies, Marshalls of Gainsborough built large numbers of aircraft at their Carr House Works on Lea Road. The first order was for 150 Bristol *F2B* fighters for reconnaissance work, followed by orders for *BE2c* and *BE2e* fighters. Such was the significance of the aircraft industry to Lincoln, that many smaller firms were involved in producing components. Penny and Porter machined metal parts for Clayton & Shuttleworth's aircraft, we have already met Kerr's propellers, and local builders and tradesmen would have met all the building requirements for factories and airparks.

With such a high output of aircraft from the Lincoln factories, it was necessary to set up testing facilities, and a centre for storing and distributing aircraft. Consequently two Aircraft Acceptance Parks (AAPs) with large flying fields were established. The first, No. 4 AAP, was built on the racecourse on West Common. A number of hangars were built along Aldermans Walk, and five *Bessoneau* hangars were added later. The Grandstand was used for accommodation and housed the officers' mess (**42**). Hutting housed workshops, offices and further living quarters. Tennis courts now occupy the site of the two main hangars and an adjoining L-shaped building shown on a contemporary plan (**43**) is probably that now serving as the Bowls Clubhouse, although constructional details in the roof, recently revealed during repairs, may suggest a later date.

Clayton & Shuttleworth also maintained a flying field for the Handley Page *0/400* and Vickers *Vimy* bombers they built at their Abbey and Tower works. This closed at the end of the war. The landing ground at West Common was never easy to fly from, so Robey's acquired a testing ground south of St John's asylum at Bracebridge Heath. This site was less encumbered by housing, was flat, and had room for expansion. By 1916, the War Office decided that this site should replace West Common, and Robey's original shed was supplemented by more sheds and by ten *Bessoneau* hangars. This new arrangement was particularly vital for the enormous Handley Page *0/400s* expected to arrive in numbers.

Overlapping with this move from West Common was a proposal to develop Bracebridge Heath into a permanent RFC/RAF station. Two triple GS hangars and an Aircraft Repair Shed (**44**) were constructed by summer 1918, with hutted accommodation on the opposite side of the main road, and personnel and aircraft began to move in along with the AAP. Only the end of the war prevented this growth. On the west side of Sleaford Road a number of huts survive. On the corner of Main Avenue are three bungalows that were carved out of a workshop building around 1924 (**45**). Two bays were removed and new additional end walls inserted, while the clerestory roof was lowered into a Dutch gable profile roof. Several other buildings also retain the telltale buttresses of single-brick buildings of this time. In the last few years, one of the triple sheds has been demolished, but the other one, though greatly modified, and the ARS survive along with later buildings on the site.

ANTI-AIRCRAFT DEFENCES

At the beginning of the First World War, the possibility of enemy aircraft bombing military targets, let alone civilian ones, in Britain was unthinkable. Not only, it was thought, was the technology undeveloped, but this was an action no civilised nation could even contemplate. Unfortunately, just over a year into the war, both civilian and military authorities were to be disabused of these ingenuous notions with the first *Zeppelin* bombing-raids of January 1916. Although searchlights existed in naval and coast defence contexts, and anti-balloon guns had been around a while, neither dedicated anti-aircraft (AA) weapons nor organisational structure existed. All sorts of attempts were made to improvise AA weapons, from machine guns clamped to wooden posts, to 1-pounder pom-poms, to high-angle coast defence guns, to 6" howitzers firing 100lb (45kg) shells vaguely skywards.

Throughout both world wars, the people on the ground were usually in more danger from unexploded AA shells, or the falling remnants of exploded ones, than they were from enemy bombs. Initially, the War Office expected that in the unlikely event that air attacks were going to happen, they would be directed at military targets. Therefore the few AA guns that were available were located at Cleethorpes W/T station, the Admiralty oil tanks and seaplane base at Killingholme, and the RNAS base at Cranwell. But even there the guns were woefully thin on the ground.

46 CLEETHORPES: a First World War private air-raid shelter erected in Yarra Road by a local pharmacist

Cleethorpes had a pom-pom and Killingholme had two pom-poms and a pair of Hotchkiss 6-pounder QF guns. One of the experiments aimed at creating a viable AA gun involved fitting a 3in (75mm) calibre sleeve to a standard 18-pounder field gun. Thus adapted, the gun could fire a 13-pound shell but with the bigger cartridge to extend its ceiling, and some were installed to defend Cranwell and the steelworks at Scunthorpe. Another stop-gap weapon was the naval 12-pounder 12cwt (610kg) QF gun, considered far from ideal, but better than nothing. By June 1916, one such, with an accompanying searchlight, had been placed on each of two sites protecting Lincoln, at Canwick and at Burton Road, both administered by Sheffield AA Command. The Burton Road searchlight site has recently been identified by oral history, and remains found on the ground suggest that it consisted of concrete platforms for the light and its generator, a shelter, probably a pre-*Nissen*-type hut on a dwarf wall, a chemical toilet and a fuel store.

The most effective AA gun was the 3", 20cwt (1 tonne) gun, developed by 1914, but only becoming available in sufficient quantity in 1916. These were certainly emplaced around the Humber, and possibly elsewhere. Another tactic was to team up searchlights with fighter aircraft, and such a combination was based at Brattleby (later Scampton), where a searchlight unit was based at Aisthorpe Farm, along with a flight of fighters of 38 Home Defence Squadron. Passive defence against aerial attack was almost non-existent. Shelters were not provided for military or civilians, so protection was left to private enterprise. At least one private individual, a pharmacist in Cleethorpes, thought it worthwhile to take precautions against bombing attacks by building his own air-raid shelter (**46**), but this was the exception.

ARMY CAMPS AND DEPOTS

The peacetime depot of the Lincolnshire Regiment at Sobraon Barracks in Lincoln had insufficient capacity for the needs of the new armies. We have already seen how the Grimsby Chums assembled at Brocklesby Park, early in 1915. Later that year the hutted camp provided accommodation for the 19th Reserve Bn. of the Sherwood Foresters, and in the summer of 1916, for the 12th Labour Bn. of the Lincolnshire Regiment. Belton Park, outside Grantham, well established as a summer camp for the Rifle Volunteers and the Territorial Force, became a much busier camp, warranting the construction of a railway spur, 2.5 miles (4km) long, off the Great Northern line at Peascliff Tunnel across to Belton (***Fig. 8***). This camp covered the entire area from the present golf clubhouse across to Belmount Tower. Local carpenters built upwards of 1,000 huts to replace the original tented camp (**47**). From August 1914, the whole 11th (Northern) Division, part of the first of Kitchener's new armies (K1), consisting mainly of battalions of northern counties regiments, but also including the 6th Bn. Lincolnshire, and the 5th Bn. Dorsetshire Regiments, assembled at Belton prior to going via Aldershot to Gallipoli in June 1915. In April 1915, the 30th Division (K4), made up almost entirely of 'Pals' battalions from Liverpool, Manchester and Oldham, had begun to assemble at Belton, proceeding to Larkhill

The First World War (1914–18) 135

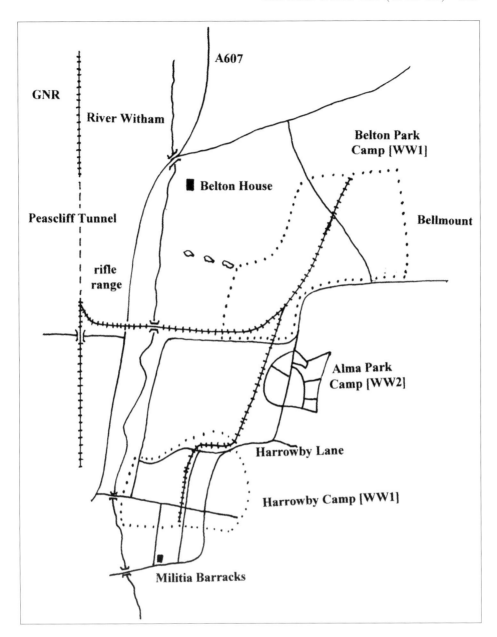

Fig. 8 Location of camps at Grantham and Belton during the two world wars

47 BELTON PARK CAMP: some of the 1,000 huts erected to accommodate initially divisions of Kitchener's 'New Army', then the newly-formed Machine-Gun Corps. Image courtesy of Grantham Museum

48 HUMBERSTON FITTIES: the oldest remaining hut to survive from the earliest days of the chalet camp that began life with the 3rd Bn. Manchester Regiment, who spent the entire war in Cleethorpes

on Salisbury Plain in the autumn before going to France. One of the limitations of Belton Camp was that there was barely room for a division's infantry elements, so the artillery, engineers and service corps units were forced to assemble and train elsewhere, making it more difficult to integrate all these units – particularly the artillery – as they went into action together.

A second camp at Harrowby, in the space now bounded by Harrowby Lane and Beacon Lane with the river on the west, was then built in order that an entire division might be accommodated in one place. This new camp consisted of six large compounds labelled 'A' to 'F', each containing a guardhouse, around thirty living huts, officers' and sergeants' messes and quarters, plus ablutions, cookhouse and stores. Vehicle sheds, canteens, a cinema and classrooms were distributed across the camp, and a spur of the Belton Camp railway, on the line of the present New Beacon Road, served the equipment stores. The main thoroughfare of the camp was later to become Hill Avenue, the main approach from town being at the south end of Belton Lane.

In October 1915, just as the third-line territorial battalions of the North Midland Reserve Division were in the process of assembling in the new combined camps, Belton Park was chosen as the HQ and depot of a totally new corps. A year of trench warfare had shown that the use of the *Vickers* machine gun had become a specialist skill, demanding more training, and more centralised organisation in the field. Infantry battalions would be equipped with the new *Lewis* light machine gun, allowing the hitherto dispersed sections of *Vickers* guns to be re-organised into companies, each with sixteen guns, and allocated on the basis of one company to each brigade. A total of 3,000 men were detached from their regiments to become the nucleus of the Machine Gun Corps. After the Palestine campaign the Lincolnshire Yeomanry, minus their horses, were absorbed into the Corps which, by the end of the war in 1918, had over 133,000 officers and men. The original Harrowby Camp had been set up with the stabling and harness-rooms that horsed artillery units needed, but these were now adapted to provide extra living accommodation for their new occupants. The sudden arrival of tens of thousands of young men had a significant effect on Grantham, whose response included a female curfew from 8pm until 7am. At the end of the war, although it was realised that the machine gun would continue to play a dominant role on the battlefield, government economies meant that the MGC had been disbanded by 1922. Belton Park Camp was demolished, but Harrowby Camp continued in use as a Ministry of Pensions hospital until 1930.

Further army camps were built as required. From late in 1914 throughout the war, the 3rd and 4th (Special Reserve) Bns., the Manchester Regiment were stationed in the Cleethorpes area with a dual role. Alongside coast defence duties as part of the Humber Garrison, they also had a training role. We have seen how 30th Division contained no fewer than eight newly raised battalions of the Manchesters, and these spent some of their time, notionally based in Grantham, in training camps at Riby Park (now Riby Grove) and at Humberston Fitties. Large camps grew up on both these sites, and troops were also billeted wherever there was space. Thirty-one men of the Manchesters were killed when a bomb fell on

138 Defending Lincolnshire: A Military History from Conquest to Cold War

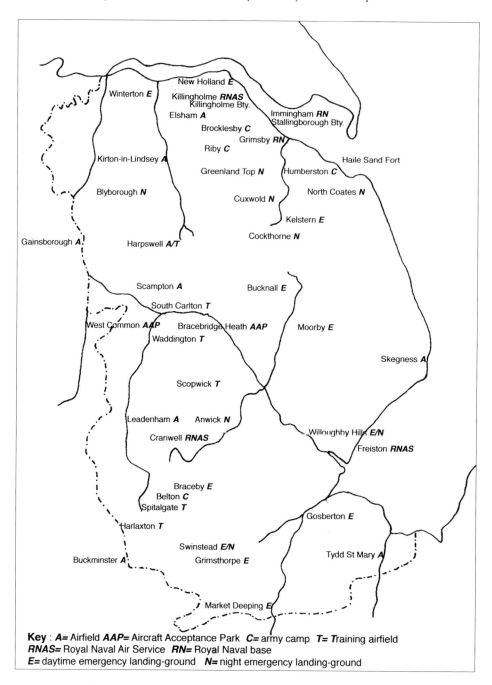

Fig. 9 First World War sites in Lincolnshire

their Baptist Chapel billet in Cleethorpes. Entrenching practice was enlivened at Riby when troops of the 4th Bn. dug up some Anglo-Saxon burials. The camp at Humberston Fitties occupied the site of a pre-war tenting-ground, and many of the huts (*48*), put up by the Manchesters, formed the basis of the chalet camp which has lasted since 1919 (**Fig. 9**).

THE DEVELOPMENT AND PRODUCTION OF THE TANK

During the last decades of the nineteenth century, Lincolnshire engineering firms were active in developing mainly agricultural machinery, such as thrashing machines and traction engines for hauling ploughs and portable steam engines. These firms included Ruston, Proctor & Co, Clayton & Shuttleworth, Wm. Foster, and Tuxford in Lincoln, Hornsby's in Grantham, and Marshall's in Gainsborough. In 1873, Foster's works in Hungary had built some torpedo boats for use on the Danube, but the output of all these firms was otherwise directed at peaceful ends. A number of products could have had military applications, such as the three-wheeled traction engines fitted with *Boydell* wheels, which had wooden boards fitted round the wheel-rim in order to spread the machine's weight over the ground. However, it was not until 1908 that the War Office began to look at the possibilities of mechanised traction.

Hornsby's won a competition in that year for a road tractor, and their oil-powered version exceeded the minimum specification laid down by the military. Hornsby then fitted their prototype chain tracks to a car with a 40hp engine to demonstrate to the army in Aldershot, adopting the term *caterpillar* as a generic descriptor. General enthusiasm, followed up by exhibitions and films, created a great deal of interest around the world, but the army's high command was dominated by cavalry officers and, unbelievably, the idea received no substantive backing from either the commercial or the military market. The idea was sold for a song, to the Holt Manufacturing Co. of New York.

In August 1914, a RNAS unit operating in Belgium, decided to compensate for their lack of aircraft by arming a number of private cars for use as reconnaissance vehicles. Favourable reports got back to Winston Churchill, the First Lord of the Admiralty, one of whose colleagues, Francis McClaren, the MP for Spalding, commanded a squadron of such cars in action at Gallipoli. Just prior to this a number of ideas for tracked artillery tractors and land battleships had come together and the Director of Naval Construction, Eustace Tennyson d'Eyncourt from Tealby, was directed to convene a Landships Committee. Not unnaturally, he turned to Fosters of Lincoln, whom he knew to be innovative. The engineer William Tritton and William Rigby, his chief draughtsman, would work with a naval liaison offcer, Lt. Walter Wilson, himself an engineer, to explore possibilities and to produce a working prototype. As soon as examples of the current technology had been retrieved from the Holt company, and from the Bullock Creeping Grip Tractor Company of Chicago, work began. By September 1915, *Number One Lincoln Machine* was moving, but not as effectively as it would need to. A number of modifications produced *Little Willie*, basically an armoured box on tracks, which was given trials in Lincoln's Burton Park. Much of the engineering was based on the Foster-Daimler heavy artillery tractor, also manufactured at the Wellington Foundry, but there remained a problem with keeping the tracks on. However, a radical improvement was suggested which consisted of a lozenge-shaped body with wrap-around tracks, with only eight of their ninety links being in contact with the ground at any one time. This was known initially at Fosters as *Big Willie*, by the Admiralty as *Centipede*, and universally as *Mother* (**49**).

D'Eyncourt suggested fitting side sponsons carrying either 6-pounder Hotchkiss QF naval guns (*Male* tanks), or Vickers 0.303 machine guns (*Female* tanks), and steering was by means of twin wheels trailed behind. An initial batch of 100 tanks was ordered by the War Office, with twenty-five supplied by Fosters at their Wellington Works in Lincoln, and the rest by the Metropolitan Carriage Co. of Birmingham at their Oldbury railway works. Soon, fifty more were ordered, completing the Mark Is.

The first completed tanks were delivered in June 1916. Within a few months, they were in action at Flers-Courcellette on the Somme front, and on the strength of their performance, Sir Douglas Haig ordered 1,000 more. Production was now spread amongst more firms with Marshalls of Gainsborough being involved. Small production runs of Mark IIs and IIIs having been completed for training purposes, around 1,200 Mark IVs, incorporating many design modifications, were built from March 1917 for active service. Metropolitan remained the main contractor, and Fosters continued both to build their allocation, and to design modifications such as the 'Tadpole Tail', incorporated in the Mark V★ model, which enabled tanks to clear wider trenches. By 1918, around 2,000 Mark V and V★ tanks had replaced most of the older models.

As well as the better-known Marks I–IV tanks, there were many others developed by Fosters. The *Flying Elephant* armed with a 12-pounder QF gun never got past the prototype stage. The real challenge now was how to exploit a breakthrough achieved by the heavier tanks. What was needed was a tank that could perform the task traditionally given to the cavalry. A medium tank, the Tritton *Chaser*, soon named the *Whippet*, was one answer. With a crew of only three, it weighed 12 tons, carried four 0.303" Hotchkiss machine guns, and could manage 7.5 mph (12kmph) on flat ground. A number of other designs followed, but the final tank in this series, the *Hornet*, incorporated many of the improvements born of all this experience, and it was regarded highly by everyone apart from the cavalry. Some thirty-six out of the initial order for 200 were produced before the war ended.

Many of the older models had been sent around the country acting as rallying points for fund-raising activities aimed at boosting munitions production. Even as late as November 1918, Horncastle was hosting a 'Tanks Week'. At the end of the war, many towns were presented with tanks as war memorials, though all but a couple of them have disappeared over the years. Grantham's lasted only until March 1929 when it was sold for scrap, realising just £26. Lincoln's souvenir tank stood

The First World War (1914–18) 141

49 LINCOLN: one of the few surviving examples of First World War tanks; this female Mark IV is in the Museum of Lincolnshire Life in the old Militia barracks on Burton Road

until 1935 in Wickham Gardens when it, too, was scrapped. Spalding's Mark IV met the same fate a couple of years later. A female Mark IV at the Museum of Lincolnshire Life is now one of only around a dozen First World War tanks to survive in Britain today. The early planning meetings of the 'land-ships project' had been held in Lincoln's White Hart Hotel, which still retains its 'Tanks Room'. Other reminders of Lincoln's contribution to armoured warfare are roads named for Tritton, a solitary wall of Foster's factory off Waterloo Street, and a plaque in Morrisons supermarket, in the retail park which occupies the land once used as a tank testing-ground.

OTHER MUNITIONS PRODUCTION IN LINCOLNSHIRE

Not only tanks and aircraft were made in Lincolnshire. Local factories produced everything from pieces of troops' personal equipment to tinned foodstuffs. The idea for tracked armoured vehicles had originated in the tractors made by Fosters and Hornsby before the war. The artillery needed traction engines and caterpillar tractors for hauling heavy guns, and these continued to be made by Clayton & Shuttleworth, along with 12" heavy howitzers. Rustons also manufactured thousands of *Lewis* guns for use in both aircraft and tanks, and by the infantry. They were unpopular in tanks, and were replaced by the French Hotchkiss machine gun.

Although there was an enormous increase in the use of powered military vehicles, much of the army's transport was horse-drawn, and local joinery firms were kept busy building carts, limbers and other specialist workshop and catering vehicles. A number of town gas-works, including those in Lincoln and Boston, produced chemicals for explosives production. Outside Lincoln, Hornsby's of Grantham supplied mines, gun-mountings, marine engines and shells for the navy. Blackstones of Stamford kept the navy's motor launches afloat by manufacturing spares, and also produced parts for submarines. Marshalls of Gainsborough built large numbers of military vehicles, shells and fuses, gun-mountings and boilers, as well as aircraft, tanks and traction engines. Grimsby's focus was on the sea, and local shipyards, such as Doig's, carried out many of the adaptations necessary to turn trawlers into minesweepers and auxiliary patrol vessels, and back into trawlers at the end of the war. There was a mine-filling plant near Gainsborough (NFF No. 22), and those mines may have been stored at the Admiralty depot in Haxey. There are a few visible remains of NFF No. 22 alongside the railway opposite Thonock Lane Farm. The concrete base of a steel-framed shed, a garage, and what may have been a pump-house still survive.

AGRICULTURE

However insatiable might have been the demands of the military for munitions, the country still had to be fed, and as enemy submarines sunk more and more ships, so a greater quantity of food had to be grown at home. Much of the local engineering output therefore continued to be steam ploughs and tractors. In 1915, County War Agricultural Committees were set up to spread best practice and encourage efficient and effective farming. They were eventually to have a controlling say in what crops were grown, but the farmers traded some of their independence for a measure of prosperity as incomes rose sevenfold over the course of the war on some farms. There was an obvious problem over manpower, however. Although many employers, such as the Earl of Ancaster, promised that jobs would be kept open for those who volunteered for the services, the industry could not afford to lose so many agricultural labourers. The Women's Land Army was constituted in 1916, but could not wholly compensate for the level of loss in the work force. From the spring of 1917, the Committee's consent would be required for any full-time agricultural worker's release to the services. There was also a state-sponsored scheme to encourage mechanisation as a further way of compensating for the loss of agricultural labour.

HOSPITALS AND WELFARE

The 4th Northern General Hospital (TF), with its HQ in offices at 6b Guildhall Street, Lincoln, was one of twenty-three such organisations across the country, set up to be mobilised in the event of war. Parts of the civilian system were also mobilised for handling the treatment of battle casualties and for their convalescence. Many organisations were involved, especially the Red Cross, who organised local volunteers into Voluntary Aid Detachments (VADs) to run local auxiliary hospitals and nursing homes. The main military hospital was set up in Lincoln Christs Hospital School on Wragby Road to act as a base hospital, with supplementary provision around the county. The Lincoln hospital had beds for forty-one officers and 1,126 other ranks. There was a small hospital at Sobraon Barracks catering only for the regimental depot staff and their dependants, and a hutted hospital with 620 beds at the camp in Belton Park. The network of auxiliary hospitals, mostly under the Red Cross and VADs, were located in large houses ranging from Brocklesby Park to the Old Palace in Lincoln, Scopwick House, the Old Hall at Horbling, Râuceby Hall near Grantham, and Holden House and Allan House in Boston. In Skegness there were two auxiliary hospitals as well as the Derby Boys' Home. In Bourne, the Vestry Hall in North Street was converted for use as a VAD hospital, and at Boultham, the auxiliary hospital for convalescent service men was run by the St John Ambulance Association. Mablethorpe's hospital was also designated a convalescent home. There were two dozen such auxiliary hospitals in the county in all.

Accommodating the increased work force in Lincoln's munitions factories caused problems. As many local families as possible were encouraged to take in lodgers, despite there being insufficient vacancies. One solution was for the employers to take the initiative, and Fosters acquired Bracebridge Hall as a hostel for workers (**50**).

50 LINCOLN: Bracebridge Hall served as a hostel for Fosters workers during the First World War; it is now a care home

PRISONER-OF-WAR CAMPS

In the First World War, the majority of PoW camps were work camps. We have seen how such a camp was set up to provide labour for building additional factory space for Clayton & Shuttleworth's Abbey and Tower plants, and there were others of this type. The majority were agricultural to get labour into the fields, or to process foodstuffs. An inventory of camps compiled by Norman Nicol lists at least three dozen camps in Lincolnshire, but these include hospitals, industrial and agricultural locations such as Boston Docks and the Pinchbeck Road agricultural depot in Spalding, as well as quite rural locations as at Rippingale Fen or Temple Bruer, suggesting bases for small work-gangs. Two groups, totalling fifty-six prisoners, were billeted in Rippingale, half in the club-room of the Bull Hotel, and half at Camp Farm in the fen. Engaged in agricultural work, these men appear to have entered into the life of the community, making decorations for their Christmas party, and performing at concert parties in the village schoolroom.

Some of the locations listed as camps, such as Belton Park with its army camp, or Bracebridge Heath with its aircraft acceptance park, must have been quite sensitive. We know that at Bracebridge Heath, PoWs were engaged in construction work. They may have been held in secure camps on the barbed wire and watchtower model, or alternatively, small gangs of trusted prisoners might have carried out building and maintenance duties, and been billeted in huts on site. Many PoWs on both sides were only too happy to have escaped the perils of the Western Front quite legitimately and were unlikely to be actively seeking ways to return there. Therefore, with ever-decreasing pools of labour available, PoW labour was valued, especially where few guards were needed.

seven

Preparing for the Next War: Rearmament (1919–38)

Once the war was over, the clearing up and the winding down began. This had been, after all, the war to end all wars, and the defeated belligerents' forces were henceforth to be drastically limited by the Treaty of Versailles, so there was no need to maintain costly standing armies. Additionally, the Depression discouraged unnecessary public spending. The Ten Year Rule, which was to stay in force until 1932, decreed that it would take that long for a potential aggressor to re-arm to the point of endangering world peace, so there was always this breathing space, making rearmament something that existed in a permanent state of postponement, or of denial, as some would have it. Britain's defence budget shrank year-on-year, hitting an all-time low in 1932. Only in 1936 would it climb back, with an increase of thirty per cent announced in the White Paper on Rearmament, and it was to be Lincolnshire, in the process of assuming the mantle of 'Bomber County', which would receive a large proportion of this increased funding.

In the intervening years, much had been dismantled. Almost before the Armistice had been signed, the Manchesters at Humberston Fitties were removing the barbed wire obstacles and filling in the trenches and dugouts. The abrupt end to the war saw the munitions factories with cancelled contracts, stockpiles of suddenly inappropriate materials, and inflated pay rolls. The lack of an infrastructure geared to design, research and development, meant that new products and new markets were needed, but after a short boom came the depression, with very little call for military or aviation production. Clayton & Shuttleworth's former Stamp End works, by 1924 being used by Babcock & Wilcox, produced some mooring masts for the new airship routes to serve the Empire, but such orders were scarce. Rustons and Hornsbys amalgamated and all the local engineering firms went through a very bad patch, as their costs rose and their traditional markets disappeared.

One of the attractions of post-war life to which the returning servicemen and women might look forward was the promise of 'homes for heroes', and there were a number of plans across the county for estates based upon the principles of the

51 LINCOLN: houses built in Swanpool by Colonel Ruston in 1919 as 'homes for heroes'

garden suburb. Colonel Ruston's 1919 proposal for Swanpool on the southwest fringes of the city (**51**) failed to survive the engineering industry's doldrums, with only 113 of the proposed 2,000 houses being built. Lincoln's St Giles estate off the Wragby road fared somewhat better. By 1920, Skegness had ninety-nine new houses on the Richmond Drive estate, while the Nunsthorpe estate in Grimsby and Scunthorpe's Henderson Avenue estate were both well under way by 1920. These houses were designed to offer a comfortable setting for the family life that many were trying to start or resume in the years following the war. Newsum's of Broadgate, the joinery firm, needed bigger premises in Carholme Road to fulfil their contracts with Scottwood Factory Built Permanent Homes, who were supplying two-storey, prefabricated timber-frame houses for London County Council's new estates in Dagenham and Becontree.

Although the Humber sea-forts had seen no service in the war, their effectiveness was immediately in doubt, and much of their armament was removed. Haile Sand lost its 4" guns in 1929, the operation being carried out by vessels of the WD fleet, probably the *Katherine* (built 1882). It was the *Katherine*, in 1933, towing the barge *Gog*, that removed the two 9.2" guns from Green Battery on Spurn Head. Each gun-barrel weighed 29 tons, and a gunner was killed when a sudden swell caused one to roll in the barge. The barrels were towed to Grimsby and off-loaded onto the *Marquess of Hartington* for the journey to Woolwich Arsenal, where they would go into storage.

THE RAF AND ITS AIRFIELDS BETWEEN THE WARS

The RAF had finished the war with thirty-four operational airfields in Lincolnshire, but by 1920, this number had been greatly reduced, Scampton closing in April 1919, for instance, and Waddington at the end of the year. An aerial photograph of Cranwell dated 1923 appears to show that the airship hangars and wind-screens had already disappeared. Spitalgate became 3 Group HQ, with an additional operational airfield at Scopwick (Digby after July 1920), mainly used for training. Cranwell, home to the RAF Cadet College and the School of Technical Training, survived, but the RAF stores depot in Lincoln was placed in care and maintenance, and the Aircraft Acceptance Park at Bracebridge Heath was leased out to private concerns, including the local bus company.

During the 1920s, the RAF under Trenchard's leadership struggled to establish itself as an independent service with clearly defined roles, development plans and organisational structures. Given the financial stringency, the plan had to be simple and skeletal. The main components of the 1923 Steel-Bartholomew Plan were a bomber force located on airfields in the Thames Valley, and a defensive screen of fighter stations protecting London, and growth, small as it was throughout the twenties, tended to adhere to this basic outline.

Lincolnshire was seen as a conveniently remote training ground. In 1927, North Coates, and in the next year, Sutton Bridge, had opened as Armament Training Camps using the ranges at Donna Nook and Holbeach respectively. The buildings at both these airfields were typical of armament training camps. The main hangars were side-opening Admiralty 'F' Sheds, recycled from First World War seaplane bases. Sutton Bridge had one, and North Coates two pairs. Those at North Coates appear to be double-banked 'F' Sheds, but were referred to as 'C' type hangars, and may represent a prototype for a design which was never put into general production, although a very similar hangar, still in use by FAA helicopters, stands at Eglinton in Northern Ireland. Much of the accommodation at both these sites otherwise consisted of huts.

In 1923, the RAF acquired a large Victorian house, St Vincents (**52**) in Grantham, as the administrative HQ for all its training units. In 1937, St Vincents became the HQ of 5 Group Bomber Command, which it remained until 1943. Spitalgate outside Grantham, after whose Spittlegate suburb the airfield was supposedly named, shows a pattern of continuous development throughout this inter-war period. Having finished the First World War with the usual complement of training depot station 'Belfast truss' hangars and a large collection of huts, the station's appearance was to change quite radically over the next two decades, being one of only a few airfields in the country to be updated with buildings to the new post-war standards. The guard-room to a design of 1923, the parachute store designed in 1925 (**53**), several type 'C' barrack blocks dating from 1923 and 1927, and the single-storey watch office with bay-window, to a design of 1926, all still sit alongside rare barrack blocks from the First World War and Expansion Period buildings such as the Airmen's Mess and Institute of 1936, and arts and crafts terraces of married-quarters. Two buildings, however, stand out even more than all these. One is the unique officers' mess (**54**) of 1928, whose architect's drawings still hang inside, and the other is the Hinaidi hangar of 1927, supplied to very few other airfields, and which replaced the earlier aircraft repair shed.

The biggest building project of the early 1930s, however, was the RAF College at Cranwell, which eventually received buildings of appropriate dignity and gravitas in 1933. Sir Samuel Hoare, Secretary of State for Air, whilst supporting the notion of the college, was dismayed by the initial designs that he felt echoed a Victorian railway station, and took the architect, James West, to visit Wren's inspirational Royal Hospital at Chelsea. West took the hint and produced the neo-Baroque building we see today, fit to stand alongside Dartmouth and Sandhurst, as a sign that the new service had arrived. Alongside large numbers of huts surviving from the First World War, the airfield received a generous provision of hangar space over the two airfields: eight 'F' Sheds, eventually supplemented, later into the 1930s by four *Bellmans* and a pair of 'C' type hangars. Daedalus House, built in 1925 as an HQ building, still survives, as does The Lodge, the residence of the Air Officer Commanding. In 1929 the Electrical and Wireless School was established alongside Cranwell's existing training establishments. There was a RAF hospital at Cranwell from 1922 until 1940, but the Apprentices Wing had moved out when RAF Halton was completed in 1926. The new 'C' type hangars replaced old wooden sheds on the South airfield and, on the

52 GRANTHAM: St Vincents, a large house acquired by the RAF in 1923 as HQ for all training units; it subsequently housed the HQ of 5 Group Bomber Command from 1937, and then 9th USAAF Troop Carrier Command until 1944

53 GRANTHAM: RAF Spitalgate, the parachute store to a design of 1925

54 GRANTHAM: RAF Spitalgate, the officers' mess, opened in 1928

North airfield, the end of lighter-than-air development meant that the vast airship hangars, along with their massive wind-screens, and all the other paraphernalia that attended their use, were demolished.

RE-ORIENTATION AND EXPANSION

Only with the recognition that Germany might pose military problems again, did the nation's defence planners move away from the tradition of regarding France as the main potential source of conflict. In November 1935, the RAF was given the go-ahead to expand, and if it was Germany who was going to become the target for bombing raids, then it must be Lincolnshire that would accommodate many of the new bomber airfields. Early glimmerings of this expansion had been seen the previous year with improvements being made to Cranwell (*55*), and a start made on a new bomber base at Waddington.

In 1936 new starts included Hemswell (**Fig. 10**), Manby and Scampton, three more bomber bases, and a makeover for Digby, which would become a sector station of 12 Group Fighter Command. The next year, improvements were carried out at North Coates and Sutton Bridge. In 1938, Kirton-in-Lindsey was started as another Fighter Command sector station on a site some way from that used in the previous war. Right up to the eve of war, the construction programmes were racing against time, and the bomber bases at Binbrook, Coningsby and Swinderby were started. Elsham Wolds, a bomber station, and Goxhill, for fighters, found themselves in the tranche of new builds that overlapped into the beginning of the war. All these stations in the Expansion Period 1934–40, were built to peacetime standards of design and craftsmanship. The advantages of this included having lots of space, comfort and order, with all of the buildings attractively built to standardised neo-Georgian designs, grouped on an easily understood grid system. Unfortunately, the disadvantage was that both aircraft and personnel were concentrated together in a relatively small area, thus increasing their vulnerability to aerial attack.

It was quickly appreciated, both by the planners in the Air Ministry and the potential neighbours, that the visual impact on the countryside of these new airfields – over a dozen in Lincolnshire alone, each the size of a small town – would be enormous. The plans therefore had been overseen by the Royal Fine Arts Commission (RFAC), advised by Sir Edwin Lutyens, and the Council for the Preservation of Rural England (CPRE). On the suggestion of the RFAC, A. Bulloch FRIBA was appointed as adviser to the Air Ministry, and a whole suite of designs for individual buildings was produced, with all the buildings on these airfields sharing similar characteristics.

Drawing numbers were allocated consecutively, with the year of production following the slash. So the 190th drawing to emerge from the Air Ministry's design department in 1936, for instance, was for a Station HQ building, hence *190/36*. This particular HQ building can be seen at Manby and is instantly recognisable wherever it appears on other RAF Expansion Period sites. Bomber stations were usually laid

Preparing for the Next War: Rearmament (1919–1938)   151

55 CRANWELL: James West's neo-Baroque main college building, designed in 1933 to impart gravitas to the new RAF

out with four or five 'C' type hangars (**56**), which were built in an arc fronting the flying field in order to reduce the possibility of their being destroyed by a single stick of bombs.

These massive, solidly built hangars could accommodate the various aircraft of the day; they were also built on fighter stations. While only two of the three planned for Digby were completed, Kirton-in-Lindsey received all three. Manby has four hangars and a similar Aircraft Repair Shed. The earlier 'C' types have big square gables as at Waddington, while Binbrook's, later in the programme, have no gables and are sometimes referred to as 'Austerity' models. The airfields in the last phase of the programme, only completed after the outbreak of war – Swinderby, Goxhill, Elsham Wolds (**57**) and Coningsby – had curved-roof 'J' type hangars substituted for the more substantial 'C' types. At Waddington where the new hangars were built on the west side of the airfield, the earlier TDS hangars were left in place, and kept in use, until the hard runways were laid in mid-1943.

The provision of watch offices was affected in similar ways. Waddington, Scampton, Digby and Hemswell all had 'Fort' types (*1959/34* in brick, or *207/36* in concrete), Binbrook, Coningsby and Swinderby had smart art-deco 'Villa' types (*5845/39* in brick, or *2328/39* in concrete), as did Waddington as an early replacement for its 'Fort'. While Manby had a one-off design, Goxhill was given the first of the wartime utility versions, to drawing number *518/40*. The other buildings of the technical area included stores of different sorts, offices, workshops, parachute stores, an armoury and photographic building, garages for tankers, fire-fighting equipment

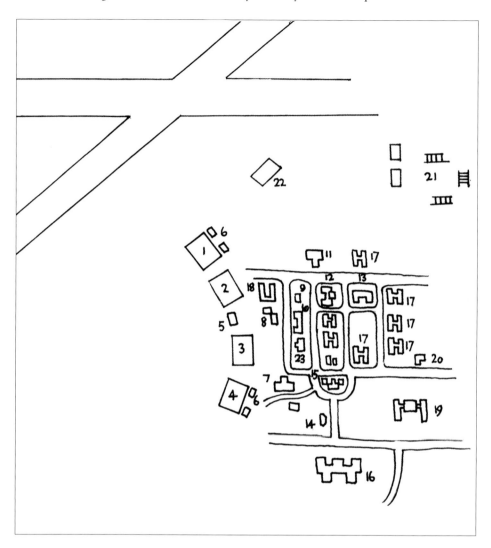

Fig. 10 Plan of Hemswell, a typical Expansion Period airfield. Key: 1–4. Hipped 'C' type hangars; 5. Watch office 207/36 and 4698/43, and extension; 6. Fuel tender sheds; 7. Sick bay; 8. Armoury; 9. Parachute store; 10. Main workshops; 11. Parachute drying tower; 12. Water tower; 13. Institute and dining room; 14. Guardroom; 15. Station HQ; 16. Officers' mess; 17. Accommodation block; 18. MT section; 19. Sergeants' mess; 20. NAAFI stores; 21. Bomb stores; 22. T2 hangar (c. 1942); 23. Main stores

Preparing for the Next War: Rearmament (1919–1938)   153

56 SCAMPTON: a 'C' type hangar, the standard design used for Expansion-period airfields

57 ELSHAM WOLDS: a 'J' type hangar built at airfields that were opening around the outbreak of the Second World War, and designed to be less costly than the 'C' type both in labour and materials

154 Defending Lincolnshire: A Military History from Conquest to Cold War

58 MANBY: the officers' mess to design 3935/35; the unusual three-storey design, enlivened by balconies and a loggia, built on only a few airfields probably reflects the large number of officers on the permanent staff of this training establishment

59 BINBROOK, three-storey barrack-block probably to drawing number 177/35

60 MANBY: Tedder Hall (3217/36), a unique design for this enormous Instructional Block. In splendid condition, it now serves as the administrative HQ of East Lindsey District Council

and tractors, and a guardroom. On a separate but closely adjacent site were messes for officers (**58**) and for sergeants, an institute (NAAFI) for other ranks, squash courts for the officers, two- and three-storey barrack blocks (**59**), canteens, a sickbay, ambulance garage and morgue, and a works building with central-heating boiler and water-tower. Nearby on the instructional site were the link trainer, bombing teacher, turret trainer, gunnery trainer and navigation trainer buildings containing machines simulating the various operations, along with classrooms.

Manby, as a station particularly dedicated to training, has the imposing Instructional Block (77/35 and 3217/36), a unique design of building with workshops and classrooms for trade training, now known as Tedder Hall (**60**). Not too far away from these domestic and training buildings, were spacious estates of married quarters, carefully stratified with senior officers in the larger detached houses, through to lowly LACs in the terraces. The whole complex was surrounded by carefully tended lawns and playing fields, providing a cordon sanitaire around the brick-built revetments of the bomb-dump and the earthed-up mounds of the underground fuel tanks. Where such a campus has retained its integrity, as at Manby or Hemswell, Scampton or Binbrook, there is still something of a sense of the old-time village community where everyone is valued, but everyone knows his role and his place. Unlike many counties, Lincolnshire still retains several of these 1930s bases as working airfields. Scampton, Waddington, Coningsby and Cranwell are all operational RAF stations, whilst Spitalgate is the national centre for TA logistics training, and RAF Digby is a centre of inter-service signals operations.

Paradoxically, at the very time that the nation's finances were at their lowest, and the country was struggling to survive the depression, flying was being popularised by the press and by local authorities. Two private flying clubs based on civil airfields took off in Lincolnshire. In 1930, a private airfield was laid out at Winthorpe, northwest of Skegness. Here, the Skegness and East Lincolnshire Aero Club operated alongside a ferry company, remaining open until just before the war. In June 1933, Waltham airfield, 7 miles (11km) south of Grimsby opened as a base for the Lincolnshire Aero Club and other small air-transport concerns. In 1938, a branch of the Civil Air Guard formed, which became No. 25 RAF Elementary and Reserve Flying Training School, to expand the pool of trained pilots in the run-up to the war. After a brief hiatus, the airfield was formally requisitioned and greatly enlarged as a bomber base in May 1940, a large civilian hangar and clubhouse forming the nucleus of the new airfield.

THE REGULAR ARMY AND THE TA BETWEEN THE WARS

From its peak establishment of nineteen battalions in 1918, the Lincolnshire regiment went back to having two regular battalions on active service, a third Reserve battalion in the depot, and two territorial battalions. Early in the 1920s, the 1st Bn. was in Ireland while the 2nd was in India until 1930, when they actually met briefly at Gibraltar, crossing while in transit. The 1st Bn. continued to India, seeing action in Shanghai in 1931, and staying in India up until the outbreak of war. The 2nd Bn. went to Catterick on its return from India in 1930, celebrating the Regiment's 250th anniversary by trooping the colour in 1935, prior to a posting to Malta and then on to Palestine.

The TA had been re-established in 1920, but on a much-reduced establishment, and the Lincolnshire Yeomanry was one of several such units never to be reformed. The enforced parsimony of the period meant that much of the army was neglected, while any resources that could be spared went to the RAF, the navy and, only finally, to the urgent programme to mechanise the army. In August 1924, 3,000 territorials from Yorkshire had camped on Wainfleet Road, Skegness for the Bank Holiday week, arriving by ten special trains from Leeds, Sheffield and Bradford. By 1932, things were so bad financially that all TA annual camps were cancelled in order to save money. Soon, however, there was a vital new role for the TA, and intensive training for it would be vital.

THE AIR DEFENCE SYSTEM

The threat of aerial bombardment necessitated the formation of an integrated anti-aircraft organisation based on the London Air Defence Area of the previous war, and spelt out in the Re-Orientation Plan of 1935. This organisation would cover the whole country and include several equally important elements. The detection of incoming bombers by the new Chain Home Radar system was represented in the county by: the Air Ministry Experimental Station (AMES) at Stenigot in the Wolds; a network of Observer Corps posts scattered across the county with their HQ in the upper floor of the Lincoln GPO Telephone Exchange in Guildhall Street, then at St Peter-at-Arches from 1938; and by acoustic sound locators attached to AA batteries. The interception of enemy bombers by aircraft of RAF Fighter Command flying from 12 Group's Sector Stations of Digby (**61**) and Kirton-in-Lindsey (with a third Sector Station, at Wittering, Cambridgeshire), was controlled from the Filter Room

Preparing for the Next War: Rearmament (1919–1938)   157

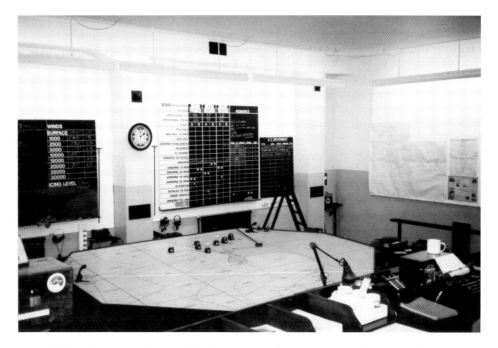

61 DIGBY: the Operations Block of this Fighter Sector Station was sealed for years and is now open to the public in a state of perfect preservation

at Watnall (Nottinghamshire), which would collate all the incoming information. The fighters would operate in a clearly defined Aircraft Fighting Zone behind the AA guns and searchlights.

This is where the TA came in, as it was to be their responsibility to man the AA defences, entailing a radical re-organisation of the force. A number of infantry units were converted for the task, and this included the 5th Bn. of the Lincolnshire Regiment, which became the 46th Searchlight Bn. of the REs, this title emblazoned over the doorway of their drill hall in Newport, Lincoln (*62*), brand new in 1938. Soon afterwards they were re-designated as 46th Searchlight Regiment RA (TA), with their HQ in another new drill hall at Westward Ho, Bargate, Grimsby, opened in January 1939. Space was needed for the territorials to practise on new equipment in specialist rooms kitted out as planetaria, and to store everything in capacious garages. Unfortunately, a counter to the novelty and complexity of the new AA guns, searchlights, sound locators, predictors and height-finders was their scarcity, as the entire system was well short of establishment up to the declaration of war. A few of the new 3.7" HAA guns, some with foreshortened barrels for indoor practice, were made available, but few units were anything like fully equipped. Mobilisation Depots, like the one on the Louth road, west of Manby (*63*), were set up to store, maintain and issue all this new kit to the TA units on their call-up or as it became available – whichever was the sooner. Another such depot has been identified on the old Great North Road, to the north of Grantham, and most recently occupied by 'Vaculug'. After the Munich Crisis, the TA had been embodied to man the new

158 Defending Lincolnshire: A Military History from Conquest to Cold War

62 LINCOLN: the Newport drill hall opened in 1938 for a new AA searchlight unit formed by converting territorial infantry of the Lincolnshire Regiment into a RE battalion

63 MANBY (TF365862): one of a network of Mobilisation Centres built for the storage of arms and equipment, particularly AA guns, for issue to territorials and reserves, on their call-up at the outbreak of war

AA defences, and this operation was consolidated from May 1939 when TA units were on continuous duties, a month at a time, providing defensive coverage, termed 'The Couverture', against air attack. Given the difficulty of managing this process, when most of the territorials were in employment and had no government protection for their jobs, a remarkable turnout of ninety-seven per cent was achieved. All credit to the terriers and their bosses. Maybe the urgency of the situation was beginning to be acknowledged.

While the 5th Bn. went off to be AA gunners, the 4th Bn. remained as infantry. New drill halls opened in Cottage Beck Road, Frodingham, Scunthorpe in 1938, and in Ropery Road, Gainsborough in 1939, along with Louth's Victoria Road hall. These provided more space for training and for storing the vehicles with which infantry units were now equipped, as well as enhanced social facilities which remained a key motivation for much recruitment. In March 1939, conscription for six months full-time compulsory service in the Militia was brought in, and a hutted camp was built at the depot to accommodate them. The RASC driver-training camp on Corringham Road, Gainsborough also served as a Militia camp. The TA was effectively dissolved as the Armed Forces Act made the members of all auxiliary forces full-time regulars.

At the same time, there began an operation whereby TA units cloned themselves to produce duplicate units. By doubling their numbers, the two Lincolnshire batteries from the former 46th (North Midland) Divisional artillery were reconstituted as the 60th Field Regiment RA (TA) with 237 Battery based at the Old Barracks in Lincoln, and 239 Battery at the Augusta Street drill hall in Grimsby. The other half of the North Midland artillery in Nottingham and Leicester produced the duplicate field regiment, by repeating the same process. The infantry were also required to go through this process. The 4th Bn. reorganised themselves, still based on Lincoln (HQ Coy), but with four companies based in Spalding (A Coy), Grantham (B Coy), Boston (C Coy) and Stamford (D Coy). The duplicate unit was based on Grantham and Sleaford (HQ Coy), Lincoln (E Coy), Spilsby and Alford (F Coy), Horncastle and Market Rasen (G Coy), and Holbeach (H Coy), becoming a new 6th Bn. and was sent to 46th (North Midland) Division, then in the process of being reformed.

THE ROYAL NAVY BETWEEN THE WARS

As soon as the war was over, naval facilities had been shut down. The 20th Destroyer Flotilla with its depot ship, the old cruiser HMS *Leander* was around only until March 1919, and many of the surviving trawlers – which had been requisitioned by the Admiralty – were returned to their owners. The Port Convoy Office had closed at the end of 1918, as had the armed merchant ships office in 1919. The RNAS had moved to Immingham in November 1918, but remained in business for only twelve months, leaving very little functioning on the naval front. In 1934 the Admiralty's Cleethorpes (or Waltham) W/T tower burned down and was replaced by five steel pylons, providing an opportunity to improve communications in the North Sea.

64 TETNEY: the Tetney Beam Station housed the transmitter for a new short wave, long-distance radio communications system inaugurated in 1926–7

Ten years earlier, a much more ambitious communications project had been implemented. In an attempt to link the far-flung reaches of the Empire in ways less vulnerable than undersea cables, a new system of wireless, using short wave transmissions over long distances, had been attempted. The Tetney Beam Station was set up in 1926–7, with the transmitter (**64**) near Grimsby (TA314028), and the receiver at Burgh-le-Marsh (TF520656). In the final years before the outbreak of war, there were government subsidies available for updating the trawlers of the Grimsby fishing fleet. In the previous war, many trawlers had been requisitioned by the navy, and this scheme was obviously intended as a way of ensuring that modern vessels would be there when their country needed them again. Until October 1939, the Humber area had come under Rosyth, but was transferred to Nore Command. One of the effects of this was to align the naval command and control boundaries with those of RAF's Coastal Command (16 Group). Flamborough Head now constituted Nore Command's northern edge.

eight

The Second World War (1939–45)

Once again, Lincolnshire was to be in the front-line of the war, both in the air and at sea. On land, the defence against an expected invasion gradually gave way to preparations for opening the Second Front. In the air, the desperate defence of the Battle of Britain was replaced by the vast operation of the bombing offensive against Germany and her allies, while the navy continued to keep open the convoy routes. Both the RAF and the Royal Navy ran large-scale training operations in the county. Total war meant total involvement for all, and as well as all those who were members of the armed services, few locals remained outside the war effort, working long hours in munitions factories or on the land, and then performing second, full-time tasks as members of the Home Guard, Air Raid Precautions (ARP), or welfare organisations.

THE ROYAL NAVY IN LINCOLNSHIRE IN THE SECOND WORLD WAR

Throughout the war, Lincolnshire was home to an unusual mixture of front-line and training functions. The roads being inadequate, and the railways overloaded, coastal shipping was an essential element in the war effort as food, fuel and raw materials for the munitions industry had to be shipped up and down the coast. These merchant ships faced the dangers of mines, submarines, bombing and strafing, in addition to all the usual perils of wind and water. A convoy system was started so that the few available escorts could work to maximum effect; merchant vessels were armed, and the Grimsby/Immingham naval complex was secured, as far as possible, against attack.

Immingham, with its large dry dock, was the base for the naval element of the Humber defences. *Beaver I* in Grimsby, with offices near the Dock railway station and a sickbay in the old YMCA building in Heneage Road, was the notional base for the seven *Halcyon* and *Hunt* class boats of the 4th Minesweeper Flotilla, but they spent more time in the Dover area where their work was even more necessary. In November 1940, the Flag Officer in Charge (FOIC) moved across the water from Hull because of the intensity of the bombing there and the volume of merchant traffic in the port, bringing with him 1,200 shore personnel. The *Dunluce Castle*, a liner launched in 1904, served as the base ship at Immingham, providing extra accommodation briefly from 1939 until early 1940. *Beaver II* at Immingham was the base for two destroyer flotillas, the 5th under Lord Louis Mountbatten in HMS *Jupiter*, and the 20th, consisting of HMS *Esk, Express, Icarus, Intrepid*, and *Ivanhoe*, which were converted for minelaying, and were to lose three of their number with great loss of life on one disastrous expedition off the Dutch coast. The brand new, 2,000-ton *Princess Victoria* was requisitioned as a minelayer in 1939, and was also lost to a mine in May 1940. The *Teviotbank* was another auxiliary minelayer based in Grimsby until 1941, when she was sent out to the Far East. *Beaver III* was the Immingham base for Coastal Forces, with MGBs and MLs, until April 1942 when it was absorbed into *Beaver II*.

During the time that the threat of invasion was at its highest, the 20th Cruiser Squadron, made up of six 'C' Class First World War cruisers re-armed as AA ships to protect East Coast convoys, was stationed at Grimsby under Rear-Admiral Vivien, who was based at the County Hotel, Immingham (**65**). Also on hand was the Auxiliary Patrol Service (APS) depot ship *Royal Charter* with eighteen patrol craft, mainly requisitioned trawlers such as the *Sheraton* (launched 1904) and armed with a QF gun and machine guns. The East Coast convoys assembled in the Humber estuary, and operated inside the East Coast Mine Barrier, accompanied by escorting AA cruisers, sloops, vessels of the APS and A/S trawlers from Grimsby. The barrier extended right the way down the East Coast from the Orkneys to the Channel, with a few gaps to allow ships out into the North Sea. Gap E was opposite the mouth of the Humber, 30 miles (48km) off Spurn Point. There was a Boom across the Humber, serviced by eight small trawlers converted into Boom Defence Vessels, with assorted motorboats as tenders. In the event of an invasion, block-ships were held in readiness to be sunk in the shipping channels. Under the guns of the sea-forts was an area for holding incoming foreign vessels waiting to be cleared for entry into the port of Hull, five drifters being used by the Examination Service to ensure that neither aliens nor contraband were landed.

In view of all the over-flying by RAF units operating over the North Sea, air-sea rescue units were based in Grimsby. The Royal Navy ran three Harbour Launches, and No. 22 RAF Marine Craft Unit (MCU) had six high-speed launches (HSLs). A further MCU, No. 1109, was based at Boston Docks. Units of the War Department fleet were based at Grimsby as 629 Water Transport Coy, RASC. These included the *Sir Herbert Miles*, still towing targets and servicing the re-activated estuary forts. The Grimsby AA defences included barrage balloons, nine of which were attached to drifters equipped with winches.

The main focus of naval activity, however, was minesweeping. Owing to the importance of the Humber estuary as both a convoy assembly area and a destination for incoming convoys, enemy aircraft, submarines and surface ships were continu-

The Second World War (1939–1945)   163

65 IMMINGHAM: the County Hotel, HQ for a number of Royal Naval units including Admiral Vivien's cruiser squadron; note the 'Mountbatten Bistro'

ously laying mines in the approaches. Ten minesweeping groups totalling thirty-five trawlers were based at Grimsby/Immingham with their depot ship, *Colonsay*. These were mainly conventional Oropesa minesweepers that cut the mine loose from its mooring cable with a towed blade, and exploded it with rifle fire as it floated on the surface, but many other methods were developed to destroy enemy mines, some more effective than others. The two mine-destructor ships – *Borde* and *Corfield* – were equipped with electro-magnets weighing the equivalent of three railway locomotives. Both of these vessels were lost to mines that they were in process of exploding. Eleven drifters were equipped either with skids employing an electro-magnetic coil on a towed raft, or pairs of LL (Double-L) cables, towed behind them on wooden floats, and giving out powerful electric pulses. All these methods were aimed at destroying the mines *in situ*, but if mines were beached, they were dealt with by an RMS (Rendering Mines Safe) party.

One such unit was based at Mablethorpe, and this was merged with its Bridlington counterpart in 1943, and re-located to Immingham. By 1944 the Grimsby M/S force consisted of eight Fleet M/S, ten BYM/S built in the USA, and fifty-six trawlers and drifters. Boston's RN base for coastal forces from September 1942 was HMS *Arbella*, located in the former workhouse, now largely destroyed. The Boston Wash Patrol used three patrol boats to maintain the anti-submarine nets in the shallow waters of the Wash. One of these patrol boats, the yacht *Ouzel*, was lost when it hit a mine while surveying camouflaged beach defences off Skegness and Mablethorpe. The *Ro-Beda* and *Wing Cliffe* carried on looking after the nets.

In 1943, twelve LCTs were stationed in Boston Docks as part of the build-up to D-Day. Immingham also became the base for a detachment of the 12th Major Port of the US Transportation Corps, with outposts in Grimsby.

In 1939 there were more than 330 steam trawlers operating out of Grimsby. At the outbreak of war, 250 of these were requisitioned by the Admiralty. Many were 'R' class (*Rose of England*, *Rolls Royce*, etc.) or 'S' class (*Sandringham*, *Sea Mist*, etc.) mainly from the Grimsby Sleight's and Standard Steam Fishing Co., with the largest number coming from Sir John Marsden's fleet of 135 Consolidated Fisheries trawlers. These boats served all around the coast, and *Rolls Royce* alone swept almost 200 mines during the war. Grimsby trawlers were involved in the Norwegian campaign, ferrying troops between ports and also in the final evacuation. They were also involved in the Dunkirk rescue operations, and with helping escapers and evacuees who came into Immingham from Texel in May 1940 and continued coming up to the end of 1942. Ships lost from Grimsby, Immingham and Boston during the war included two destroyers, one mine-layer, two mine-destructor ships, twenty-five trawlers and drifters, four yachts, one tug and one LCT, with over 700 personnel killed.

On 4 September 1939, Billy Butlin's Skegness holiday camp, actually in Ingoldmells, was requisitioned by the Admiralty as HMS *Royal Arthur*. This became a RN Initial Training base with 4,500 ratings in each intake, with a total throughput of 250,000 during the war, including recruits from the Dutch and Norwegian navies. There was a permanent staff of 750, including 110 officers. The Viennese dance hall became the armoury, the Tyrolean beer garden the sickbay, and the trainees were housed in wooden chalets. York, Kent and Gloucester dining rooms became the Forecastle, Top and Quarter-deck Divisions. The Gaiety Theatre building had only just been bought by Butlin from the British Empire Exhibition in Glasgow, and recently delivered on site as a steel frame and not much else. One of the first jobs to be done by the navy was to assemble it as the base lecture hall. The navy also increased the stock of chalets, especially after ninety had been destroyed by bombs. The Admiralty calculated Butlin's lost income on the basis of the 1938 season's profits, so he could be compensated at the end of the war, withholding only a small proportion of the cost of improvements they had carried out. The camp's status as a stone frigate was somewhat lost on the German propaganda machine, when it was announced by Lord Haw-Haw as sunk. It underwent bombing raids and one attack in January 1942 caused much structural damage, and four men were killed. Butlins Funcoast World continues to thrive at Ingoldmells, and a token pre-war chalet has been preserved on site.

THE ROYAL AIR FORCE IN LINCOLNSHIRE

Although much progress had been made by the developments of the Expansion Period, it quickly became clear that the rapid wartime growth of the RAF would soon outpace the existing building programme. When Waddington returned to operational status in 1939, for instance, the 1927 Officers' Mess, Newall House was inadequate, having to be supplemented by eight large tents, and it was also necessary to retain the old First World War hangars. A new programme of construction was quickly initiated.

The particular topographical features of especially the Lincoln Cliff made it a perfect take-off point for sorties across the North Sea to targets in northern Europe. To the bomber stations already established would be added many more over the course of the war, built on green-field sites: North Killingholme, Kirmington, Ludford Magna in the north; Cammeringham, Dunholme Lodge, Wickenby, Bardney, Faldingworth, East Kirkby, Kelstern, Skellingthorpe, Fiskerton and Spilsby in the centre of the county; Blyton, Sandtoft and Sturgate in the northwest; and Folkingham, North Witham, Woodhall Spa, Fulbeck, and Metheringham in the south. Waltham, with its pre-war facilities that included a large side-opening hangar, was converted from a civil flying field into another bomber station. The fighters at Kirton-in-Lindsey had satellites at Caistor, Goxhill and Hibaldstow, and those at Digby had Wellingore. Sutton Bridge and Harlaxton retained operational training roles throughout the war, whilst North Coates along with Strubby were part of Coastal Command, and also used by the Fleet Air Arm. Folkingham had started life as a decoy for Spitalgate but, by late 1942, was itself needed as an airfield. Coleby Grange opened as a night-fighter station and later flew *Mosquitos*.

As the build-up to the Second Front gained momentum, the troop carriers of the 9th USAAF were allocated Fulbeck, Folkingham, and Barkston Heath, with Goxhill going to the fighters of the 8th USAAF. Early in the war a network of Emergency Landing Grounds serviced a number of major airfields such as Waddington. These ELGs included Sturton, Hykeham and Ludborough, but by 1942 they had gone. The Theddlethorpe and Holbeach ranges had their own emergency landing-grounds, the former marked only by a single small brick building. Bracebridge Heath, the the First World War AAP, was brought back into service in 1941 by A.V. Roe, who established a repair depot, primarily for their *Lancasters*. Built partly with German PoW labour, it provided a facility between those on airfields, and the factory repairing 4,000 aircraft which would probably otherwise have been scrapped. One of nearby Waddington's hangars was taken over for final assembly prior to delivery to airfields, and aircraft were towed there down the A15. The factory site, beside the railway between Dunston and Nocton, now used by a manufacturer of double-glazing units, is said to have served as a store for these replacement aircraft.

At the beginning of the war, the number of active airfields in Lincolnshire was in single figures, but by the end of the war there were forty-five, of which thirty-four were, or had been, operational bomber bases (**Fig. 11**). All this massive building operation took place into 1944 in conditions of some urgency. During 1942, a new airfield opened every three days somewhere in Britain, and Lincolnshire alone, across 1942 and 1943, saw a new one every month. These new airfields were very different from those of the Lutyens era, built to a much-reduced aesthetic. In place of the well-proportioned and elegant neo-Georgian architecture there were mass-produced utilitarian buildings, intended to enjoy only short lives. Indeed, the

Fig. 11 Second World War airfields in Lincolnshire

The Second World War (1939-1945)   167

66 COLEBY GRANGE: the night-fighter style watch office

official descriptor for the hutting, with walls of a single-brick's thickness, supported by buttresses and covered in cement-render, was 'temporary brick' (tb). As well as their construction, the layout of these wartime airfields was very different. Now everything was to be dispersed, the aircraft in hangars, pens or on hard-standings scattered around the perimeter. Technical, administrative and instructional sites were all separated, and messes, gymnasium and living or communal sites were quite widely dispersed, some distance from each other. If you were to get around you had to have a bike. An almost complete detached communal site with gymnasium, squash court, canteen, kitchens and living huts may be seen at Ludford Magna, at least a mile from the technical site, with others at Strubby and Metheringham, similarly distant from the business end of those airfields.

Wartime designs for watch offices started out as function-specific. Thus Coleby Grange (**66**) has a night-fighter station tower (*12096/41*), as did Dunholme Lodge and Fiskerton for some reason, but Hibaldstow's was to a different design (FCW 4514); Bardney and Fulbeck had bomber-satellite towers (*13726/41*); Harlaxton (Type 'A' *15898/40*), and Blyton, Cammeringham and Waltham (Type 'B' *7345/41*) were all towers for OTU satellites; Wellingore had a fighter-satellite tower (*2658/42*). Skellingthorpe's original tower was apparently unique. It must soon have become obvious that as airfields' functions changed, so their watch offices became inappropriate; a general purpose tower was thus developed, first a design numbered *12779/41*, then the universal *343/43*, as at Barkston Heath, East Kirkby, Sandtoft, Sturgate, North Witham, Wickenby and Strubby, all seven being extant, with that at Sandtoft – like Hibaldstow's – having been converted into a house.

168   Defending Lincolnshire: A Military History from Conquest to Cold War

67   NORTH KILLINGHOLME: a *T2* hangar at this bomber airfield

68   BRACEBRIDGE HEATH: the B1 hangar built by the Ministry of Aircraft Production at this aircraft repair facility run by A.V. Roe

All these towers were built to specifications that anticipated short working lives. Wartime hangars, too, were very different from the monumental 'C' types of the 1930s. The *Bellman* had been designed in 1937 to be easily erected, and, if necessary, easily dismantled and moved to another location. North Coates got four of these before the war, and others went to Cranwell and Hibaldstow. As soon as wartime conditions prevailed, all those new airfields needed hangars that were cheap, quickly manufactured out of minimal materials, easily erected and re-deployable. The answer was the *T2*, which met all those criteria, the 'T' standing for 'Transportable' (**67**). Most bomber airfields required a pair of *T2*s, and an aircraft repair hangar, usually a *B1*, designed by the Ministry of Aircraft Production (MAP) and manned by their civilian employees (**68**), and nearly all the airfields built between 1941 and 1944 had these hangars.

Good examples of *T2*s can be seen at Waltham, Wickenby, North Killingholme and Swinderby. East Kirkby had six *T2*s, and Barkston Heath had ten, many of which accommodated gliders prior to the airborne operations of D-Day and Arnhem, as did five more at Fulbeck. A *T1* still stands at Coleby Grange. Ludford Magna became a Base Major Servicing Unit alongside normal operations, receiving four extra *T2*s. Examples of *B1*s stand at Spilsby, Faldingworth, North Killingholme, Waltham and Strubby. A number of airfields were given *Blister* hangars, low curved shelters for fighters, eighteen of which were erected at Harlaxton, and one can still be seen at Caistor. These also often served as Free Gunnery trainers on bomber airfields. The USAAF constructed six *Butler Combat* hangars at its Air Depot at North Witham, where only their concrete bases survive.

Many of the airfields' functions were contained in prefabricated huts: the ubiquitous *Nissen*, and its larger cousins, the *Romney* and *Iris*; the *Handcraft* with its heptagon-profile asbestos roof; the plaster-board *Laing*; the Air Ministry hut of timber sections; the *BCF* and *ORLIT* of concrete panels; and huts made of hollow tile-bricks, asbestos cement and corrugated-iron. Some large buildings, like Main Stores or Workshops, were made up of a pair of *Romney* huts with a tb link, as at Kelstern, but there were designs for specific purposes as well. At Metheringham, *Romney* huts may be seen serving as the Briefing Room and Station Office next to the Operations Block, as the station's Sick Quarters, as well as on the technical site.

Several different Parachute Stores were designed in tb, examples standing at Spitalgate, Sandtoft and Waltham, and the Gymnasium/Church/Cinema (*14604/40*) can still be seen at Metheringham (**69**), Strubby, Hemswell, Ludford Magna and East Kirkby. Tractor and trailer sheds and fire-engine sheds (*10868/40*) usually accompanied the watch office. This trio of specialist structures could be seen at Goxhill until recently, and survives today at Sandtoft, Cammeringham and Sturgate. By the time North Killingholme opened in November 1943, *Nissen* huts served for both these functions. Specialist training buildings are also recognisable, a good example being Bombing Teachers (*47/40*) seen at Metheringham (**70**), Turret Trainers, or the Navigation Trainer (TD49), examples of which can be seen at North Killingholme and Swinderby. Several airfields had detached wireless stations. That at Manby, now demolished, had a brick and earth traverse around it with a pillbox at each corner.

Coningsby's at Tattershall Thorpe is now a training centre for RAF police dogs. In ruins, and fast disintegrating alongside the B6403 at Londonthorpe, is the wireless station for Spitalgate and St Vincents. One distinctive feature of the wartime airfield was the *Braithwaite* water-tank, holding 40,000 gallons (180,000 litres) on its skeleton steel tower. Examples include North Witham and Metheringham (**71**).

Building these new airfields was an enormous task, particularly as at the same time, concrete runways were being laid at the existing ones, in order to be able to operate the new heavier bombers such as the *Lancaster*, with its weighty bomb-load. Until mid-1943, Waddington, for instance, had only grass runways. A third of all the country's construction resources went into the job, with hardcore being brought in by train from the bombed cities, and timber being brought into Brayford Pool by barge. The Air Ministry Works Department, responsible for supervising all these projects, was based first at 10 Upgate, then at Eastfield House, Louth, with a staff of over 100 in four area offices across the county. Barry Holliss has shown how dependent on the railways all these new airfields were for their initial construction, for their supplies of food, spares and munitions, and for the movement of personnel. Each airfield represented a small township of around 2,000 souls, completely dominating the surrounding rural settlements, and putting pressure on local services. At Waddington, it was necessary to divert a major road, and many other rural by-ways were sealed off for the duration.

As well as new buildings, the RAF took over a lot of old ones. At Woodhall Spa, Lady Grace Weigall, daughter of the Maples furniture retailer, had built and furnished Petwood House. For a while after the First World War, the house had served as a hotel, but when the airfield opened in 1942, it became the officers' mess. It has now reverted to being a hotel. At the other end of the scale, the semi-derelict Ashfield House served as billets for Waddington. In 1941, Blankney Hall became the off-site Operations Room for Digby. West Willoughby Hall near Ancaster was wrecked by RAF occupation, then by the army, then finally used for bombing practice by *Mosquito* pilots, probably from Spitalgate, where 17FTS operated from May 1945 until June 1947. Now, only the stables remain. St Vincents, a large house near Spitalgate in Grantham, was used by the RAF for a variety of functions from 1923. It was home to HQ 5 Group Bomber Command until October 1943 when its transfer to Morton Hall near Swinderby, made St Vincents available for the 9th USAAF Troop Carrier HQ.

The electronic war also needed terrestrial anchor-points. The existence of a German beam for directing bombers onto known points was discovered over Spalding, and a British equivalent, *GEE*, was developed, first transmitted from the Stenigot radar station, and then from Nettleton to the end of the war, the signals being picked up by a receiver in the aircraft. A radar-based system called *OBOE* also operated to confirm the distance that bombers travelled to their targets. With a range of 270 miles (430km), the *Cat* and *Mouse* components were located 100 miles (160km) apart in Norfolk and Kent. The *ASPIRIN* station at Holton-le-Moor confused enemy pilots by picking up the German signal and transmitting it repeatedly. Louth W/T station acted as a *MEACON* to jam the German beam, with a

The Second World War (1939–1945)   171

69 METHERINGHAM: the Gymnasium/Church on a communal site at this bomber station

70 METHERINGHAM: a Bombing Teacher on the synthetic training site; recently beautifully restored for use as the offices of a haulage company

71 METHERINGHAM: the 40,000-gallon Braithwaite water tank on its tower

transmitter at South Elkington and a receiver at Legbourne. Louth then operated as a *BUNCHER* station helping aircraft to get into formation in cloudy conditions, and as a *SPLASHER* station transmitting signals to enable allied aircraft to get home. The USAAF ran a similar fixer operation from Skidbrooke, picking up distress calls and enabling the ASR services to respond. Most airfields and selected ROC posts were equipped with Homers codenamed *DARKY* that enabled aircraft to be guided onto a cone of searchlights (*SANDRA*), by triangulation on the ground. Hibaldstow was one of the first to receive this facility. A pre-war German system, *LORENZ*, known here as Blind (later Beam) Approach Beacon System (BABS) was used to land aircraft in cloudy conditions. Along with low cloud making landing difficult for returning bombers, and rain turning grass strips into quagmires, fog was a major problem. This was solved to some extent by the *Fog Investigation and Dispersal Operation*, (FIDO), later changed to the more obvious, if ungrammatical, *Fog, Intensive, Dispersal Of*. This was a system that placed petrol burners alongside runways to burn off the fog. It demanded eighty per cent alcohol in the mix to avoid excessive smoke, and used enormous amounts of fuel, stored in capacious tanks. Fiskerton, Ludford Magna and Metheringham all operated the system, but Sturgate received it too late for use.

The well-known operations dealing with *Ultra* at Bletchley Park were dependent for their raw material on the Y Service, which intercepted enemy radio transmissions and fed through anything that might interest the code-breakers, as well as picking up a great deal of material in clear. There was a Y Service filter room at Immingham, and a Y Station at Branston, with its WAAF operators billeted possibly in East Mere House or Canwick House.

RAF TRAINING

Skegness was, from February 1941, the home of 11 Recruit Training Centre, but unlike the navy, which was concentrated on one campus, it was scattered across the town. Many of its buildings were requisitioned from the holiday trade, and many still operate today as hotels. The station HQ was in the Seacroft Hotel, now called the Renaissance (*72*), with a Wing HQ in the Grand, and a guardroom at the railway station. The Central Drafting Office, staffed by WAAFs, was the South Dunes Hotel. The sickbay started in the Dorchester, then transferred to the Seacroft Boys' school, now the Seacroft Court care home. The officers' mess was in the County Hotel (*73*), and there were airmen's messes in the Tower Gardens Pavilion, the Casino, now the North Parade social club, the Tower Café, the Imperial/Grosvenor House Hotel (*74*), and the Notts Poor Boys' Home, while NAAFIs operated in the Queen's Hotel and the ground floor of the Crown. The Arcadia and the upper floor of Marks and Spencers were used for lectures and training films. Drill was carried out on the Tower Esplanade, the flag was raised daily on the Pier, and assault courses, involving crossing the Waterways, were constructed on some of the adjacent open spaces. Airmen's billets occupied the Abbey, Dorchester, Grand, Grosvenor House and Savoy hotels, with WAAFs billeted in the Quorn Hotel. Some 80,000 recruits

72 SKEGNESS: the Seacroft Hotel, now the Royal Renaissance, once the HQ building of No. 11 RAF Recruit Training Centre

73 SKEGNESS: the County Hotel, once the officers' mess of No. 11 RAF Recruit Training Centre

The Second World War (1939–1945) 175

74 SKEGNESS: the Imperial and Grosvenor House Hotels, once one of several airmen's messes of No. 11 RAF Recruit Training Centre; the cream building to the left is the Queen's Hotel, which served as one of two NAAFIs

75 GRIMSTHORPE PARK: a Quadrant Tower from which observers could observe the accuracy of aircrew on this bombing range

passed through in batches of up to 7,000 at a time, and all these, plus the large permanent staff, had to be accommodated. Amongst other similar incidents was the bombing of the Red House Hotel in which nine airmen were among the twelve fatalities.

Flying training was a continuous activity, ranging from the basic at a Flying Training School – such as 12 SFTS at Spitalgate with its relief landing ground at Harlaxton, or RAF College SFTS/17 SFTS at Cranwell – to the OTUs (e.g. Sutton Bridge) and HCUs (e.g. Blyton and Swinderby) to be found periodically at a number of airfields. Manby's specialist training in the use of particular bits of kit like the Sperry Bomb-sight, or techniques such as using BABS, also had to be accommodated while causing as little disruption to normal operations as possible.

With so much of the bomber force stationed in Lincolnshire, and the Air Armament School at Manby, there was a need for ranges. To the established bombing and gunnery ranges of Donna Nook, Holbeach, Theddlethorpe and Wainfleet Sands, were added local ranges used by individual airfields. Examples include Alkborough, Fenton, Bassingham Fen, Grimsthorpe Park, Leverton and Manton Common. Theddlethorpe was the scene of the early trials of the 20mm *Hispano-Suiza* cannon manufactured by BMARCo in Grantham. Some of these ranges remain in use, but others cannot even be identified. A quadrant tower survives in Grimsthorpe Park (**75**).

THE RAF REGIMENT

As will be seen later in this chapter, finding sufficient manpower to defend the RAF's airfields proved a constant problem. While it would be competing for the same recruits, the RAF nevertheless felt that a discrete force composed entirely of RAF personnel, to be dedicated to airfield defence, would be the most effective solution. Thus in February 1942, existing ground defence officers, trained AA Ground Gunners, and newly recruited infantrymen were organised into ground defence squadrons. A regimental depot and an officer training unit (OCTU) were established at Belton House outside Grantham, sharing a new hutted camp at Alma Park, now an industrial estate, established on a different site from either of those occupied in the First World War.

With the help of instructors from the Royal Marines and the Guards, a training programme was established which produced a peak establishment of 50,000 officers and men in 240 squadrons in July 1943. Alma Park consisted of over 200 buildings ranged around an oval of access roads, with specialist training facilities and all the domestic accommodation for a permanent staff and continuous intakes of trainees. Local training areas included Gibraltar Point, with an AT gunnery range and a musketry range shared with the Skegness recruits, an AA practice camp at Anderby Creek, and a Battle School at Swayfield. At Gibraltar Point, the targets moved round on a narrow-gauge railway track. Squadrons and Independent AA Flights of the RAF Regiment served on virtually every airfield in Lincolnshire during the second half of the war. A large number of units served abroad, and many of the AA gunners were involved in the *Diver* operations (see below), particularly on the South Coast.

THE ARMY IN LINCOLNSHIRE

Local units in the Second World War

The outbreak of war found the Lincolnshire Regiment's 1st Bn. in India, and it was to spend the entire war fighting in the Far East theatre, ultimately in Slim's 'forgotten' Fourteenth Army in Burma. The 2nd Bn., stationed on the Isle of Portland, immediately sailed for France, landing in Cherbourg on 3 October 1939 as part of the BEF. After the Dunkirk evacuation, it stayed in the UK preparing for the assault landings in Normandy of June 1944. From there it fought as part of the 3rd Division's 9th Bde., until the ceasefire found it near Osnabruck. The 3rd Bn. was at the depot in Lincoln, which became an Infantry Training Centre (ITC) for recruits, putting them through basic training. Accommodation was at a premium, so the old RAF Stores complex in Longdales Road was taken over while new hutted camps were built at Sobraon Barracks. The 4th Bn. became part of 146th Infantry Bde. and saw action in Norway, prior to being part of the garrison of Iceland. It then landed at Le Havre as part of the 49th (West Riding) Division, and fought through northwest Europe. The 4th Bn's. duplicate unit, now the 6th Bn. was sent to France in 1939 to carry out labour duties and further training. After Dunkirk, it spent time re-equipping and training, while manning anti-invasion defences, first in Norfolk, and then for a year on the South Coast at Romney Marsh, subsequently serving in Tunisia, Italy and Greece, from January 1943 until its disbandment in February 1946. A wholly new 7th Bn. was raised in July 1940 at Tollerton Park near Nottingham, then stationed in Skegness, Mablethorpe, Marsh Chapel, North Coates and Donna Nook on coast defence duties until the end of 1941, when it was re-trained to become the 102nd LAA Regt RA. It served in the UK before landing in Normandy, fighting through to Holland. Newly-equipped with rocket-projectors, it fought to the end of the war and was then assigned to Occupation duties. In autumn 1944, both the 2nd and 4th Bns, along with the 102nd LAA Regiment, now attached to I Corps HQ, were all part of Montgomery's 21st Army Group.

Hartsholme Hall, the home of the Shuttleworth family, was taken over by the 6th Holding Battalion, a composite unit receiving semi-trained recruits from the Lincolnshires, Sherwood Foresters, East Yorkshires, and the York and Lancaster Regiment. The Hall became the officers' mess, whilst the recruits, up to 4,000 of them, lived in huts and tents in the grounds, which also accommodated training facilities. When this unwieldy unit was broken up in autumn 1940, the Lincolnshire component became first the 50th Bn. then the 8th Bn., serving in Norfolk as coast defence troops. It was then converted to become the 101st AT Regiment RA in early 1943. Most of it was then cannibalised into other below-strength units, but one battery served in Normandy, fighting alongside fellow Lincolnshires at one point. The 60th Field Regiment RA served in the Western Desert and Italy with the Eighth Army. Cadres from the locally recruited 17th/21st Lancers were taken as the basis for the 24th Lancers, one of six newly created armoured regiments.

ANTI-INVASION DEFENCES

After Dunkirk, a German invasion of the UK had become a certainty, but the small numbers of trained troops available and the almost total lack of arms and equipment made it very difficult for General Ironside to be confident in his plans. Given that enemy landings could take place virtually anywhere on the east and south coasts between Orkney and Cornwall, the forces available would be spread very thinly on the ground. Ironside's strategy was simple. The Coastal Crust, fortified with heavy guns in concrete emplacements, pillboxes and blockhouses, mobile artillery, wire, minefields and anti-landing obstacles, was intended to delay enemy landings and confine them to the beach-heads for as long as possible. It was hoped that the RAF, with home advantage, would be able to resist the efforts of the *Luftwaffe* to dominate the skies.

The secret of a successful amphibious assault would lie in the enemy's ability to reinforce and re-supply the first assault troops, so it was down to the Royal Navy, with adequate air cover, to sail down from Scapa and Rosyth and to disrupt the enemy lines of supply. Some way back from the coast were formidable anti-tank barriers, natural watercourses and artificial ditches, reinforced with concrete pillboxes, and prepared demolitions. Behind this obstacle, known as the GHQ Line, lay the army's striking force, the GHQ Reserve, poised to respond wherever they were needed. What few tanks there were, accompanied by infantry in requisitioned lorries and buses, would attempt to throw the invaders back into the sea. As the autumn evenings drew in, the sea grew stormier and the enemy failed to materialise, then things became more optimistic for the defenders. The factories were by now turning out more tanks, guns, vehicles and aircraft, and it became possible for Alanbrooke, Ironside's successor, to modify the defence plan. As the army gained mobility, many of the static defences, a heretical notion in the eyes of the army's leadership could be thinned down. The construction of fixed defences, except on airfields, virtually ceased, and defences were to be based on nodal points, where defended localities (DLs) would prevent the enemy from carrying out the *Blitzkrieg* tactics used in France.

Coastal artillery
Lincolnshire was seen as a likely avenue of invasion, either as a diversion, or as the main event. With the removal of the 4" guns from Haile Sand Fort, there were no active coast batteries on the Lincolnshire coast. The solution lay in the construction of Emergency Batteries. These consisted of old 6" naval guns, from scrapped First World War cruisers, mounted in brick and concrete gun-houses with overhead cover against air attack. Each battery had a pair of gun-houses flanked by 90cm coast

The Second World War (1939-1945) 179

76 FREISTON SHORE: the right-hand gun-house of this coast defence battery armed with two 6" guns

artillery searchlights (CASLs) in canopied emplacements, with magazines, communications and control room behind. A short way away was the camp, with office, workshops, hutted accommodation for the guns' crews and guardroom, the whole complex being surrounded by wire, slit-trenches and pillboxes. The magazines were segregated into three sections for shells, cartridges and fuses. Such batteries were built at Grimsby Docks, Mablethorpe, Crook Bank, Gibraltar Point and Freiston Shore (**76**), this last one being the Examination Battery for Boston Haven. These emergency batteries were usually given a purpose-built Battery Observation Post (BOP), but none seem to have survived in Lincolnshire. That may be because existing structures were used, as at Freiston Shore, where it would appear likely that the top floor of the adjacent pre-war Plummers Hotel proved adequate. The battery at Stallingborough was equipped with two naval 4.7" guns. In October 1941 a new battery was established at Jacksons Corner, possibly utilising the guns from Gibraltar Point. Many of these batteries were camouflaged, with that at Mablethorpe, according to contemporary observers, having 'Welcome to Butlins' emblazoned across the gun-houses.

As well as these guns in fixed emplacements, a significant number of smaller guns were made available for beach defence. At Horseshoe Point and elsewhere, some 4" and 12-pounder naval guns were emplaced in gun-houses, and others were mounted on open platforms, or given a mobile role mounted on the backs of trucks. Several positions were prepared for use, but never armed. The operation to arm naval trawlers and merchant ships required the very same weapons that were being allocated to beach defences, so an alternative had to be found by the army. Fortunately the

180   Defending Lincolnshire: A Military History from Conquest to Cold War

US Army released some 900 First World War vintage 75mm field guns, and around twenty of these were used in Lincolnshire to replace some of those 4" naval guns reclaimed by the senior service.

Also deployed in the beach defences were numbers of 6-pounder Hotchkiss QF guns which had been mounted in First World War Marks I–IV tanks, and stored since then at Woolwich Arsenal. Some were mounted in gun-houses, as at Boston Haven and Pyes Hall, and others were given wheeled carriages for mobile use (see table below). Old First World War guns were given a new lease of life. A battery of 60-pounder howitzers was stationed outside Louth, for instance, in order to bring fire to bear on routes from the coast and potential landing grounds. Good use was also made of the county's generous provision of railway lines. A batch of twenty-three First World War vintage 12" railway howitzers had been reconditioned at the LMS works in Derby, and three of these were located on railway lines at Whitton Ness, Grimsby and Stallingborough. They had a range of 6–8 miles (10–13km), fired a 750lb (340kg) shell, and had 120 degrees of traverse each way. A turntable loading platform accommodated the crew, and outriggers were provided for stability.

Another way of exploiting the mobility of the rail network was by using armoured trains. In July 1940 the 1st Guards' Bde. was responsible for the defence of the south bank of the Humber and set up an armoured train in Grimsby. Two 10-ton flat trucks were given concrete sides pierced by loopholes for riflemen firing in standing and kneeling positions, while an open hexagonal hatch in the steel roof gave scope for AA fire. One truck was placed each side of the locomotive that was armoured with steel plate. This train operated around Grimsby Docks, and a second train was under construction for use in Immingham, but was apparently never completed.

A much more ambitious programme had been set in motion in May 1940 which involved the construction of a fleet of twelve armoured trains to operate down the east side of the country from Inverness to Eastbourne. Railway experts such as Sir Nigel Gresley were consulted and a standard train was designed consisting of an armoured locomotive and four armoured trucks. The open trucks at front and rear each mounted a 6-pounder Hotchkiss QF gun, a Boys 0.55" AT rifle, and three Bren guns. The two closed trucks either side of the locomotive had rifle-loops, closed by sliding steel shutters. Given the scarcity of steel plate, concrete was used for some of the trucks' armour, and from 1941, many of the trains were crewed by Polish troops. Train M patrolled Lincolnshire and was based variously at Louth, Spalding, Boston and Grimsby, visiting Cleethorpes, Skegness, New Holland and Mablethorpe.

Lincolnshire coastal artillery in the Second World War

Whitton Ness	SE915245	1 x 12" railway howitzer
Killinghome	TA164202	2 x 12 pdrs on towers
Stallingborough	TA224147 TA224147 TA184117	1 x 4" No. 705RGF 2 x 4.7" QF installed 6/40 4 x 3.7" + 4 x 5.25" DP; 1 x 12" railway howitzer. NB Sunk Is. Guns, 2 x 4.7" QF removed 1943 (357 Coast Bty)
Immingham Dock	TA168166 TA205151	182165, 194169, 207161, 201157, 196148, 193165; 7 x 6 pdrs around perimeter of docks 1 x 6 pdr on railway truck
Grimsby Docks	TA285112	2 x 6" (318, 319, 320 Bty of 513, 545 Regt + HG); 1 x 12" railway howitzer
Haile Sand Fort	TA349061	2 x 6pdr, 276 Bty (513 Regt)
Church Lane, Humberston		2 light guns manned by 154 Bty RA
Northcoates Point	TA370035	1 x 6pdr
Horseshoe Point	TA381017	1 x 12 pdr then 1 x 4" or 1 x 4.7" in gun-house
Pyes Hall	TA407006	1 x 6pdr in gun-house (927 Defence Bty /RAF Regt)
Red Farm		1 x 6pdr
Somercotes Haven	TA410006	1 x 3pdr
Donna Nook	TF428998 TF430996	1 x 2 pdr 1 x 2 pdr
North Somercotes	TF439977 TF441972	1 x 12 pdr 1 x 12 pdr
Howdens Pullover	TF449951	1 x 4" or 1 x 4.7" in gun-house
Saltfleet	TF446948 TF447946	2 x 4" (mobile) 2 x 4" (mobile)
Toby's Hill	TF457943	1 x 3 pdr
Seaview Farm	TF463924	1 x 4" (mobile) then 1 x 6 pdr
Rimac DL	TF467917 TF469919	1 x 6 pdr also 2 x AA lmgs 1 x 6 pdr
Olivers DL	TF479901	1 x 4" (temporary mobile) then 1 x 6 pdr

Location	Grid Ref	Armament
Theddlethorpe St Helen	TF484893	1 x 4" (mobile)
Crook Bank	TF489884	2 x 6" BL Nos. 1142 and 1870 (318/9 Bty)
Mablethorpe	TF507855	2 x 6" BL (319 Bty)
Trusthorpe	TF515840	1 x 4" (mobile)
Sandilands	TF530809	Unoccupied gun position for 1 x 4"
Huttoft Bank	TF541789	1 x 4" (mobile)
	TF548772	1 x 2 pdr
Anderby Creek	TF552763	1 x 2 pdr
Sea Bank	TF560746	1 x 2 pdr
Chapel Point	TF562734	Unoccupied gun position for 1 x 4"
Chapel St Leonards	TF562723	1 x 4" (mobile) then 3 x 6 pdrs
	TF563710	1 x 2 pdr
Ingoldmells	TF575688	Unoccupied gun position for 1 x 4"
Jacksons Corner	TF573667	2 x 6" BL guns Nos 1183 and 2052 from 10/41 (545 Regt)
Seathorne	TF572657	1 x 4" (mobile)
	TF572653	Unoccupied position for 1 x 4"
Skegness RNLI	TF570631	1 x 4" (temporary mobile)
Skegness Vine hotel	TF569620	1 x 4" (temporary mobile)
Gibraltar Point	TF554577	2 x 6" BL; No. 1192 + ? (320/1,349 Bty, 545Regt)
Wainfleet Sands	TF525567	Unoccupied gun position for 1 x 4"
Friskney	TF485534	Unoccupied gun position for 1 x 4"
Benington Sea End	TF423457	Unoccupied gun position for 1 x 4"
Boston R Witham/rwy	TF321456	1 x 2 pdr
Butterwick Sea Bank	TF407441	Unoccupied gun position for 1 x 4"
Freiston Shore	TF397424	2 x 6" BL; Nos. 1190 and 1245 (320 Bty, 437 Bty, 545 Regt)
Scrane End	TF392407	Unoccupied gun position for 1 x 4"
Fishtoft Bank	TF364398	1 x 2 pdr then 1 x 6 pdr in gun-house
Sutton Bridge	TF484212	1 x 6 pdr or 1 x 75mm
Nene Outfall	TF494256	1 x 2 pdr
Lundys Farm	TF396341	1 x 2 pdr

NB. Some designated 6 pdr positions may have been occupied by US 75mm guns; 8/1940: three batteries of 21 A/T Regt deployed in Boston Area, Immingham, and Chapel St Leonards, and H5 Bty with 8 x 6 pdrs at Skegness; there were a total of 9 x 2 pdrs at Claxby, Grange Farm (Louth) and Langton.
Sources: Unit War Diaries, some via Tim Hudson

Units defending Lincolnshire
In the summer of 1940, the 1st Division, previously part of the BEF and evacuated from Dunkirk, was assigned to Lincolnshire, with its HQ at Canwick Hall (*77*), south of Lincoln. The 1st Guards Bde. was given the north of the county, with its HQ at Louth. Its men were spread so thinly though, that at one point, the whole Grimsby and Immingham area was defended by a single company of the 2nd Coldstreams. The Boston and Spalding area was held by 131st Bde. with 3rd Bde. in between, and 2nd Bde. in reserve. At a later date, 145 Bde. was centred on Horncastle, and the 144th Bde. was in the Skegness area with one of its battalions around Burgh-le-Marsh. Also in Lincolnshire at about this time was the 44th (Home Counties) Division, a first-line TA formation, from which 131st Bde. had been detached. Both these divisions went on to serve in North Africa.

In May 1941, the Lincoln Division was formed from three independent infantry brigades, 204th, 205th and 212th, without divisional troops, specifically for anti-invasion duties. Until their posting abroad, the 1st and 2nd Divisions alternated between training while remaining part of the GHQ Reserve and coast defence. After December 1942, the 48th (South Midland) Reserve Division took over until the end of the war. This was a formation that could supply drafts to other units, thus allowing other complete divisions to train for overseas service with the field force without interruption or depletion. Skendleby Hall was taken over as 3rd Brigade HQ and an underground bunker was dug. Stanton shelters and concrete roofs are still visible alongside the hall (*78*).

Brackenborough Hall, near Louth was the location for a Battalion HQ. For a few months in summer 1940, Holbeck Hall, between Louth and Horncastle, was taken over by 1st Bn. the Loyal North Lancashire Regiment. The main house accommodated the officers and their mess; the guardroom was in the stables, the sickbay in the dairy and the chaplain's room in the laundry. Rank and file slept under canvas in the park. Properties all over the county were taken over by the military. Fulbeck Hall (*79*), requisitioned in 1940, hosted battalions of both the Gordon and the Argyll and Sutherland Highlanders, the Lancashire Regiment and the Royal Welch Fusiliers, prior to becoming an airborne forces' HQ. In Lincoln, Coldbath House near the hospital served as an ammunition store for the army, and then as a base for REs until it was bombed in 1942. Lindum House (*80*) in Canwick was built by Pumphreys of Gainsborough as the RE Northern Command HQ, and was transformed by the local architect Sam Scorer into a spectacular home for the Wright family in 1966. Army camps were established at Trusthorpe, Wellingore, Scawby and Osgodby, and even Humberston Fitties was pressed into service once more with bungalows being occupied as HQ, offices, stores, officers' mess and living accommodation for troops manning coast defences.

184   Defending Lincolnshire: A Military History from Conquest to Cold War

77 CANWICK HALL: served as HQ for 1st Infantry Division after its evacuation from Dunkirk and assigned to guard the Lincolnshire coast; other units were subsequently based here throughout the war

78 SKENDLEBY HALL: HQ of 3rd Infantry Brigade; these shelters, alongside the Hall, were used for ammunition storage

The Second World War (1939–1945) 185

79 FULBECK HALL: requisitioned in 1940 it served as HQ for a number of infantry units; from October 1943 it became HQ of 1st Airborne Division under General Urquhart, whose staff planned the Arnhem operation from here

80 CANWICK: Lindum House started life as the Northern Command HQ of the Royal Engineers and was cleverly converted into a family home in 1966

81 THEDDLETHORPE-St-HELEN (TF482895): a coastal observation post attached to a *RUCK* pillbox, one example among several along this coast

The Second World War (1939-1945)

Defending Lincolnshire's beaches: the Coastal Crust

The survival of the odd pillbox gives a misleading impression of the effective strength of the Coastal Crust defences. Every effort was made to ensure that enemy landings would be as difficult as possible by integrating the various elements of the defences. Ready-made jetties were made unusable, Cleethorpes Pier being breached in May 1940. Skegness Pier, whose central section had been removed and replaced by a catwalk, was occupied by all three services. Potential invasion beaches such as Tetney Fitties were mined, and continuous lengths of tubular scaffolding, sometimes festooned with anti-personnel mines, were erected to stop invasion barges grounding, along with slanted steel stakes embedded in concrete rafts which would rip the bottoms out of landing craft. Concrete AT cubes were laid in lines to obstruct beach exits. Observation posts (*81*) and pillboxes (*82*) were built at least every 800 yards so that their fields of fire would interlock, but many were built in particularly vulnerable spots much closer together to create DLs with all-round defence. Where natural drains or outfalls were lacking, AT ditches were dug, further to impede enemy vehicles attempting to get off the beaches. There were great entanglements of barbed wire, with gaps deliberately left to channel the enemy into the fire of machine guns laid on fixed lines. Many British beaches were equipped for flame-warfare, and there is no reason to believe that Lincolnshire's were any different. Surviving plans, drawn up by the County Council in 1945 to chart the clearance of these defences, show just how formidable they were. As in the First World War, reliance was put on the Coastguard service to watch out for signs of an impending invasion. A conference of scout-leaders was held in Lincoln in 1939 to allocate a group of eight scouts, aged 14-18, to each coastguard station as signallers.

82 NORTH SOMERCOTES (TF443961): a Lincolnshire pattern 3-bay pillbox provided with wide machine-gun loops in its short sides in order that it might enfilade the beach

188   Defending Lincolnshire: A Military History from Conquest to Cold War

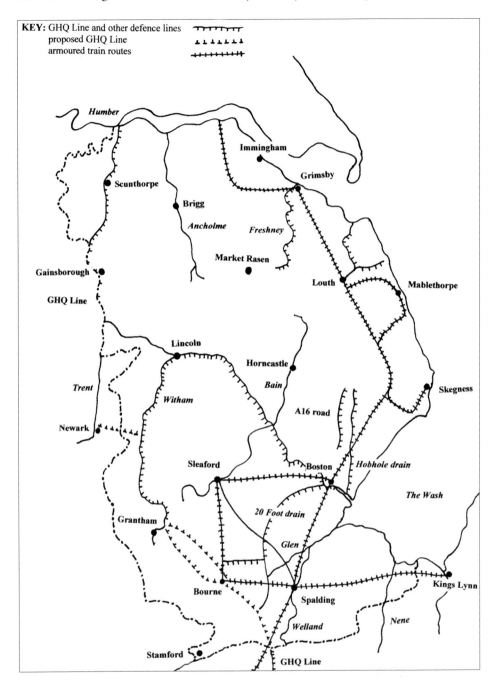

Fig. 12 Second World War defences of Lincolnshire

The war diary of 23rd Field Coy. RE, attached to 3rd Infantry Bde. gives a flavour of the task faced by the defenders in 1940. Based at Grebby Hall near Spilsby – but living in tents as there were no billets available – during July 1940, their tasks included the mining of the foreshore at Skegness, Chapel St Leonards and Gibraltar Point, building gun positions for 4" naval guns, constructing and camouflaging pillboxes, digging AT ditches, mining bridges and making a start on erecting huts for winter quarters. That was just the first week. More of the same followed relentlessly with the additional tasks of building concrete Anderson shelters for ammunition storage at the gun positions, constructing railway blocks consisting of rail wagons reinforced with concrete and filled with ten tons of rubble on the Boston-Wainfleet-Skegness Line, and laying Dannert Wire pyramids on the foreshore. This last was a thankless task, as high tides or storms tended to demolish these obstacles as fast as they could be built. By August they had moved to Wainfleet Hall with billets in the village (**Fig. 12**).

Defence in depth: the GHQ Line
The Coastal Crust was only a veneer, and it was vital that any enemy breakthrough should be contained. It had been Ironside's intention that the GHQ Line should extend north from the River Welland along the Cross Drain and the Bourne Eau, and on through Lincolnshire to hit the Witham at Barkston and then along the Trent to the Humber. The original reconnaissance report for the Line, dated June 1940, records a problem in selecting the best defensive line in the southern part of Sector 4 (Bourne to Newark-on-Trent). There being no natural obstacle between Bourne and Barkston, it was suggested that the Line could follow the A15 road past Morton and Rippingale to Folkingham, keeping to the eastern face of the higher ground, and then branch off west to Heydour and thence across Barkston Warren to the Witham. This route would have required a considerable amount of digging to produce an effective AT ditch. The alternative was to follow the River Glen to Lenton, then go across country via Ropsley, Belton Park and Syston Park to Barkston. This was felt to be unsatisfactory, however, because although it would entail less digging, it would be dominated from the heights of Bourne Woods in the Edenham area. In the event, neither route was taken, and the Line was never consolidated. It should be noted though that Henry Wills includes two pillboxes on the hills northwest of Ropsley in his gazetteer. From Barkston, it was intended that the Line would follow the Witham, joining the Trent above Newark to the west of Winthorpe, but it was more likely that an AT ditch would have been dug parallel to the Grantham-Newark railway line, as neither the Syston copses, nor the Witham itself, were deemed to provide sufficient obstruction.

It would appear that the GHQ Line north of the Welland was still at the planning stage when the policy regarding fixed defences was changing. However, it was still policy to deny the enemy ease of movement, and any bridge close to the coast and not vital was blown up by the REs. Inland, bridges were prepared for demolition. The bridge carrying the railway over the South Forty Foot Drain northwest of Donington underwent a major reconstruction in 1988, and a number of tunnels, 3ft (1m) wide, were found leading under the supporting girders. They were clearly intended to contain explosives, and were angled to achieve maximum destructive effect. Similar 'tunnels for military purposes' had previously been found in the bridge over the Trent at Gainsborough, and when the Spalding-Boston line became the A16 road, one of the bridges was found to have demolition chambers in its abutments, and these had to be filled in to ensure its stability. Those bridges that were vital to the defence – either because they carried essential services, or were necessary for the swift deployment of counter-attacking forces – were given a defensive pillbox, manned by troops detailed from their local brigade. A system of signals was devised so that all those tasks could be co-ordinated by a central control, rather than being prey to rumour or mis-information. A green rocket indicated that enemy ships had been sighted, Golden Rain meant 'SOS enemy are landing', a red rocket reported that the enemy had already landed, and a white one meant 'I require assistance'. As well as the universal code words such as 'Cromwell' – an instruction to take up Action Stations – many areas had an additional local code. 'Haig' was the signal that invasion was imminent on the 1st Division front.

Defence in depth: other defence lines
Between the Coastal Crust and the GHQ Line there were a number of additional linear obstacles, designed to prevent an enemy surge across the county. Part of the strategy was an attempt to confine the enemy even if he had achieved a break-out from the beaches. This consisted of defined linear AT obstacles carving up the county into boxes. In the north, the River Ancholme, the River Freshney from Grimsby down to Ludford, the canal from Tetney Lock to Louth, and the adjacent waterways around North Somercotes, all provided north–south barriers. Strong points, such as Louth, Saltfleetby and Market Rasen, could seal off these pockets. In the centre of the county, the Witham from Boston across to Lincoln, and then the Fossdyke Navigation to the Trent at Torksey, provided an east–west barrier to free movement. There was also a suggestion that an AT ditch linking the Witham to the Ancholme via the Barlings Eau might be dug to complete the north–south barrier. In the south of the county, the South Forty Foot Drain linked Boston to the putative GHQ Line at Rippingale. Two parallel lines of defences based on the A16 road between Boston and Keal and the Hobhole Drain ensured that an enemy force would not easily cross the flat fenland behind the beaches north of Boston. Along the Hobhole Drain, every crossing is defended by a concrete pillbox, and the rail crossings, in addition, are defended by AT blocks, once bound together by steel hawsers. Along the line of the A16, there were at least eight large concrete emplacements of which six survive (*83*), designed to house 6-pounder QF guns. Boundaries between formations were always vulnerable, so a mobile reserve force consisting of a battalion with tracked *Universal* (Bren gun) carriers and trucks, was stationed each side of the River Welland. Other survivals from these defence lines, including pillboxes and AT blocks, may be seen along the South Forty Foot Drain west of Boston, and along the Witham near Tattershall Bridge. All these planned defence

83 STICKNEY (TF344583): four pairs of these emplacements for 6-pounder QF Hotchkiss guns, straddled the A16 road between Sibsey and Keal Cotes, so placed as to cover the open ground behind the defensive line of the Hobhole Drain

lines, actual and notional, would have provided a coherent framework to which the county's defences might be fixed (**Fig. 13**).

The fen terrain of south Lincolnshire fortunately was particularly hostile to tanks, so the strategy of 131st Bde. in the summer of 1940 was to identify key points – particularly bridges and road junctions – and to fortify them with pillboxes, roadblocks and weapons pits. They called these positions 'BASES', and these ranged from a single roadblock on the bridge over the Nene at Sutton Bridge, to seventeen roadblocks and twenty-four planned pillboxes around Boston, manned by a whole battalion. Spalding, too, was heavily defended, as another entire battalion was committed to its defence. Once the immediate threat of invasion was past, a more considered strategy could be implemented.

References to mobile reserves, and an emphasis on movement and the disruption of the enemy's room to manoeuvre – using pre-set demolitions amongst other tactics, particularly in Northern Command – had been a foretaste of things to come. The decision had been taken back in July 1940 to confine the fixed defences of the River Trent to the bridges – Gainsborough, Dunham and Keadby, for instance – in Lincolnshire, rather than to attempt a continuous concrete barrier that would be wasteful of labour, materials and manpower, and tactically of questionable value. At the eastern end of the railway bridge across the Trent at Torksey are several rows of sockets into which steel rails would have been inserted, blocking the whole width of the permanent way. Keadby was a swing bridge and Dunham's fragility was seen as a bonus, as it would clearly be unable to support the weight of armour, and

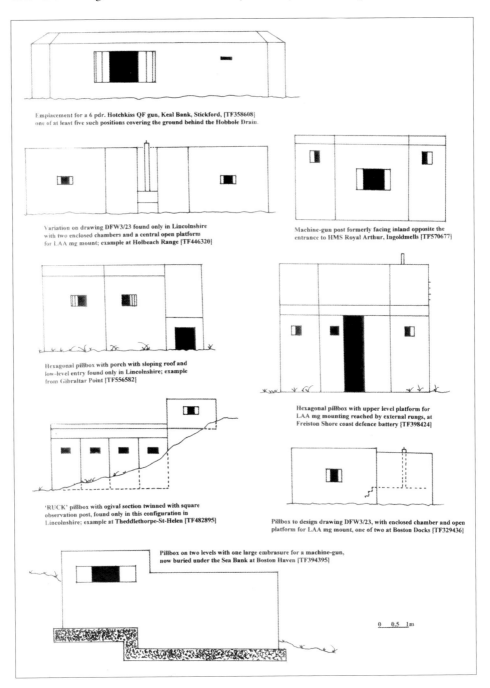

Fig. 13 Second World War pillbox designs in Lincolnshire

could be easily blown up by explosives attached to the girders. Gainsborough was a different matter and needed careful preparation (see below). One novel element of mobility was introduced by the creation of the Trent River Patrol, itself an example of the way in which the army and the quickly-evolving Home Guard were beginning to work together under a unified command with distinct but complementary functions.

Defence in depth: nodal points
We have already seen how 1st Division's strategy was applied by 131st Bde. around Boston (*84*) and Spalding. By the end of 1940, there were thirty-five such defended towns and villages in Lincolnshire. Their purpose was to hold up an enemy advance until larger forces could be brought to bear. Lincoln was clearly the largest of these strongholds (**Fig. 14**), and by July 1940, the city was enclosed by thirty-one roadblocks and 600 yards of AT ditch was being dug. Lincoln's perimeter was 3 miles (4.8km) around and required a large force to man it. The CO of the ITC doubled as garrison commander, and was able to call on his permanent staff and the training battalion at the barracks, plus the three battalions of the City of Lincoln Home Guard, probably around 4,000 men in all.

The defensive perimeter utilised a mixture of existing obstructions such as the railway embankments on the south of the city and terraces of houses, specially dug

84 BOSTON (TF327433): one of a pair of such pillboxes, to drawing number DFW3/23, with closed chamber for three Bren guns, and an open platform for mounting an AA light machine gun

194 Defending Lincolnshire: A Military History from Conquest to Cold War

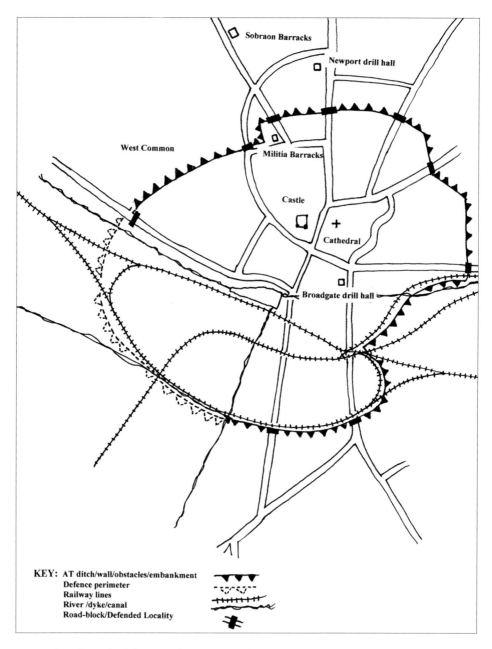

Fig. 14 Plan of Lincoln defences in the Second World War

AT ditches on the east and west, lengths of 4ft-thick (1.1m-thick) concrete AT walls, and a barricade of felled trees, all these elements being linked together into a continuous barrier round the city's inner core. Those roads that pierced the defences and had not been completely sealed off by obstacles were closed by roadblocks. These consisted of a reduction of the road down to the width of a single vehicle creating a narrow gap which could be closed by a combination of vertical steel rails dropped into prepared sockets and cylindrical concrete AT blocks that were rolled across the road. Houses, such as the Arboretum Lodge, and other buildings that overlooked such sites were prepared for conversion into defensive positions. Weapons were kept in purpose-built stores such as that behind the Peacock Hotel on Wragby Road. Garden walls that ran along the perimeter were loop-holed to enable riflemen to fire onto the approaches. The AT ditch was 12ft (3.7m) deep and 20ft (6m) across. Sometimes a ditch was dug inside a garden wall, with the earth being used to reinforce the wall, and the ditch providing a secondary, unseen obstacle. Short lengths of the AT wall can still be seen at the junction of Mill Road and Long Leys Road (*85*), and near the Boultham Street crossing of the Witham (*86*). The in-filled loopholes in the wall at Eastcliff Road are visible as differently coloured bricks, and there may be evidence of further loopholes in the wall of Newport cemetery, and in a house on Yarbrough Road above West Common. AT cylinders lie near Dixon Street and off Carholme Road, and five sockets for AT rails remain in the pavement on Nettleham Road (*87*).

Grantham and Gainsborough were similarly fortified, if on a smaller scale. In Grantham, the remains of road and rail blocks can still be seen under the railway bridge on Dysart Road, and on the embankment above the road by the railway bridge on Springfield Road. Wartime photographs show very narrow gaps between the AT walls, with steel rails laid out on the ground for instant insertion once the order to close had been issued. There was a clearly-laid out protocol for closing road-blocks which involved allowing as much friendly traffic as possible through, de-mobilising vehicles left on the wrong side, destroying stocks of fuel which could not be moved inside the defended perimeter, and only at the very last moment closing the roadblock. Bitter experience in the retreat to Dunkirk had impressed these principles deeply in the minds of these troops now preparing to defend their homeland.

In Gainsborough, the defences had two main aims. The first was to safeguard the town with its important munitions factories from attack, and the second was to deny the enemy access to the vital bridge over the Trent. Roadblocks of large, brick-shuttered concrete blocks were erected on the A631 on the east side of the town, at the west end of the bridge, and on the Lincoln road, south of the railway bridge. In addition, sockets for steel I-beams were installed in the A631 and the A156 where they went under the railway embankment, and also further out on the Corringham road beyond the RASC depot. The Trent road bridge was prepared for demolition by Gainsborough UDC staff who excavated shafts in the eastbound carriageway down into the main bridge piers, sealing the tops of the shafts at road level with heavy-duty manhole covers.

85 LINCOLN: a short stretch of anti-tank wall, part of the City's defended perimeter, at the corner of Mill Road and Upper Long Leys Road behind the old Militia Barracks

86 LINCOLN: a length of anti-tank wall on the west bank of the Witham off Boultham Street, more or less at the spot where the defended perimeter was taken over by the railway track

The Second World War (1939-1945)   197

87 LINCOLN: slots for the insertion of vertical anti-tank rails in the pavement where the city's defended perimeter crosses over to the west side of Nettleham Road

88 SALTFLEETBY: the Prussian Queen public house, a local defence HQ with a Home Guard store behind and standing at the centre of a quadrilateral of pillboxes and anti-tank blocks

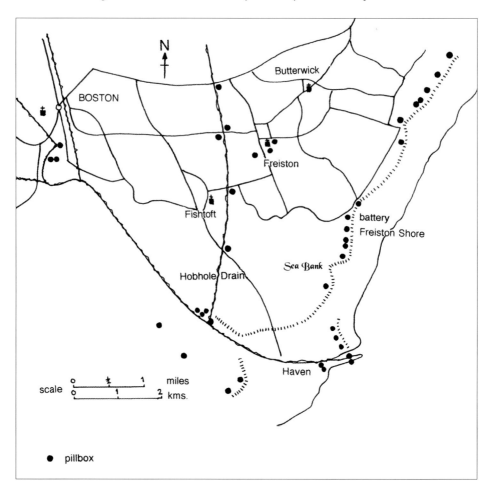

Fig. 15 Map to show coast defences in the Boston area

In contrast to those urban centres were smaller settlements that marked important road- or rail-junctions. The village of Sutterton, between Sleaford and Holbeach, where the A16 and A17 roads cross, is a good example. Here there is a Lincolnshire pattern pillbox to east and west of the crossroads, the one in the cemetery being painted with gravestones as camouflage. On the old Boston road is what appears to be a fifty-person air-raid shelter that may have been adapted as an explosives and inflammables store for the defenders. Nearer to Algarkirk, covering the railway (now the A16 road) is a hexagonal pillbox. Had these fixed defences been linked by field defences, trenches, wire and weapons pits, then they would have made an effective contribution in a delaying action. At Saltfleetby between Louth and the coast, two parallel roads could bring invading troops away from the beaches. A complex of four rectangular pillboxes, roadblocks of concrete AT cylinders, and the Home Guard HQ (*88*) in the pub, with a store behind it for explosives, acts as a DL astride these routes. At Burgh-le-Marsh, a road-block across the road inland from Skegness and controlled from an OP in the fish and chip shop, consisted of AT cubes, either side of the road, into which could be inserted a horizontal RSJ to close the road. Similar arrangements existed all over Lincolnshire. Sometimes relics of this time come back in unexpected circumstances. Market Deeping had AT blocks on Stamford Road, and AT rail sockets and more blocks in the market place. At the end of the war, the AT blocks were sawn off at ground level, but enough mass was left over the next sixty years to sink down onto a gas-main, finally fracturing it and blowing out the back wall of a house. Other towns and villages with surviving defences include Boston (***Fig. 15***), Halton Holegate, Spalding, Spilsby, Stamford and Uffington.

Airfield defence
In addition to precautions against invasion from the sea, measures were taken to guard against airborne landings. In the beginning, many flat spaces seen as potential landing grounds for enemy transports or gliders were obstructed by vertical poles strung together with wires, trenches dug across open spaces, and immobilised cars and farm-carts filled with rubble spaced out in open fields, all designed to prevent aircraft from landing. An example of rows of poles has been recorded in Welbourn. The most obvious places for enemy landings to take place were on established airfields, which by their very nature are vulnerable to attack from land, sea, and, especially, from the air, and any defence scheme had to take into account several eventualities. One was the possibility of a direct assault on the airfield itself by airborne troops. Another was an attack by troops landed elsewhere by air or by sea. A third involved being over-run in the course of a general invasion, and a fourth envisaged the involvement of fifth columnists supporting clandestine attack.

In summer 1940, Major General Taylor, Inspector General of Fortifications at the War Office, laid down the manning levels and the works requirements for airfield defence. He decided that location should be the key criterion for deciding the level at which fixed defences should be provided. Hence all airfields within 20 miles (32km) of a designated seaport would be deemed Class 1, qualifying for the highest level of defence provision. In Lincolnshire, Boston and the Humber estuary were classed as seaports that might become targets in the course of an enemy invasion, so any airfield within the agreed radius was to be given this level of fixed defences. This was set at between twenty and thirty-two pillboxes, some facing inwards to repel an enemy air landing, and others facing outwards, to defend against external assault. Provision was also made for dummy pillboxes to draw enemy fire and mislead enemy dive-bombers. The majority of Class 1 airfields were also provided with *Pickett-Hamilton Forts*, the so-called 'disappearing pillboxes'.

Given the shortage of manpower, an attempt was also made to determine the optimum manning level for the garrison of an airfield. For Class 1 airfields, this was set at 274 men. This was only the army contingent. It was expected that the RAF would organise defence platoons from their ground staff and any other available personnel, under the command of supernumerary or under-employed RAF officers. Rudimentary armoured vehicles were extemporised from trucks and civilian

89 SWINDERBY (SK886614): the airfield's Battle HQ suitably perched on a hummock overlooking the flying field

cars, in order to provide some element of mobility in the defence, however basic. The defence was co-ordinated from a Battle HQ, in the early days a converted building or adapted pillbox, but from 1941, a standardised purpose-built structure (**89**), built to Air Ministry drawing number *11008/41*.

Also in 1941, the RAF Regiment was formed, primarily for airfield defence. The defence of airfields against air attack was usually the responsibility of AA Command, but AA guns were normally integrated into the general defence, with gunners being taught how to engage ground targets. Since, in the early days at least, no AT guns were issued, the 3.7" HAA gun was the only available weapon effective against armour. It was also common for RAF personnel, especially on bomber-stations, to put some aircraft machine guns or cannon on improvised mountings in an AA role. Some of these were mounted on trucks or jeeps, turning them into versatile additions to the ground defence's armoury as well. While the initial defence layout tended to be linear with two concentric rings of pillboxes circling the airfield's perimeter, as tactical ideas developed, there was a move toward the establishment of strong-points with all-round defence, distributed around key points of the airfield, an analogue to the DL in other defence systems. Many of these ideas were taken up and developed by the squadrons of the RAF Regiment as they came on stream throughout 1942 and early 1943.

Possibly owing to the urgency involved in carrying out the construction of airfield defences, many of the pillboxes are based on the simplest DFW 3/22 design, and examples may be seen at Barkston Heath, Digby, Sutton Bridge and Wellingore (seven), but there are also examples of quite individual approaches to fixed defences in the county. At Spitalgate, there are three larger hexagonal pillboxes, at least one with a three-leaved cantilevered blast-wall inside, and another apparently built without benefit of concrete other than in its roof, which is now trying to slide off. At Digby and Wellingore there are several fighter dispersal pens with outward-facing walls loop-holed as musketry galleries (*90*), and Sutton Bridge formerly had a semi-sunken rectangular pillbox with eleven loopholes. The loopholes of some of the pillboxes at Wellingore and Digby (*91*) are fitted with *Scarff* mountings that may have originally been manufactured for First World War aircraft. At Binbrook is a single example of a shellproof hexagonal pillbox installed on many other airfields across the country. Manby had a unique W/T station which lay within an earth traverse with a concrete machine-gun post set at each corner. As with the other contexts in which pillboxes were employed, they were part of a complex system of trenches and weapons pits, wire and other obstacles, and mines. The Allan Williams turret is a small, steel, dome-shaped two-man turret that revolved over a pit allowing the two mounted weapons – Bren or Lewis lmgs – to engage targets on the ground or in the air through 360 degrees. Only 200 or so were ever manufactured, but examples survive in Lincolnshire at Spitalgate, Harlaxton (*92*), and two *ex situ* at Gosberton (TF221301).

The disappearing pillboxes, or Pickett-Hamilton forts, were allocated to most Class 1 airfields, and this included fourteen in Lincolnshire, only one of which – Sutton Bridge – was in a high priority group nationally. The Pickett-Hamilton fort comprised a concrete loop-holed cylinder that sat inside a slightly larger cylinder set in the ground. When in the down position, the roof was at ground level. Action stations saw the crew of two sprint across the grass, go in through a hatch in the roof, and raise the fort by means of pneumatic pressure from a compressed air bottle, or manually if that system failed. In a raised position, the trio of forts installed at the junctions of runways could command the landing area with automatic fire. The key concept was that when friendly aircraft landed, the forts were sunken, and when the enemy were trying to land, they were raised. Churchill was greatly impressed, but although 335 were constructed by the New Kent Company of Ashford, Kent and installed on 124 airfields, they were considered neither reliable nor even particularly useful. One of three installed at Woodhall Spa by the end of February 1941 can be seen at Thorpe Camp. For some reason the prefabricated sub-structure was unavailable so it was set in a solid mass of concrete, making the operation to secure its retrieval particularly difficult.

There are a number of examples in Lincolnshire of the standard Air Ministry drawing number *11008/41* Battle HQ design. This consists of several sunken rooms for PBX, messengers, etc., with a concrete-roofed cupola with 360-degree observation slit, which enabled the garrison commander to co-ordinate the defence of the airfield with benefit of all-round visibility over the flying field. It is entered through a hatch next to the cupola, with another entrance at the other end down stairs to the messengers' room. Examples of these may be seen at Binbrook, Hibaldstow, Spitalgate, Swinderby, Wellingore and Wickenby; others of this pattern existed, but have been demolished. At Goxhill the otherwise standard BHQ has had its

90 DIGBY: one of several defended fighter dispersal pens with loop-holed revetments; similar structures may be seen at Wellingore

91 DIGBY: the interior of one of several hexagonal pillboxes defending the airfield's perimeter; a *Scarff* mounting, similar to those in the First World War aircraft is fitted for a Lewis gun, and a removable concrete bung is supplied to seal off particular embrasures, presumably in response to an Air Ministry ruling that pillboxes should have fewer loopholes

92 HARLAXTON (SK901331): an Allan Williams turret, sited to defend the northern approach to the airfield

cupola heightened, and quite uniquely, there are two more cupolas attached to sunken Stanton shelters located on the northern edge of the airfield, and unusually described on the official Air Ministry plan *(641/45)* as 'Observation Posts'.

Attempts to inject mobility into airfield defence started with the *Armadillo*, a generic term for armoured trucks. A wooden box structure with loop-holed hollow walls filled with shingle was bolted onto the truck's flat bed, creating a compartment for two or three men with rifles and a Lewis gun, but lacking overhead cover. They replaced the wholly impracticable *Bison*, which was basically a concrete pillbox on wheels, one of which can be seen at East Kirkby, one of only a handful of survivors. Small family saloons like the Standard 14 hp were fitted with steel sheets over oak planks to produce a rudimentary armoured vehicle. These, the first such models to be produced in quantity, were named *Beaverettes* after Lord Beaverbrook, Minister of Aircraft Production, who first commissioned them. Given that the evidence on the ground would suggest that nowhere were pillboxes built in the numbers that the Taylor Report seemed to require, it is possible that the numbers were made up by use of these mobile defence posts, always in conjunction with fieldworks. Official airfield plans seldom record fixed defences, but usually include open blast shelters that may have been regarded as defensible, and the boomerang-shaped slit trenches that were also dual-purpose.

The defence of Vulnerable Points (VPs)

We have seen how important bridges were usually incorporated into defence lines in order to ensure their security, and how searchlight sites were often defended because they were regarded as integral parts of the ground defences. Other sites that sometimes merited fixed defences were buildings serving as formation HQs. Possibly owing to its proximity to the coast, Brackenborough Hall, a Battalion HQ, was quite strongly fortified. Three large loop-holed blockhouses, two of them under a single roof, an observation post, and a defended perimeter with weapons pits camouflaged as compost heaps can still be seen. Louth Park, a 'Diver' AA Regimental HQ, retains a close-defence pillbox.

Pillbox designs and defensive tactics

Pillboxes developed out of the static trench-warfare of the First World War's Western Front, and were seen as a way of giving a degree of protection to machine guns and their crews. They were always just one component in a whole system of field fortification that included trenches and weapons pits, wire, mines, AT obstacles, and the use of camouflage. On their own, they were little more than death traps. The Directorate of Fortifications and Works at the War Office (DFW3) produced a number of drawings, which enabled RE officers in the field to brief civilian contractors whose tenders for the work had been accepted, with a limited number of RE field companies working alongside them. There was also scope for locally designed types to be constructed.

93 HOLBEACH DROVE (TF315109): a hexagonal pillbox built to drawing number DFW3/22, defending a searchlight site

Examples of some DFW3 models are quite common in Lincolnshire. The design based on drawing number *DFW3/22* was a bullet-proof pillbox, a regular hexagon in shape, with five loopholes and a door in the back wall, often protected by one or two pistol loops. Examples may be seen on likely former searchlight sites such as Weston, Holbeach Drove (**93**) or Willoughby, on defence lines such as the Hobhole Drain, and defending roads as on the A152 near Wrangle, where there are four. These are not the most numerous across the country, but they are the most ubiquitous.

A local variation on this model provided a porch with a sloping roof, examples of which can be seen at Skegness near the boating-pond, at Gibraltar Point, and on the old road above the A17, east of Sutton Bridge. A further modification, found south of Freiston Shore battery, provided buttresses thickening the lower walls below the loopholes. Also at Freiston Shore is a Type 22 pillbox with an open upper floor holding a LAA machine gun on a timber post, and accessed by rungs built into the external wall. Another official design was that to drawing number *DFW3/23*. This is a square, roofed pillbox with three loops for light machine guns, with an open enclosure to the rear, also loop-holed and holding a post-mounting for a LAA lmg, two examples of which can be found at Boston. A local variation of this design provided a second closed square chamber, thus placing the open section in the centre. At least fifty of these were built only in Lincolnshire, with one sitting plumb on the Lincolnshire/Norfolk border. Although mainly confined to the coast defences, there was once one at Pode Hole guarding the pumping station. One step further on from this local design is a version found at Saltfleetby, Theddlethorpe St Helen and Shorts Corner, where the central open platform is roofed over to produce a rectangular pillbox with two chambers each having three loopholes. The *DFW3/26* is a square chamber with four loopholes and a low door, and examples can be seen at Boston Haven and Fosdyke Bridge.

The War Office also produced a drawing (*DFW3/28a*) for a shellproof gun-house specifically to hold the 2-pounder AT gun, but these guns being in very short supply, a modified version was developed in the eastern counties, to hold our old friend the Hotchkiss 6-pounder QF gun. This had a narrower-than-normal front embrasure, and a pedestal mounting for the gun with an iron ring to which the gun could be secured by nine bolts. Five out of the eight built in the Stickney/Sibsey area survive, but it is doubtful whether any of them ever saw guns mounted. These were pre-prepared fallback positions that were thankfully never needed.

Northern Command commissioned large numbers of a prefabricated pillbox called the 'Ruck', after its designer. This consisted of a skeleton vault of concrete ribs, with the spaces filled in with concrete paving slabs, and some gaps left in sides and roof for loopholes. On the Lincolnshire coast this was sometimes used in conjunction with a small square concrete OP with four observation slits. Examples of this pairing survive on the golf course south of Skegness, near Rimac, and at Tetney Lock. A single Ruck stands at Lawyers Creek, and mere traces of others at Freiston Shore. Another rectangular pillbox is almost unique to Lincolnshire. This has three rifle-loops in each long side, and a loop and a doorway at each end. Built onto each end are various combinations of mortar-pits, or LAA lmg mountings. Around ten

94 NORTH SOMERCOTES (TF442972/3): in the foreground is a rectangular pillbox with eight loopholes and a mortar pit at each end; on top has been built a 1960s *ORLIT* Royal Observer Corps aircraft-spotting post; beyond is a Lincolnshire 3-bay pillbox; in the distance is a building associated with the bombing range

95 SUTTON BRIDGE: a Turnbull mount set in the loophole of a pillbox

The Second World War (1939–1945)   207

of these survive on the Lincolnshire coast, and one at Donna Nook has had a Cold War ROC aircraft-post built on top (*94*). Across the county are various one-off designs which probably seemed good ideas at the time but never attracted enough interest to be replicated elsewhere. One near Boston Haven has two levels, and another is rectangular with a pentice roof. Many pillboxes were fitted with Turnbull mounts (*95*), designed to hold a machine gun steady while allowing it to traverse freely.

Shortages of cement and of timber for shuttering, coupled with the inaccessibility of many sites and the scarcity of transport, often made the operation of constructing pillboxes and other defences very difficult. The scale of the achievement is therefore astonishing. At the end of the war, a thousand AT blocks were removed from Skegness alone, probably representing no more than ten per cent of the county's total. A total of 500 would be a conservative estimate of the number of pillboxes built in the county, and most of this construction took place in the period May to November 1940. We have seen how the arrival of replacement munitions enabled the generals to change from a static to a mobile approach. An instance evidencing this change can be seen in Gainsborough where, as early as August 1940, roadblocks whose concrete had barely had time to set were being demolished as they were now regarded as a potential hindrance to the mobility of the defending forces. Fixed defences continued to be valued on the coast where it was felt that their strength allowed for reduced manning levels, freeing troops for training, whereas in inland positions there was more ambivalence. Provided the existing pillboxes were integrated into a wider defence plan then they were tolerated but, apart from on airfields, very few were built after the early months of 1941. Some were camouflaged as rocky outcrops on the shore, as cottages with false gabled roofs, as shelters on the esplanade, and as pigsties and other agricultural buildings. Others were left deliberately exposed as decoys.

While the primary object of the troops was to delay the enemy's advance, every opportunity to destroy his armour was to be seized. The roadblock would stop the tank, and the machine gun in the pillbox would pin down the accompanying infantry while the tank was disabled with grenades and mines. Simplistic, possibly suicidal, but desperate times demanded desperate measures.

PREPARATIONS FOR THE SECOND FRONT

The East Midlands were selected for much of the preparation involved in the airborne aspects of D-Day. Several Lincolnshire airfields were taken over by the troop carriers of the 9th USAAF including Fulbeck from late 1943, and Folkingham and Barkston Heath in early 1944. North Witham provided maintenance and repair facilities for the transports, gliders and their tugs. Many of the troops who would land in aircraft or gliders or by parachute were also based in south Lincolnshire around the turn of 1943/4 for the D-Day operations of June 1944, and later for the Arnhem adventure. Easton Hall had been requisitioned by the War Office in 1939 and was occupied by 2nd Bn. Parachute Regiment; the house was demolished in 1951. In October 1943, Fulbeck Hall became HQ of the 1st Airborne Division, earmarked for post-D-Day strikes, but destined to land at Arnhem in September 1944, under General Urquhart. Some training took place at Belton Camp, and units were scattered across the area using a variety of large houses, including Stoke Rochford Hall, Caythorpe, Belton House, Casewick Hall, and Shillingthorpe Park. Harlaxton Manor was used by the 1st Airborne Division, whose Pegasus badge forms a memorial in the Old Stable-yard. Uffington Hall and Rectory were also used, where troops – among them RASC drivers destined for the Mulberry Harbours – were under canvas in the Park.

THE LINCOLNSHIRE HOME GUARD

On 14 May 1940, the formation of the Local Defence Volunteers was announced, mainly to pre-empt the piecemeal efforts of free enterprise and the consequent proliferation of private armies across the land. The task of organising what soon became officially titled the Home Guard was given to the county Territorial Associations. Elderly officers appeared from the Retired List to lead a combination of old soldiers, men in reserved occupations, and schoolboys too young yet to be called up. The official histories record twenty-three battalions of Home Guard in Lincolnshire, totalling 25,000 men at Stand-down in 1945, but TA papers in the County Archive list the officers for only twenty-one battalions. Working from the higher total, Lincoln City and Holland raised three battalions each, Kesteven raised four, whilst the much larger and populous Lindsey raised thirteen. The county was split into sectors with three or four battalions defending each sector under a commander. Thus the Scunthorpe Sector was defended by Lindsey Home Guard's 1st–4th Bns (Scunthorpe and District, Scunthorpe Works, Epworth and Brigg), Grimsby and district by the 5th–7th Bns (Grimsby Town, Cleethorpes Town and Grimsby Rural/Laceby), and the Alford Sector by 8th–10th Bns (Caistor, Louth and Skegness).

In Kesteven the CO of the four battalions was Colonel Mountjoy-Fane of Careby Rectory. The 4th Kesteven Bn. covered the area around Stamford and Bourne, with 'C' Coy. commanded by Major Hoare of Holywell Hall. Each village raised a platoon relative to its size, so 'E' Coy, numbering around 100 men, and led by Major Bates was drawn from Rippingale, Dowsby, Dunsby, Haconby and Morton, with a fifteen-strong mobile platoon on bicycles armed with rifles and two Lewis guns. Until recently, a store for ammunition stood at the north end of Dowsby village. Local HQs used whatever buildings were available. There was a Bn. HQ in the Toll Bar School at New Waltham, and there were Company HQs at: Barton-upon-Humber in the drill hall on Butts Road; at Saltfleetby in the Prussian Queen public house; in Grimsby in the Augusta Street drill hall; in Cleethorpes in the old Woolworths building on the High Street; in Sleaford (2nd Kesteven Bn.) in the billiards room over Colonel Chambers' garage in Westgate; and in Skegness it was recorded in the official Invasion Plan as being in Bolingbroke House on Scarbrough Avenue, although there is little local knowledge relating to this address.

The specific tasks assigned to Home Guard units were to give depth to the beach defences by establishing strong-points to deny the enemy mobility, to intercept enemy airborne forces at their point of landing, and especially to provide in-depth inland defences to protect industrial centres and the approaches to ports. All these activities were to be performed in tandem with the regular forces that would co-ordinate their joint operations. Additionally, key VPs would be guarded by the Home Guard, and it is said that the Admiralty W/T station at Waltham was under the wardship of a platoon of the local Home Guard, all survivors of the Grimsby Chums, and known as the 'Pyloniers'. Home Guard training was vital, but could only be taken seriously once appropriate weapons became available. Rifles were obtained from the USA but something a bit more powerful was needed, so the concept of sub-artillery was born.

The Home Guard was equipped with the Northover Projector, a drainpipe on legs which fired Molotov Cocktails; the Smith Gun, a 3in (75mm) smooth-bore cannon that traversed on dustbin-lids doubling as wheels when it was towed behind an Austin Seven, with another pair of wheels forming a limber for the shells; and the Blacker Bombard or Spigot Mortar which could throw a 14lb (6.5kg) anti-personnel, or a 20lb (9kg) anti-tank bomb a couple of hundred yards. The Spigot Mortar could be fired from a field mounting with tubular legs and spade grips for stability, or from a permanent mounting. This permanent mounting consisted of a framework of iron bars called a 'spider' set in a thimble-shaped concrete block the size of an oil-drum, from whose domed top protruded a stainless steel pintle. The thimble was set in a brick-lined pit with brick ammunition lockers let into the sides. The spigot mortar was kept in a safe, dry place, usually one of the Home Guard stores (**96**) that are dotted around the county, and brought into action to be

96 LOUTH (TF340849): a standard-pattern Lincolnshire Home Guard Explosives & Inflammables store

mounted on the thimble at 'Action Stations', when the rockets went up and the church bells were rung.

It would appear that in Lincolnshire, spigot mortars were mainly used on mobile field-mountings, as only three thimbles are known: in Sutton Bridge, in Long Sutton, and in Stamford. These improvised weapons may have been makeshift, but they provided much needed fire-power in desperate times. The Home Guard were taught all sorts of street-fighting skills by instructors who had served in the Spanish Civil War with the International Brigades. Many of these techniques were concerned with enticing tanks into ambushes where they could be disabled by sticky bombs and incendiary grenades. Home Guards used their own rifle ranges such as Hubbards Hill in Louth, or the rifle club in the Crown Brewery in Norman Street, Lincoln. There were also battle schools where battle drills could be practised realistically, and Appleby Hall was completely destroyed in such exercises. Improvisation was the order of the day, and much ingenuity went into producing armoured vehicles by applying steel plate to civilian cars and mounting machine guns in them. More traditional was Sleaford's solution to the mobility problem. To its east, out on the heath, there was a dearth of north–south roads, and this made it difficult for patrols in wheeled vehicles seeking out enemy parachutists. Brigadier Adlercron of Culverthorpe Hall therefore had the idea of recruiting a mounted unit, providing hunters from his own stables, and drilling the unit in the park. Groups of these mounted Home Guards carried out patrols and liaised with neighbouring units in areas that would otherwise have been inaccessible.

The auxiliary units
More controversial than Home Guards as cavalrymen would have been Home Guards as guerrillas, if anyone had known about them. The British Resistance Organisation (BRO), or the auxiliary units as they were usually referred to, were small cells of undercover members of the Home Guard. They were generally located in rural areas near the coast, and recruited from countrymen who were in their element living off the land and familiar with fieldcraft skills. Successful poachers were ideal candidates. Their task was to establish underground operational bases (OBs), or hides, stocked with food, arms, ammunition and explosives, so that in the event of an invasion, they might emerge to sabotage the enemy's supply lines, disrupt his communications, and tie up fighting troops in guarding the rear areas. They were trained in silent killing, setting booby-traps and bomb-making techniques. Each cell, or patrol, was independent and had no knowledge of others. In order to give room for manoeuvre, patrols sometimes built multiple hides, and there are no less than six such structures in Brocklesby Park.

The county HQ, with a permanent staff of seven officers and NCOs, was first located at Wellingore Hall, but moved to Blankney Hall, with a northern HQ at Normanby Hall, where there was a hide in the cellars, and a southern one at Dalby Hall. Key personnel were sent away for training at Coleshill House in Berkshire, but local training took place at Dalby Hall (**97**) and in many other appropriate locations, such as woodlands and quarries. There were over thirty patrols in Lincolnshire with

The Second World War (1939-1945) 211

97 DALBY HALL: the British Resistance Organisation's southern HQ and county training centre

a total membership of nearly 200. The standard OB was a buried Nissen-type hut containing bunks, an arms rack, food and ammunition storage, and a chemical toilet. It was entered down a shaft whose hatch might be hidden under a tree-stump, and a tunnel exiting in a different direction provided an escape route. In order to maintain secrecy, very few contractors were used, just Clarke & Sons in Lincolnshire, who were responsible for the construction of at least nineteen hides. As well as using couriers for conveying news, a separate wireless net was established so that local Zero Stations would receive orders that could be passed on via dead-letter drops or distributed by patrol leaders. The centre of this network was in Lincoln with Zero Stations at Barton-upon-Humber, Brocklesby, Mablethorpe, Skegness and Wainfleet. To keep the system secure, no wireless operator was aware of any other. At Wainfleet All Saints, the radio receiver was in an outhouse of Batemans Brewery, with the aerial in a copper-beech tree next to the windmill.

Local defence plans
Once many of the emergency organisations were in place, there was a need for an integrated plan that sought to ensure that they were working together. The Invasion Committee in Skegness formulated such a plan, probably early in 1941. The main task of the defending forces was to deny the enemy the use of the beaches and the main exit routes from the town, and to maintain civil and military services from disruption. In the event of invasion, the local military commander at Battalion HQ in Burgh-le-Marsh would take control and employers would release Home Guard personnel to join their units at their pre-determined battle stations within

two hours on the signal 'Action Stations'. Alford was the HQ of the local 10th Bn. Lindsey Home Guard, whose 'D' Coy. was based in Scarbrough Avenue. The ARP reporting centre and CD Divisional Control was at the bathing pool in Grand Parade until it was bombed out when a move was made to Pembroke House, now the Masonic Hall, in Rutland Street. Civil Defence had a rescue and de-contamination centre at the Richmond Drive depot.

Empty railway carriages were held in sidings at the station in case mass evacuation became necessary. Facilities for dealing with casualties at first-aid posts, at the local hospital, and at the RAF sick quarters on Seacroft Esplanade, along with a mortuary, were all detailed in the plan, as were general welfare provision, emergency food supplies, water, sewage, salvage, road repairs and burial arrangements. The immobilisation of vehicles, the cutting off of gas supplies and destruction of petrol stocks were also included. Instructions to the residents who had not hitherto been evacuated were to be relayed via the police mobile broadcasting car. Skegness was generously supplied with air-raid shelters, having places for 4,500 in public shelters, and 3,000 in Morrison shelters in private houses. The 100-place shelter in the High Street banana store and the communal surface shelter in Lumley Avenue were fairly typical. At the south end of Drummond Road and on Seacroft Esplanade there were full roadblocks closed by steel rails and cement barrels. Opposite Dean's Farm on the Wainfleet road, on the Burgh road beyond the water tower and at West Brick Pit Corner near the golf course on Roman Bank, there were checkpoints that could be upgraded to roadblocks. The principal duty of the police was to control the civil population, to keep specific roads open for military use, to enforce precautions against espionage, sabotage, and rumour-mongering, and to ensure that petrol stocks could not fall into enemy hands As early as 1938 the Skegness Wheelers cycling club had volunteered their services as messengers for the ARP. In 1943, parts of the beach were re-opened from 6am–9pm for the summer season, but locals were aware of fatal accidents the previous year when people had strayed into beach minefields.

AIR DEFENCE OF LINCOLNSHIRE

Lincolnshire contained plenty of naval and military targets, as well as industrial ones, so the full repertoire of air defence measures, both active and passive, were put into effect. Fortunately the county suffered less than some areas, but nevertheless underwent several heavy attacks and lived under the constant threat of aerial bombardment. During the course of the war there were over forty air raids on the Grimsby/Cleethorpes area, and thirty more on Skegness/Mablethorpe. One raid on Grimsby in June 1943 unleashed hundreds of small *Butterfly* bombs, which caused 163 casualties – mainly after the 'all-clear' – had sounded, as people disturbed them. Bombs caused around 200 fatalities in other towns, including Scunthorpe, Gainsborough, Grantham, Boston and Lincoln. Somewhat surprisingly, daylight raids on coastal farms were recorded in AA unit war diaries.

Anti-aircraft artillery

For the majority of the potential targets for bombers in Lincolnshire, anything approaching adequate AA cover was a long time coming. In 1939, both effective AA weapons – the 3.7" HAA gun and the *Bofors* 40mm LAA gun – were in very short supply. Those few targets, mostly RAF airfields, deemed worthy of AA cover at all, had to make do with mainly obsolete weapons. In October 1940, Sutton Bridge had two 3" guns and nine Lewis guns, while at North Coates there were two mobile 40mm guns and two Lewis guns. Both these airfields were armament training camps felt to be in vulnerable coastal sites. Manby, in no less vulnerable a location, made do with just 14 Lewis guns, two fewer than Binbrook, Cranwell and the Admiralty W/T station at Waltham. This last site had warranted the despatch from Norwich of a detachment from 78th HAA Regiment specifically to man eight Lewis guns in August 1939 as a stopgap measure. Hemswell and Kirton-in-Lindsey had a pair of 3" guns and fifteen Lewis guns each, and Digby, Waddington and Scampton each had two static 40mm guns and a handful of Lewis guns. The vital Chain Home radar station at Stenigot was defended against air attack by three mobile 40mm guns and six Lewis guns. If the fatalistic notion that the bomber would always get through was to prove true, then precious little was being done to prevent it. The civilian munitions factory targets of Grantham and Lincoln had no AA protection at all at this time, in fact HAA guns that had hitherto been protecting Grantham were moved to Derby. Scunthorpe was favoured with twenty-four HAA guns in August 1940, but by November they had been re-deployed, probably to London, and replaced by seven static 40mm guns and thirty-four Lewis guns.

There were a few AA sites covering the Humber estuary with one on Grimsby sea wall near the docks, and others at Stallingborough, Immingham and Humberston. There appears to have been an endless juggling act performed to make best use of scant resources. The war diary of 39th AA Brigade, based at Scawby Camp near Brigg, the parent formation for many of Lincolnshire's AA units through to 1942, records constant movement of units between airfields, factories, VPs and the AA practice camp at Weybourne in Norfolk or, in the case of RAF Regiment AA squadrons, their new practice camp at Anderby Creek. Other locations for unit HQs appear to be Elsham Hall, the Militia camp in Gainsborough, the Grange at Bishop Norton and Hibaldstow airfield. Throughout 1941, many targets had only LAA cover, but the Home Guard crew of a twin-20mm *Hispano-Suiza* gun at BMARCo in Grantham nevertheless shot down a *Junkers 88* bomber on 27 January 1941, receiving the congratulations of Lord Beaverbrook, the Minister of Aircraft Production, whose factory in Springfield Road, had been one of the targets that night.

It was not until 1942 that more AA guns had been emplaced. Grantham's four HAA sites were still equipped with only two pairs of 3" guns in June 1942, but by the end of the year, eight 3.7" HAA guns had been added, manned by 570 (Mixed) HAA Regiment, as well as a dozen 40mm guns. This was partly because the town's munitions plants were under constant attack, and because the rail junction – rated '*Bargain*', i.e. in the second tier of importance – had necessitated this upgrade of provision. Lincoln, too, was given three batteries, each of four mobile 3.7" HAA guns, one of which had accompanying GL radar. These batteries were at Riseholme, Reepham and Sharps Farm. In addition there were six LAA sites in Lincoln: at the Water Tower in Chapel Street; at Boots in Clasketgate; at Rustons Sheet Ironworks in Melville Street; at the Hovis factory at Brayford Wharf; the Ritz cinema on High Street; and the Usher Gallery on Lindum Road. In June 1942, there were twelve sites around Scunthorpe, but only two were armed, each with four static 3.7" HAA guns with GL radar. The Humber Gun-defended area (GDA) was relatively well protected by 1942. There were a total of thirty-seven sites, just under half of which were armed. Weapons mounted included 3.7" and 4.5" HAA guns. There were a dozen or so sites on the Lincolnshire side, of which maybe half were armed. One of these was Little London (H20) near Stallingborough, which had been equipped with four 3.7" guns in 1942, but by November 1944 had been rebuilt as a completely new battery with four electrically-operated, radar-controlled 5.25" HAA guns. By 1943, the standard issue for airfields was generally four power-operated, mobile 40mm Bofors guns, although Hemswell still had only 12 AA lmgs on 1 May that year. Vulnerable points continued to be defended by whatever was available, and RAF trainees in Skegness remember a pair of Browning 0.5" machine guns mounted by the boating lake near Seacroft. As a new weapon, the 3" un-rotated projectile or 'Z' Battery began to appear in the AA arsenal, a rocket-firing practice range opening at Sutton-on-Sea in January 1942.

Just when the bombing threat appeared to be over, a new terror weapon emerged in the shape of the *V1* 'doodle-bug'. As the launch sites for these flying bombs moved northwards, then the AA defences were extended. The code for these bombs was 'Diver', so the defences consisted of designated areas of sky in which guns or fighters would operate. To the south were the Coastal Gun Belt, the 'Diver Box' around the Thames Estuary, the 'Diver Strip' up the East Anglian coast, and then finally the 'Diver Fringe' from Ingoldmells Point to Filey in North Yorkshire. Every available AA gun was deployed to these defences, and there were thirty-nine HAA batteries in the Fringe sector. Twelve of these batteries were in Lincolnshire, crewed by 144 (Mixed) HAA Regiment RA, with HQ at South Elkington Hall, and a Sector Operations Room at Louth Park. There were Battery HQs at Trusthorpe Camp and The Camp, Marsh Chapel. Three batteries were in Mablethorpe, two each side of Saltfleet, four between Donna Nook and RAF North Coates, and one at Cleethorpes, close by a pre-existing AA site.

A typical 'Fringe' battery consisted of four 3.7" HAA guns mounted on 'Pile Mattresses', firm platforms of railway sleepers and rails in which sat the hold-fast for the gun fed by all the electrical cabling which powered it. There was a GL radar set, a tracker tower, and huts housing generators, magazines, crew-shelters and a command-post. Behind this was a camp with more huts for workshops, offices, canteen, mess, living accommodation and gun-stores. The 'Fringe' was complete by the end of December 1944, and the last *V1* hit London a fortnight later. As well as the guns, groups of four searchlights were spaced at 1,500–2,000-yard intervals inland on the Lincolnshire coast, manned by 69th S/L Regiment with HQ at Fulney Park,

Spalding. The regiment's batteries were stationed around Mablethorpe with HQ at Trustville Holiday Camp, at Sibsey, and just over the Norfolk border at Terrington St Clements. In 1944 Digby's sector HQ for 50th AA Brigade was at Ashby Hall in Ashby-de-la-Launde.

Searchlight sites
Alongside the AA guns were searchlights, particularly important in the early part of the war before GL radar had been sufficiently developed. We have already seen how the 5th Bn. Lincolnshire Regt. had been converted into the 46th Searchlight Regiment with its HQ at the Westward Ho drill hall in Grimsby. Its 383rd Coy. was based in the Butts Road drill hall in Barton-upon-Humber in 1939, with a section HQ at New Waltham, and was manning S/L positions at Beelsby Top, Ashby-cum-Fenby, Holton-le-Clay, Humberston Fitties, Cleethorpes Boating Lake and Pyewipe. In April 1940 it was moved to Northumbria. Other such units came from further afield. Units of the 58th (Middlesex) AA Bn. from Harrow were stationed at Haugham Slates south of Louth and then at Edenham near Bourne. This sort of dispersal was normal at this time as the strategy was to fill a zone, parallel to the coast, with a lighted area in which the AA guns were able to operate. Sites were usually spread out at intervals of 3 miles (5km) to form a two-dimensional grid. Later in the war all sorts of groupings were tried, but early on, S/L sites were seen as being permanent enough to be designated strong points and given defences, often a pillbox.

Isolated pillboxes, not obviously related to other defences, can often be explained by this practice. Pillboxes spaced at three mile intervals can be traced along lines from Skillington through Corby Glen to Haconby, and from Pinchbeck through Weston, Saracen's Head, Holbeach Hurn and Gedney Dyke, these west–east lines representing transects across the Lights Zone. One final piece in the active air defence structure was the provision of barrage balloons. The Humber area was organised from No. 17 Balloon Centre, Sutton-on-Hull, with seventy-four balloons in use, including twenty-four waterborne around the ports on both sides of the estuary.

Radar sites
The Chain Home (CH) system of Radio Direction Finding (RDF) was brought into commission just in time to detect enemy aircraft. Stenigot (Station 34) AMES (Air Ministry Experimental Station), as these installations were named, had been planned in November 1937, and opened in the spring of 1939 as the link in the chain between Staxton Wold (Yorkshire) and West Beckham (Norfolk). It had a standard East Coast layout of four steel 350ft-high (107m-high) transmitter towers in a square, and four wooden 240ft-high (73m-high) receiver towers in a line. The receiver and transmitter blocks were semi-sunken with earth traverses, as was a generator building. On the surface of the site were a warden's house, a guardroom and some huts for offices and living accommodation. All this was surrounded by a fence and close-defence pillboxes, those at Stenigot being triangular with the angles cut off. It was felt that these secret sites, particularly those on the East Coast, were vul-

nerable to attack, so they were given LAA guns, as well as being well defended with wire, weapons pits, trenches and, it was recommended, a double ring of pillboxes. Living sites were dispersed to protect them against bombing, and Stanton shelters provided for personnel not in the buried works.

The CH stations were unable to detect low-flying aircraft so, in the early months of the war, Chain Home Low (CHL) was developed in conjunction with a project which sought to provide the army Coast Defence (CD) radar for detecting maritime targets. Two discoveries were quickly made. Firstly that it was wasteful to develop parallel systems with similar purposes and, secondly that for technical reasons, CH and CHL would not easily co-exist on the same sites. While scratch equipments provided temporary cover for the Humber area, Ingoldmells (Station 33) CHL station was built to complement Stenigot, opening in February 1940, but to be replaced by Skendleby (Station 34A) within six months. Instead of high towers, CHL sites had aerial gantries constructed astride the huts that housed the instruments, and the machinery, either manual or powered, which rotated the aerials. A standby-set and some living huts completed the complex.

The next problem to be solved was that of the fighters being able to intercept enemy aircraft at night, and there were two elements to the solution: AI radar in aircraft which could detect enemy aircraft, and GCI radar which enabled ground controllers to direct fighter pilots onto their targets. Airborne Interception (AI) radar and Ground Control Interception (GCI) radar developed separately but in tandem. Mobile GCI equipment was installed at Orby (06G) to work with the fighter operations room at Digby, entering service in January 1941. The Intermediate Transportable design installed at Orby consisted of a steel gantry supporting a 10ft (3m) aerial array, with timber hutting, and brick generator building. By mid-1943, Langtoft (08G) was in operation using similar equipment to that at Orby, and both were scheduled to achieve 'Final' status once this highly sophisticated system with its complex engineering and structural requirements could be fully developed. The layout of the Final GCI station, as built at Orby and Langtoft, included an operations block known as the Happidrome, which contained all the information-processing elements, and the aerial array over its underground operating room.

Although the Air Ministry had avoided the duplication inherent in parallel CD and CHL systems, the army continued to attempt its own system of ship detection, which was itself different from Coast Artillery (CA) radar. Known as Triple-Service, a chain of CD/CHL stations were planned in April 1941, which initially included four proposed sites in Lincolnshire: Donna Nook (M57), Mablethorpe (M58), Huttoft Bank (M59) and Chapel St Leonards (M60). Of these, Donna Nook and Mablethorpe were built, and a brand new station at Humberston with a 184ft-high (56m-high) steel tower was built as a prototype, coming on air in December 1941. The tower straddled the timber operations block (**98**), with a brick standby-set house next door. This technology was rapidly overtaken by the new centimetric system, Chain Home Extra Low (CHEL), which was installed at Skendleby (K161), and Mablethorpe was declared redundant by the end of 1942, followed by Donna Nook during 1943.

The Second World War (1939-1945)   217

98 HUMBERSTON: the operations block of this proto-type Triple Service Coast Defence/Chain Home Low (CD/CHL) radar site opened in December 1941

Few remnants survive of Lincolnshire's Second World War radar network. Stenigot retains one of its steel masts, one of only a handful nationally, and used by the trainee aerial riggers from RAF Digby. Orby and Langtoft retain much of their wartime fabric, but in amongst later Cold War remains, all submerged within a stock-car racing track and a scrapyard respectively. Skendleby exists only in its later form, but Donna Nook retains features of a CHL station, and Humberston has retained its timber operations block, amongst other structures on the Tertia Trust site.

The (Royal) Observer Corps in Lincolnshire

The Observer Corps (Royal from 1941) began the war with its organisational structure established and a number of full-scale dry runs under its belt. In 1940, there was a move for 11 Group's Lincoln operations room, from the top floor of the GPO to St Peters Chambers, Silver Street where there was more space. The Observer Corps' Midland HQ moved from RAF Spitalgate to Mostyn Lodge, Grantham in June 1940. Around the county there were fifty-five posts for spotting enemy aircraft, grouped into threes with telephone or radio links to Lincoln. There were thirty-nine such triads reporting to 11 Group, while some posts in the north of the county reported to York, and others in the south to Cambridge. These posts had all been built to individual design, although there was an optional standard model available. The only common components of an aircraft post were the Mickelthwaite Height Correction Attachment, which was fixed atop a tripod, and some other very rudimentary bits of kit. The standard design was known as the 'rabbit hutch' and was a wooden shed with an open section attached. A survivor from Tetford may be seen at the museum at Thorpe Camp. Some posts, such as Alford, were simply open squares of sandbags, while others occupied the tops of raised structures, such as Sleaford's, on top of the water-tower at the town's maltings. At Boston, an open timber platform on stilts was built on the concrete plinth, which can still be seen.

The Midland Area HQ had moved to Watnall (Nottinghamshire) in 1942, and in October 1943 the Lincoln Operations Room moved into St Martins Hall in Beaumont Fee. Towards the end of the war, improvements were made to some of the aircraft posts. At Mablethorpe, a brick post was built on top of a substantial concrete building in the sandhills. Epworth is a brick post with a covered half and an octagonal opening over the other half. This opening could be covered by a plexiglass skylight, and posts to a similar design were built at Bourne and Billingborough. The post at Barton-upon-Humber on Beacon Hill is described as being built of brick and reinforced concrete, 15ft (4.5m) square, and with an open upper storey. There are references to other observation posts, particularly in windmills, such as at Gosberton, Wainfleet and Welbourn, but these were not necessarily linked into the official ROC organisation. Some ROC posts were assigned tasks in addition to aircraft spotting. Two Lincolnshire posts, Louth and Old Leake were equipped with GL Radar sets that enabled them to identify friendly aircraft through their IFF systems, thus isolating enemy intruders, and also helping lost aircraft to land safely. Another system for homing aircraft in trouble was *Darky*, which was installed at Wainfleet and Fosdyke. They were able to direct aircraft to an airfield where a cone of three searchlight beams (*Sandra*) awaited them. *Granite*, installed at Blyth, over the Nottinghamshire border, was a safety measure whereby red flares were launched when the cloud-base was down to 1000ft in areas of high ground.

Bombing Decoys
One alternative to shooting enemy bombers down was to trick them into dropping their bombs away from their real targets. This was achieved by building decoys a few miles distant from real airfields, and this idea was later extended to civilian and industrial targets. The programme was under the control of Col. Turner's Department at the Air Ministry, and was activated in the last weeks of peace, initially providing decoy sites for RAF airfields. There were 'K' sites that were simulations of satellite airfields with dummy aircraft designed to be seen in daylight. These dummy aircraft were manufactured mainly by the Sound City film studios at Shepperton (Middlesex). In Lincolnshire there were 'K' sites at Hemswell and Manby with *Whitley* bombers, Waddington and Spitalgate with *Battles*, and North Coates with *Blenheims*. The 'K' site at Swayfield served Cottesmore (Rutland). Airmen were based on each site as ground crew, moving aircraft around and generally simulating the day-to-day activities of a working airfield. A shelter was provided for them in the event of an attack. For nighttime purposes, the 'Q' site was developed with lighting, and at the approach of enemy aircraft, the runway lights would be dowsed but only after the enemy pilots had had time to notice them. A *Chance* light, mounted on

The Second World War (1939–1945)   219

the control blockhouse, simulated the lights of an aircraft on the ground, and sometimes vehicles were driven around to add to the apparent activity. A much smaller crew was needed, mainly to control the lights electrically from the blockhouse. Most airfields in eastern England were provided with a pair of 'Q' sites. In the first tranche, nine airfields – including Scampton, Waddington (**99**) and Digby – were given fifteen decoy sites. Subsequently seventeen more decoys were provided for eleven more airfields. As more airfields were required, the fake became genuine, as happened at Folkingham – initially a decoy for Spitalgate. A very few decoys were dual-purpose from the start. Hagnaby was a 'K/Q' site for Manby/Coningsby, and two airmen who served there from January 1940 have described life on this site. They tell how they went, under the strictest secrecy, to the depot in London where they assembled dummy aircraft, prior to being posted off to rural Lincolnshire with their fake *Whitleys*. At night they started up the generators and lit the flare path. They also, naturally enough, tell the story of the enemy dropping wooden bombs on their decoy site.

As the war progressed, a range of specialist decoys was included in Col. Turner's repertoire. The most common were 'SF', Special Fires, known as *Starfish*. These were extensive networks of braziers containing fires, oil-fires and built-in sudden surges of flame. These were meant to simulate the effects of bombs falling on urban areas of housing and factories. They were ignited as soon as the bombing stream was heard, in order to indicate where the bombs should be dropped. Oil Depots were provided

99 GAUTBY (TF164718): the control blockhouse of a Bombing Decoy built to entice enemy raiders away from Waddington

with QF decoys ('P' Series), which simulated burning fuel. Killingholme had such a decoy at East Halton near Goxhill. The Navy's 'N' Series included *Starfish* and lights (SF/QL) decoys for Immingham, Killingholme and Grimsby and another for Tetney Haven, controlled from the Admiralty post at the seaward end of North Sea Lane, Humberston. A Civil QL site covering Lincoln was located at Branston Fen.

Large civilian targets were usually provided with Permanent SF sites, and Scunthorpe had three at Risby, Twigmoor and Brumby, active from at least mid-1941, and well into 1943. Both Lincoln and Grantham had Temporary SF sites, Lincoln's near its Branston Fen QL site with another at Canwick, and Grantham's at Boothby Pagnell. The greatest ingenuity went into the QL programme activated in October 1942, which sought to provide site-specific simulated lighting effects. Various combinations of lights to signify marshalling yards (MY), locomotive glows (LG) and factory lighting were installed at Risby for Scunthorpe's Northern Iron & Steel Co., and at Twigmoor for the Appleby, Frodingham Steel Co. Grantham's Boothby Pagnell decoy was up-graded with similar effects. Despite the inherent problems in assessing the effectiveness of preventative measures, enough decoys were actually bombed to suggest that this must have reduced the bomb-load falling on real targets.

Civil Defence

The fear of aerial bombardment was prevalent from the war's first days. Soldiers of Lincolnshire's TA units reporting for duty in September 1939 were ordered via War Office telegram to bring their civilian respirator with them as there were not yet enough of the military model available. Centres of population were provided with enough public shelter places for the ten per cent of the population who might be outside as a raid began. Employers were meant to ensure that they had adequate provision, and homes were allocated Anderson shelters, on a means-tested payment system, or Morrison shelters for indoors. Lincoln had public spaces for 7,000, plus a similar number in schools, supervised by 1,000 ARP wardens. The cathedral precinct was under the care of wardens based in Eastgate School. Shelters in commercial premises could be used by neighbours, and the inhabitants of Newsum's Villas in Carholme Road, for instance, were allowed to use the cellars under the adjacent factory. Skegness had public spaces for 4,500 including 100 in the High Street Banana Store and around 200 other shelters, including communal shelters in Lumley and Scarbrough Avenues, and 3,000 Morrison shelters were distributed. Boston had a total of forty-six public shelters, some of them in cellars and others as surface shelters. Many of this latter type – as built down the middle of Oxford, Cambridge, Harrow and College Streets in Grantham, for instance – were built with insufficient mortar, and were known to collapse in a near-miss bomb-blast. Sirens to sound the alarm and all clear were mounted on prominent structures (**100**). There were first-aid posts, emergency temporary shelters for the homeless, fire stations and sub-stations, and emergency water supplies.

The whole operation was co-ordinated from the ARP reporting centre. At Skegness, this was at the Bathing Pool in Grand Parade, and when this was destroyed

The Second World War (1939–1945) 221

100 DEEPING St NICHOLAS: an air-raid siren mounted on a railway building adjacent to the level crossing on the Spalding road

by bombing, it was in the Pembroke House in Rutland Road, now the Masonic Hall. At Barton-upon-Humber, the Civil Defence Control was in a concrete bunker with a steel door behind the former Council Offices, now St Peters Court. Mablethorpe's reporting centre was still standing at last sight, and Grantham's was under the Library/Museum. Many families built their own shelters, an example being that at the Old Vicarage in Caistor, built of barrel-vaulted brick and measuring 25–30ft (8–10m) long, 10ft (3m) wide, and around head-height. Rustons of Lincoln manufactured some steel one-man shelters for firewatchers and sentries, and one stood on Monson's Farm in Skellingthorpe until recently. A number of other vital functions were protected against bombing. By the station at Metheringham is a brick and concrete blockhouse with steel-shuttered windows, which was the railway control centre for the region, one of twenty-five such structures nationally. Tattershall Castle was one of many locations to which art treasures and museum collections were evacuated for safekeeping, away from their vulnerable homes in the cities.

MUNITIONS DEPOTS IN LINCOLNSHIRE

The RAF's bombing operations required a correspondingly extensive logistical support structure to keep it going. Aviation fuel came via a pipeline from the Humber, with depots at Torksey and Stow. There was an Equipment Park (207MU) at Scunthorpe, and Broughton Wood, Brigg was 209MU's air stores park for 1 Group, Bomber Command. There were Air Ministry Works Department depots at Honington and Holton-le-Moor (*101*), where buildings remain at both sites. Although individual airfields had their own ready-use bomb-stores, these were only the final links in a long supply chain. The major underground stores supplied Forward Ammunition Depots such as Norton Disney (93MU), at Swinderby station with subsidiary depots at Tumby Woodside and Fox Covert, serving 5 Group Bomber Command. The depot of 100MU at South Witham, supplemented by roadside storage around Stretton, served 1 Group. Market Stainton was the depot of 233MU with a capacity of 20 kilotons, and sub-sites at Orby and Wragby. Very little of these sites now remains. At South Witham, many hut bases remain in Morkery Wood, while most of the administrative and domestic functions were accommodated in Stocken Hall and its outbuildings. North of Market Rasen, little remains of the bomb-dump beside the railway at Nova Scotia bridge.

Munitions production
Many of the county's firms took up where they had left off at the end of the First World War, two specific projects underlining this continuation. Ruston-Bucyrus, commissioned by Churchill in 1939, to design a trenching-machine capable of cutting through the German defences of the West Wall, came up with 'Nellie', an acronym for Naval Land Equipments. This was an 80ft-long (24m-long) tracked plough that could dig a trench 5ft (1.5m) deep and 7ft 6in (2.25m) wide at a speed of 0.4–0.7 mph (0.6–1.1 kmph). It underwent initial feasibility trials at Skellingthorpe, followed by more intensive trials of the production model at Clumber Park (Notts).

101 HOLTON-le-MOOR: the guard-room/HQ of the RAF Works Depot between the railway and the A46 road

At this stage in early 1942, doubts as to the usefulness of such a machine were beginning to creep in, but it was not actually cancelled until May 1943. The other project involved Fosters & Co. who designed an experimental 70-ton tank carrying a heavy gun, code-named *TOG2STAR*, 'TOG' being an acronym for 'The Old Gang'. A prototype, carrying a 17-pounder AT gun, was tested in the Skellingthorpe road gravel-pits in November/December 1941, but, weighing in at 80 tons, was judged unsuitable for the type of warfare now evolving, especially given that even the heaviest mark of the new Bailey bridge was designed for a maximum weight of only 70 tons.

Of more use to the war effort were the large numbers of diesel engines built by Ruston & Hornsby. These were used in small naval craft, in locomotives in Admiralty depots such as Ditton Priors (Shropshire), and in munitions factories. Along with Bucyrus they built tanks and armoured gun-tractors. Additionally, Lincoln factories made searchlights, AA guns, radar parts, depth charge casings, gun mountings, mines and shells. Smith Clayton Forge manufactured components for Rolls Royce, Bristol and Armstrong Siddeley aero engines, as well as other aircraft parts. In Grantham, Ruston & Hornsby made parts for naval vessels including gun mountings, while Aveling Barford built tracked Bren gun carriers. BMARCo on Springfield Road made 20mm cannon for *Spitfires*, *Seafires*, and, later on, for *Sea Furies*, along with millions of cannon-shells. Some of this work was carried out in shadow factories at Hungerton Hall and Stoke Rochford. In Gainsborough, Marshalls had had a contract with the Admiralty since 1936 to build naval Twin 4" and 4.7" gun-mountings for cruisers and destroyers, as well as AA guns and pom-poms. They also built midget submarines (X-craft), one of which – X-24 – survives in the Gosport submarine museum. Rose Brothers made *Bofors* LAA guns and powered gun-turrets for *Lancaster* bombers, designed by Group-Captain Rice of 1 Group, Bomber Command, and Alfred Rose. Bomber Command's 5 Group came to treat the factory as their own workshop. Rose Bros. established a shadow factory at Saxilby and set up de-centralised workshops to avoid bombing. The steelworks and allied engineering firms in Scunthorpe produced everything from tank landing craft to the tanks to go in them.

To meet the navy's insatiable demand for small escort and mine-sweeping craft, the ship-building yards were kept busy. In Grimsby, J. S. Doig built fifteen MFVs, and five *Fairmile* 'B' class MLs, Humphrey & Smith built six MMSs and twenty-one MFVs, and E. Bacon & Co. and Beeley & Sleight built a number of small landing craft. Clapson & Sons of Barton-upon-Humber built three MFVs, and GL Watson of Gainsborough, five Torpedo Recovery Vessels for servicing the ranges. Appleby-Frodingham in Scunthorpe built large tank landing craft (LCTs).

THE HOME FRONT

This section records a number of non-military but nevertheless important aspects of life in wartime Lincolnshire.

Agriculture
Acting very much on the experience gained in the previous war, a number of measures were taken early on. In September 1939, a directive from the Ministry of Agriculture required ten per cent of grassland to be ploughed for use as arable land. The Women's Land Army (WLA) had re-formed in June 1939, attracting casual female labour but later bolstered by conscription. Although agricultural work counted as a reserved occupation, many male workers had joined up as territorials. War Agricultural Committees were formed in Lindsey, Holland and Kesteven, and had implemented official policy smoothly without having to resort to dispossessions. PoWs were made available for carrying out heavy work, such as drainage or lifting sugar beet alongside the WLA, many of whose members were doing quite heavy work themselves without the benefit of PoW help.

In each of the years 1939–41, a quarter of a million rats were killed as hitherto derelict land was brought into use. The production of bulbs and flowers was reduced to a quarter of the pre-war level. After D-Day, freed Russian prisoners were brought in to help as well, with school children attending farmwork camps. Children also gathered hedgerow fruits, particularly rose hips for Vitamin C-rich syrup, and blackberries for jam; schools closed for the potato harvest. Food-processing plants were particularly important in ensuring that fresh food was not wasted and that both servicemen and women and civilians benefited from the increased production. Processed vegetables went into   soup, provided as emergency supplies for those bombed out.

102 USSELBY: this building is remembered locally as the NAAFI for the troops guarding the PoW camp (Camp 407), most likely situated in the former army camp

Productivity – in terms of the effectiveness of labour – rose by nine per cent during the war. Although firms like Marshalls of Gainsborough continued to build tractors and threshing machines, generally the manufacture of agricultural machinery was subordinate to munitions production, and many of the diesel tractors, graders, caterpillar tractors and so on developed by engineering firms were put to use in building airfields rather than in farming. Between September 1938 and April 1943, farm income saw a net rise of 400 per cent. WLA members lived on farms or in collective billets known as Land Army Hostels. There were such hostels, for instance, in Leverton village hall (The Three Horseshoes), at Billingborough, Wellingore, and two surviving examples at Whaplode Drove and Honington. The YMCA ran camps for foreign volunteers, such as that at Horbling.

Hospitals
The original RAF hospital was at Cranwell, but this proved inadequate and Rauceby mental hospital near Sleaford was taken over in 1940. Nocton Hall was also converted into a casualty clearing station until 1943 when the USAAF took it over. In Lincoln the Sobraon Barracks hospital served the needs of the army, and civilian hospitals met local needs, but with a new mortuary in the Burton Road Institution. In August 1942, the County Hospital and Nurses' Home were damaged by bombs.

PoW Camps

As the war progressed, more and more PoWs had to be accommodated, and some large camps were built to a common plan with compounds for the administration, for the guards, and for the prisoners who were generally housed in brick huts with separate ablutions blocks and communal eating facilities. Pingley Camp (Camp 81) outside Brigg was a well-preserved example, as was Moorby (Camp 79) near Horncastle, until their recent demolition. At Usselby (Camp 407), a brick building, thought to be the camp NAAFI, survives (*102*). Fragments also remain at Potterhanworth and at Low Fulney near Spalding (Camp 153), but the majority of the twenty or so camps in the county have vanished, as at the former Wellingore picnic site, where only some concrete hut-bases remain, or where now stands the Danish Invader PH on the Oakham road out of Stamford (Camp 106)

nine

The Cold War (1946–93)

As soon as the Second World War ended, the military presence in the county was quickly run down, with the majority of camps and airfields closing within twelve months. Given the county's traditional reliance on tourism, a programme for demolishing the coastal defences was soon under way: piers and beaches were re-opened, seaside landladies went back to their customary clientele, the Admiralty made good any damage and paid compensation for lost wartime profits, and Butlins, Skegness was restored to the Redcoats. The Navy retained very little interest in Lincolnshire but the RASC coasters *Sir Evelyn Wood* (built 1896) and the *Marquess of Hartington* (built 1886) continued to be brought from the west coast of Scotland for their annual refit in Grimsby, until they were scrapped in 1957, this being the only place with the appropriate facilities for coal-fired vessels. Requisitioned houses were restored to their owners, although some, such as Easton Hall, had been so badly damaged that demolition was the only option. The army maintained a presence at the barracks in Lincoln with TA detachments dotted around the county, but really it was only the RAF that was represented in any strength. The Home Guard was re-formed for a short while at the time of the Suez crisis in 1956. Although aircraft of the V-force were in the air with armed nuclear weapons at the time of the Cuban missile standoff in 1962, mercifully the possible escalation was avoided. Fortunately, the only local call-out had been in response to a natural disaster when 4,000 troops were involved in helping out in the east coast floods of 1953, and RAF North Coates itself had to be evacuated.

THE RAF IN LINCOLNSHIRE DURING THE COLD WAR

The possession of nuclear weapons formed the basis of Britain's defence strategy throughout the Cold War period (***Fig. 16***), resulting in the theory of deterrence summarised as Mutually-assured Destruction (MAD), in which all participants in any exchange of nuclear weapons would be guaranteed instant annihilation. The RAF's contribution lasted from the end of the war until 1969 when the Royal

228 Defending Lincolnshire: A Military History from Conquest to Cold War

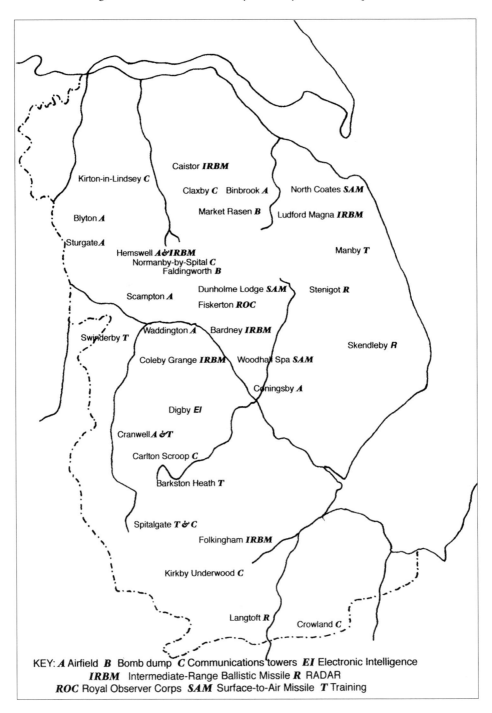

Fig. 16 Cold War sites in Lincolnshire

Navy's *Polaris*-equipped nuclear submarines took on the responsibility for Britain's share of NATO's nuclear deterrent.

The RAF deployment

Forming the basis of the new post-war RAF were the fast jet-bombers of the V-Force: *Victors, Canberras, Valiants* and *Vulcans*. The prototype *Vulcans* had been assembled in the workshops of A.V. Roe at Bracebridge Heath in 1952, and ultimately many were to be based at Scampton and Waddington between 1957 and 1981, with others at Coningsby in the 1960s, and a dispersal for two aircraft at Cranwell. Binbrook, Hemswell, Scampton and Coningsby provided bases for *Canberra* squadrons at various times during the early 1950s. These aircraft carried a variety of nuclear weapons over the period up to 1969, including US bombs, and the British *Red Beard, Blue Danube, Yellow Sun* and *Blue Steel*. Prior to the production of these British aircraft, the *Canberra* first appearing in 1951, RAF squadrons equipped with US *B-29 Washington* bombers had been based on a handful of British airfields, including Coningsby and Waddington. To protect the bombers and to intercept foreign intruders, fighters were based across the county – first *Hunters* and *Javelins* (1962–5), and later *Lightnings* (1966–87) at Binbrook, *Meteors* at Blyton (1952–4), and at Coningsby, *Phantoms* (1969–77), *Tornados* (1988–2003) and currently the new *Typhoon* Euro-fighter. Woodhall (no 'Spa' on the signs now) remains in service as a satellite of Coningsby, providing aspects of technical back-up for the *Typhoons*. Sturgate was reactivated by the USAF in 1952, operating as an occasional base for *Thunderstreak* jet-fighters of the Strategic Air Command, but only until 1964. Since 1991, Waddington has been home to the AEW electronic warfare aircraft, initially *Nimrods* and subsequently Boeing *E3 Sentries*.

Lincolnshire has continued as a training venue with Cranwell consolidating its position as the RAF's officer-training college. The Central Flying School has been co-located there since 1992 and most aircrew training takes place there. It was the only airfield in Lincolnshire earmarked for use by the USAF in any future conflict involving NATO forces. Barkston Heath provides a second airfield for the College's flying-training operations. Spitalgate was involved in training until 1975 through its Central Gliding School, and was the main venue for WAAF training from 1960–74. Swinderby was No. 7 School of Recruit Training (RAF and WRAF), and the location for Flying Selection Training until 1993. Manby has hosted both the College of Air Warfare and the School of Refresher Flying amongst other flying-training units up to 1974 with use of Strubby until 1972. Blyton was an Advanced Flying School until 1954, flying *Meteors*. Bombing ranges continue in use at Wainfleet Sands, Donna Nook and Holbeach St Matthew. A RAF hospital opened at Nocton Hall in 1947, remaining in use until 1983, listed in its latter years as a 500-bed USAF contingency hospital for handling casualties in any potential European nuclear exchange.

Adapting the airfields for the nuclear age

The major requirement of the new aircraft was longer runways. Scampton and Waddington were each given a 9000ft (2750m) runway by the mid-1950s, that at

103 MANBY: the watch office to drawing number 2548c/55

Scampton necessitating a re-alignment of the (Roman) A15 road. Concrete runways were finally laid at Cranwell's south airfield in 1954. Coningsby has a single 9000ft runway equipped with arrester gear at each end. Although, chiefly for reasons of economy, every attempt has been made to adapt existing buildings to new uses, there have had to be new builds as well. New control towers were built at Manby (*103*) and Scampton (2548c/55) and Swinderby and Waddington (7378a/55), although Waddington retains its original, but modified, watch office for local control. Coningsby received a new Control Tower in 2005 as part of its upgrade for use by the *Typhoon*. A VCR was added to Strubby's existing tower during the time it served as Manby's satellite. In 1960 Cranwell's College Hall finally received its fourth wing in the style of West's original building, and in 1962 Whittle Hall, in a similar style, was added, followed by Trenchard Hall in 1966, built to accommodate the technical training facilities being transferred from Henlow, but in a style more suited to a modern technological world.

Although the 'C' Type hangars, present on so many of Lincolnshire's airfields, were spacious enough to lend themselves to most modifications, there have been a number of instances where new specialised hangars have had to be built. Coningsby's 'J' Type hangars were supplemented by a *Gaydon* hangar (*104*), designed in the 1950s to accommodate the V-force *Vulcans* based there from 1962–4. At Binbrook there is a QRA hangar (*105*) that was designed to shelter a pair of *Lightning* interceptors, sitting on the end of the runway ready to take off at a moment's notice. In the early 1980s, Coningsby was provided with HAS for its *Phantoms* (*106*). The AEW aircraft at Waddington enjoy the luxury of an enormous purpose-built hangar (*107*),

The Cold War (1946–93) 231

104 CONINGSBY: the *Gaydon* hangar built to house *Vulcan* bombers

105 BINBROOK, the QRA (Quick Response Alert) hangar that housed a pair of *Lightning* interceptors

106 CONINGSBY: a Hardened Aircraft Shelter, originally built in the early 1980s, to house *Phantoms*

107 WADDINGTON: the purpose-built hangar in which AWACS aircraft are maintained and serviced

108 SCAMPTON: the *T2* hangar and sheds providing fuelling facilities for up to ten *Blue Steel* standoff bombs at a time

which was erected in 1990 and dominates the airfield. It is designed to hold two aircraft for maintenance operations, with parking for seven additional aircraft on the concrete apron outside. An adjoining mission support centre holds a flight simulator, mission simulator and software support. Bombs were stored at the Permanent Armaments Depot (PAD) at Faldingworth and in specialist bomb-storage facilities at Coningsby, Scampton and Waddington. A Supplementary Storage Area was added to Coningsby's existing nuclear weapons store, but constituted Scampton's only such provision. Waddington had USAF 'igloos' to house US atomic weapons on loan to the RAF, but under US guard.

Scampton's appearance as a wartime airfield has probably changed the most. The introduction of the aircraft of the V-force imposed a complex ground operation to maintain the electrical and electronic flight systems, and this necessitated the construction of the avionics building. Scampton was also one of only two airfields to be equipped with *Blue Steel*, a standoff missile that could be launched from an aircraft some distance from its target. It became operational in 1962 and a large, prefabricated storage and servicing building, composed of two modified *T2* hangars with an attached two-storey office building, was connected to the avionics building. Some distance away another *T2* hangar with double gabled sheds alongside (***108***) provided fuelling facilities for the missiles, ten of which could be accommodated at one time in separate bays. Both the avionics and fuelling buildings still survive, but the servicing facility has gone. At Digby, new buildings have been added to those remaining from two world wars to accommodate the signals/electronic intelligence units based there.

The THOR *IRBM missile system*

The intrinsic vulnerability of bomber aircraft led to a search for alternative delivery systems. While the British *Blue Streak* was already under development by de Havillands, it could not be available for at least another five years, so a ready-made US Intermediate Range Ballistic Missile, *THOR*, was adopted for joint USAF/RAF use until an ICBM could be developed, entering service in 1958. Its limited range of 1,500 miles (2,400km) meant that Russian targets were only attainable

109 COLEBY GRANGE: one of the massive concrete blast-walls that formed the launching pad for a *THOR* intermediate-range ballistic missiles in the early 1960s

from European launch-sites. Four groups, each of five airfields, were identified in eastern England as *THOR* bases, one group with Hemswell as HQ comprising Bardney, Caistor, Coleby Grange and Ludford Magna. An additional Lincolnshire location was Folkingham, part of a group based on North Luffenham in Rutland. Each site held three *THOR* rockets, kept on long canvas-covered trailers, which could be raised by means of a gantry into the vertical firing-position. Thick concrete L-shaped blast-walls (**109**) protected the crew and the sensitive services from the blast, but most of the site's infrastructure – including the tanks for the volatile mix of kerosene and liquid oxygen that fuelled the rockets, and the theodolite platforms used for setting the rockets' compasses – was quite exposed. Some of the installation was organised by works services based at RAF Sturgate. Underlining the stopgap nature of the operation, by mid-1963 the sites had been closed down and the missiles returned to the USA. The massive concrete blast-walls may still be seen at Coleby Grange, but those at Ludford Magna have recently been reduced to rubble.

The RAF Regiment

In 1945 the RAF Regiment had been run down, reduced to a strength of only 3,000 officers and other ranks, and most squadrons had been disbanded. Only in 1947 was the post-war establishment decided, setting a level of 8,000 officers and men in forty-seven squadrons, and this had been achieved by 1952. The permanent establishment was supplemented by squadrons of the Royal Auxiliary

Air Force Regiment, one of which was based at Scampton in the early 1980s, moving to Waddington in 1985 and soon to be joined by a further part-time squadron, armed with captured Argentinian 35mm LAA guns and their accompanying *Skyguard* radars.

DEFENCE AGAINST NUCLEAR ATTACK

Britain finished the Second World War with a sophisticated and comprehensive network of radar sites that facilitated the detection and interception of hostile aircraft. Much of this network was closed down after 1945, but coverage of the east coast was maintained and formed the nucleus of the air defence programme known as *ROTOR*, which began operations in 1950. The programme included radar sites, underground GCI stations and control rooms that co-ordinated a defence comprising interceptor fighters, surface-to-air AA missiles and AA guns. The UK Warning and Monitoring Organisation (UKWMO) included a re-vamped Royal Observer Corps, and Civil Defence was charged with minimising civilian casualties. A military communications system based on a network of microwave towers was designed to ensure that current information quickly reached those with a need to know. Civil government would continue from underground bunkers, and emergency food and fuel supplies were stockpiled for controlled distribution as necessary.

ROTOR *in Lincolnshire*
The existing Chain Home station at Stenigot returned to service in 1953 essentially as it had finished the war, but with some additional buildings; the GCI station at Langtoft, on the other hand, was modernised by the addition of a two-level semi-sunken *R6* bunker entered from a standard bungalow guard-house. Three of its five plinths for Type 13 Mark 6 height-finding radars also survive (**110**), as does its remote wireless station between Langtoft and Baston. Skendleby had been a wartime CHEL site and soon resumed this role, re-opening in 1953, but now housed in an *R3* two-level underground bunker reached by stairs from the guard-house (**111**). It was also equipped to function as a GCI station if needed. It, too, has a detached wireless station near Ulceby Cross. Aircraft needed to establish their exact position prior to being vectored onto targets by the GCI stations, so VHF Fixer Stations were established, two in Lincolnshire being at Lutton and Skidbrooke. The Humberside GDA was controlled from the AA Operations Room at Wawne. Although various components continued to function, the increased speed of intruder aircraft and the relative slowness of reporting systems meant that *ROTOR* had ceased to exist as an integrated system by 1958, AA Command having stood down as early as 1955.

110 LANGTOFT: one of three surviving plinths for Type 13 Mk 6 height-finding radar, part of the *ROTOR* air defence system

111 SKENDLEBY: the standard *ROTOR* radar-site guardhouse in the guise of a civilian bungalow; the large rear extension housed the access ramp which descended to the underground bunker

AA missiles

The demise of the army's AA Command transferred the responsibility of active air defence to the RAF, who built a network of surface-to-air missile (SAM) sites stretching from North Yorkshire to Suffolk and equipped with *Bloodhound* missiles. The test site for the programme was North Coates. Sites had two fire units each containing sixteen missiles, but North Coates, the Tactical Control Site for Lincolnshire with Dunholme Lodge and Woodhall Spa under command, had three fire units. A target would have been identified by the early warning radar at Patrington (Humberside), whose Type 82 *Orange Yeoman* radar would track it until it came within the 55-mile (88km) range of the Type 83 *Yellow River* radar located on each SAM site. Then one or more missiles would be launched and an on-board computer would calculate the point of interception.

As well as the thirty-two launch pads, these sites had a complement of a dozen or so buildings, ranging from the large shed for servicing the missiles and their ramjets, to the octagonal tower for the radar, through to stores, offices and a canteen. Accommodation was off-site. This trio of sites operated with *Bloodhound Is* (**112**) between 1958 and 1964, with Woodhall Spa – where the missile-servicing building still stands (**113**) – being used until 1967 for training on *Bloodhound II*. Following a deployment to Germany, the *Bloodhound II* units returned to Britain and sites were set up at North Coates again (1975–90) and at Barkston Heath (1983–90). These new missiles were more mobile, so fewer permanent structures were needed, the Type 86 radar being mounted on a skeleton steel tower. In 1991 the *Bloodhound* units were stood down. Since the late 1960s, the close defence of airfields has been the responsibility of the RAF Regiment with their *Rapier* AA missiles, which are designed to need only minimal structures for their operation and therefore seldom leave evidence on the ground.

The Royal Observer Corps in Lincolnshire 1945–91

So successful had been the operations of the observers in the Second World War that they were seen as an essential part of future air defence systems. The wartime aircraft-spotting posts had been built on an ad hoc basis and by 1950, many were unserviceable, so the Orlit company of west London, specialising in prefabricated concrete structures, was contracted to design and produce a standard post. This was a rectangular box measuring 10ft x 7ft (3 x 2m), half of which was roofed as a store while the other half was open to the sky and contained the table and plotting equipment. Some (Type A) – such as still stand at Burgh-on-Bain and Sturton-by-Stow – stood on the ground, while the elevated version (Type B) – as surviving at Swallow (**114**) – stood on four concrete posts and was entered via an integral ladder. One Orlit A has been built on top of a wartime pillbox at North Somercotes.

Within a few years, threats of a nuclear attack had materialised and the network of ROC posts was seen as the most appropriate way of recording the fall of nuclear bombs and of monitoring the spread of radiation. Orlit was again contracted to produce an underground post with surface instrumentation. This consisted of a larger rectangular box measuring 19ft x 8ft 6in (5.8 x 2.6m) with an interior height of

112 A *Bloodhound* (the army called them *Thunderbirds*) surface to air missile (SAM), photographed at Thorpe Camp

113 WOODHALL SPA: the missile assembly sheds for *Bloodhounds*; on the left is the corner of the characteristic SAM-site guardhouse, and centre-stage is taken by a fine example of the ubiquitous *Yarnold sangar*, a pre-fabricated guard-post still found at most RAF establishments

The Cold War (1946–93) 239

114 SWALLOW (TA177024): the elevated version of the Orlit aircraft-spotting post introduced for Royal Observer Corps use in the early 1960s

240 Defending Lincolnshire: A Military History from Conquest to Cold War

115 BISHOP NORTON (TA982922): the partially-exposed Orlit underground Royal Observer Corps post for monitoring radioactive fall-out after a nuclear bomb strike

116 FISKERTON: the semi-sunken regional Royal Observer Corps control room; here were collated and interpreted data from the network of underground monitoring posts

7ft 6in (2.3m) buried under 3ft of earth. Inside were two bunks, a chemical toilet, storage for a week's supply of food and water, and an area 7ft (2m) square of working space. All that is visible on the surface is the top of the entrance hatch, air vents and the Fixed Survey Meter, which measured ambient radiation levels. Two other instruments were provided: the Bomb Power Indicator which allowed the crew to record blast, and the Ground Zero Indicator, a very simple shadow-graph for pin-pointing the direction of a nuclear explosion by projecting its flash onto light-sensitive paper.

These underground posts were linked in threes by 'phone, with one in each triad equipped with radio to report to a central filter and control centre. By 1955 it had become apparent that a combination of the high speeds at which aircraft were now flying, the impossibility of reporting sightings quickly enough for action to be taken, and the increased efficiency of the new radar sets, rendered the traditional aircraft-spotting role of the ROC redundant, so it was therefore finally decided in 1965 that the nuclear monitoring role should become the ROC's primary function. Many of the underground posts remain, some like Holbeach being maintained in pristine condition. The Bishop Norton post has been partly exposed so that the external features are visible (**115**). There were fifty-four underground posts in Lincolnshire in 1965, of which forty-nine were part of 15 Group (Lincoln), four were part of 18 Group (Leeds), and one belonged to 7 Group (Bedford). By 1968, some twenty-seven of these posts had been closed down.

Since 1947, the ROC control centre had been at RAF Waddington, but in 1960 a new purpose-built protected Group HQ was opened on the former airfield at Fiskerton (**116**). This building is semi-sunken and had a control room on two levels, with incoming information from the posts transferred visually onto screens and an operations table in a sunken well overlooked by galleries where the controllers sat. As well as this 'pagoda' style building, with its secure entrance and projecting ventilator shafts standing proud of the enclosing earth mound, offices and ancillary buildings were accommodated in *SECO* huts. Closed in 1991, the Fiskerton centre is now used by a commercial cartridge-filling company.

Ballistic Missile Early Warning System (BMEWS)
A number of systems were developed through the 1960s to attempt to detect incoming missile strikes and to give sufficient warning, up to a generous seventeen minutes in Britain, to get the retaliatory nuclear-armed aircraft airborne and to sound the sirens at home. One such system was *ACE HIGH*, which enabled radio waves to be beamed at the troposphere from whence the resultant scatter could be picked up at enormous distances. This overcame the problem of having to build repeater stations at frequent intervals in order to cater for the curvature of the earth. This facility was the basis for 'over the horizon radar' and 'tropospheric scatter communications systems'. Britain had five *ACE HIGH* sites, of which Stenigot was one. Here, four large antenna dishes were built, along with a thirteen-bay-long electronics building containing the transmitters and receivers along with offices,

crew-rooms and workshops for servicing and maintaining the sensitive equipment. The whole complex was housed within high security fences with guard-posts, adjoining the old CH radar site. Although the wartime site has been given protected status by EH, the later structures, stood down in 1990 owing to both political and technological developments, have sadly been demolished.

Communications and infrastructure
The Admiralty W/T station at Cleethorpes was re-named Waltham in 1948, then New Waltham. It closed down in 1980 and was demolished. From 1961–79, the USAF, in the form of 2166 Communications Squadron, maintained a chain of radio relay stations at Crowland, Kirton-in-Lindsey, and Spitalgate. That at Crowland has recently been demolished to make way for a new road. An essential part of the early warning system was a network of microwave towers, of which the best known is the GPO Tower in London's Tottenham Court Road, opened in 1961. Three examples can be seen in Lincolnshire at Claxby, Carlton Scroop and Kirby Underwood (*117*), with a TV tower at Belmont, inland from Skegness. A further system of radio stations, known as *Hilltop* was run by the Home Office for use by the police, emergency services and ROC, examples of which include Kirkby Underwood (co-located with the microwave tower), Fulnetby, and Grange Farm. Campbell also lists Normanby-le-Wold as a *Hilltop* station. The monster golf-ball standing on its candlestick-shaped tee at Claxby is part of the civil air traffic control system (NATS). The RAF radio transmitting station at Normanby-by-Spital near Hemswell, recently demolished (although its security fence remains), transmitted regular half-hourly messages to airborne V-bombers.

Throughout the 1960s and 1970s a network of Essential Service Routes was constantly under review, with amendments being made up until at least 1979. These were roads, exclusively for military use in the event of a nuclear strike, which would be controlled by the police to ensure that civilian traffic – particularly refugees – would be prevented from using them. In Lincolnshire they included a route linking Newark-upon-Trent and Grimsby (A46, A158, A157 and A16), the A57 westwards from Lincoln, the A15, A16 and A151 between Peterborough and Boston, and the whole length of the A1 (code-named 'Stag' and linked to the Humber ports by 'Bat', now the M62). In order to keep the railways running, it was intended to build a network of bombproof control bunkers, as had been done during the Second World War when that at Metheringham had been constructed. However, after the completion of only two of the new batch, it was decided to use mobile centres housed in railway carriages. While the nuclear warheads were generally moved by road convoy with RAF police out-riders, at the time of the Vietnam War, 250lb (114kg) and 500lb (228kg) HE bombs were put on trains at Market Rasen and shipped out to the USA from Immingham.

Despite the anticipated devastation that a nuclear strike would obviously cause, there was still an intention that the operations of both national and local government might continue. Britain was divided into Regions that would be administered by a commissioner under the conditions of martial law. Lincolnshire fell into

The Cold War (1946-93) 243

117 KIRKBY UNDERWOOD: the Microwave Tower that formed part of a national network of emergency communications, whose spine was, appropriately if obviously code-named *Backbone*, and whose best-known exemplar stands in London's Tottenham Court Road

Region 3, the East Midlands, controlled from an underground bunker set up in the 1950s within the government buildings complex of Nottingham's Chalfont Drive. This Regional Seat of Government incorporated a 'war-room', a communications centre and a BBC studio. By the 1960s, more remote and more secure Sub-Regional Controls were established. In Region 3 these were SRHQ 3.1 in the former *ROTOR* bunker at Skendleby, and SRHQ 3.2 in a former Second World War cold store at Loughborough (Leicestershire). The Skendleby bunker was completely re-modelled for this new role, its latest equipment dating from 1985. Local government offices were encouraged to construct some form of bombproof bunker, usually with air locks on the doors, in order that operations might be continued during emergency situations. As late as 1987, the Thatcher government was offering 100 per cent funding for Home Office-approved schemes for local authority bunkers. There is an emergency centre in the basement of Lincoln's City Hall, and another under the council offices in Brigg. The post-war AAOR at Wawne functioned for a while as Humberside's county control.

Another concern of the government was the stockpiling and distribution of emergency food supplies, and MAFF set up a network of Buffer Depots. These tended to be away from the most likely targets for enemy strikes so only one, at Fiskerton airfield, was built in Lincolnshire, but there were military fuel depots at Killingholme and Immingham, both of which were identified by the US forces as Defense Fuel Support Points. The North Hykeham NAAFI distribution depot – serving all the local RAF airfields – was demolished in 1995, to be replaced by a new centre on Grantham's A1 Triangle Park business complex.

Munitions storage and production
At the end of the war, many Lincolnshire airfields were used to store the great stocks of bombs that were suddenly no longer needed. Faldingworth, however, was singled out for a specialist role storing and servicing the atomic weapons that would be carried by the V-force. A five-sided enclosure with double fences, guard-towers at the angles, and free-roaming, semi-wild police dogs, contains a group of buildings each having a very specific purpose. A picket post, MT garage and stand-by generators flanked the outer gate, while the guards' barrack-room and mess, together with the dog compound, were grouped around the inner one. Within this securely fenced inner compound, three Atomic Bomb Stores, surrounded by high earth traverses each holding twenty bombs on racks, were spaced around an oval loop road. *Blue Danube*, for instance, using the old *Tallboy* casing, was 24ft (7.3m) long and weighed 10,000lbs (4,650kg), so each store had a lifting gantry in front.

Also accessed by this road were the Fissile Core Stores, sixty-two in total, in groups of six and eight. These were small buildings, the size of garden sheds, which held the initiators for the bombs, codenamed *Gauntlet*, without which the bombs were effectively harmless. The buildings had doors with combination locks on a rotating cycle, and the cores were stored in stainless steel pits in the floor sealed with further combination locks. When the bombs were transported, the cores travelled separately, and the bombs went in three parts – nose, centre and tail – as they were only allowed to be assembled fully on the airfields themselves. Other buildings around the loop road included workshops for servicing, maintaining, possibly using X-ray equipment, and practice in assembling the bombs. Other workshops were used for servicing the fissile cores, and for maintaining the bomb-trolleys. Two reservoirs held emergency water supplies. Like its near-identical twin at Barnham (Norfolk), the Faldingworth site is virtually complete.

It would seem that in two world wars, Lincolnshire's industry responded with vigour when the occasion demanded it, but generally its factories were more geared to ploughshares than to swords. One exception has been BMARCo/Astra Holdings, a subsidiary of Oerlikon, whose factory at Springfield Road, Grantham manufactures 20mm and 30mm cannon for the Royal Navy. When the facility at Faldingworth was no longer needed for atomic weapons storage, it was taken over as an indoor testing range for these guns. One of the targets is set into a sizeable chunk of metal that came from the German battle-ship *Tirpitz*, disabled by bombers from Bardney and Woodhall Spa, accompanied by the RAF Film Unit from Waddington, in September 1944.

Camps, drill halls and barracks
Sobraon Barracks, Lincoln remained the home of the Lincolnshire Regiment until it was absorbed into the 2nd East Anglian Regiment in 1960, when it became a TA Centre. Except for the Keep and some newer buildings occupied by the territorials, the barracks itself has been replaced by housing. Only Westward Ho in Grimsby is currently occupied by an active TA unit, but other former TA premises are used by ACF detachments. Stonefield House in Church Lane, Lincoln, now a school, was the TA's administrative centre from the 1950s until 1968. In 1961, its responsibilities extended to eighteen active drill halls and nearly thirty cadet detachments. These included units of the 4/6th Lincolns, just in the process of becoming the Royal Anglians, the RA, RE, REME, RASC and WRAC. New facilities for ACF detachments at Brigg (1993) and Frodingham (1991) have been built to a common design found in the Yorkshire and Humberside RFCA area. Between 1965 and 2004, Kirton-in-Lindsey airfield served as a barracks for Royal Artillery units, although gliding continued throughout the Army's occupation. It has now been returned to RAF use. Spitalgate airfield is the national training centre for TA logistics personnel. Beckingham Camp is still in use for training and was one of two such establishments that were converted into overspill prisons during the prison officers' strike of 1980. It has been suggested that it had previously been earmarked as an internment camp for enemy aliens and those holding unacceptable political beliefs during times of heightened tension that might have escalated into nuclear war during the Cold War period.

As it happened, the Cold War threat suddenly disappeared, and although the peace dividend has been used to justify a reduction in armed forces personnel, the perceived threat of international terrorism has ensured that high levels of security are maintained around Lincolnshire's active defence installations.

Bibliography

Balfour, G., *The Armoured Train*, 1981, London
Beckwith, Ian, *The Civil War in Lincolnshire*, in Bennett, S. and Bennett, N., *An Historical Atlas of Lincolnshire*, 2001, Chichester
Beckwith, Ian, *The Lincolnshire Rising*, in Bennett, S. and Bennett, N., *An Historical Atlas of Lincolnshire*, 2001, Chichester
Beresford, G., *Goltho: the development of an early medieval manor c.850–1150*, 1987, London, E. H. Archaeological Report no. 4
Blake, R., Hodgson, M. and Taylor, B., *The Airfields of Lincolnshire since 1912*, 1984, Earl Shilton
Brown, H., 'The Mounted Home Guard', 2005, in *Lincolnshire Poacher*, Vol. 6, No. 3
Brown, J., *Farming in Lincolnshire 1850–1945*, 2005, Lincoln, History of Lincolnshire Committee
Bryant, G.F., *The Early History of Barton-upon-Humber*, 1994, Barton-upon-Humber
Bryant G.F., and Tyszka, D., *Barton Remembered 1939–1945 Part 2: The Home Front*, 1998, Barton-upon-Humber
Campbell, D., *War Plan UK*, 1982, London
Campbell, D., *The Unsinkable Aircraft Carrier*, 1984, London
Chapman, P., *Grimsby's Own, the story of the Chums*, 1991, Beverley
Chorlton, M., *Danger Area: the complete history of RAF South Witham*, 2003, Cowbit
Cocroft, W., *RAF Langtoft survey report*, 1998, Cambridge, RCHME
Cocroft, W. and Thomas R., *Cold War, Building for Nuclear Confrontation 1946–89*, 2003, Swindon
Coleman, E.C., *The Royal Navy in Lincolnshire*, 1991, Boston, Richard Kay
Colyer, C., *The western defences of the lower town*, 1975, Ants. Jnl., LV
Cooley, R., *The Unknown Fleet: The Army's Civilian Seamen in War and Peace*, 1993, Stroud
Coulson, C., *Hierarchism in Conventual Crenellation*, 1982, Med Archaeology, 26
Coulson, C., *The Castles of the Anarchy*, in ed. Liddiard, R., *Anglo-Norman Castles*, 2003, Woodbridge
Creighton, O., *Castles and Landscapes*, 2002 and 2005, London
Creighton, O. and Higham, R., *Medieval Town Walls*, 2005, Stroud
Curzon, Marquis of Kedleston, and Tipping, H.A., *Tattershall Castle*, 1929, London
Davies, C., *Stamford and the Civil War*, 1992, Stamford, Paul Watkins.
Davis, A., 'The Fight at Gainsborough', 1995, in *Civil War Times*, 51, Leigh on Sea
Davis, P., 'English Licences to Crenellate 1199–1567', 2006/7, *CSG Journal*, 20
Delve, K., *The Military Airfields of Britain: East Midlands*, 2008, Marlborough
Dobinson, C., *Twentieth Century Fortifications in England: II Anti-invasion defences of WWII*, 1996, York, CBA; *III Bombing Decoys of World War II*, 1996, York, CBA
Dobinson, C., *AA Command*, 2001, London

Dorman, J., *Guardians of the Humber*, 1990, Hull
Dowling, A., *Humberston Fitties*, 2001, Cleethorpes
Dransart, P., 'Fetternear' (moat excavation), in *British Archaeology*, September 2009
Embleton, W., *The English Civil War Day by Day*, 1995, Stroud
Everson, P., 'Belleau Manor', in *Lincolnshire History and Archaeology*, 14, 1979
Everson, P.L., Taylor, C.C., and Dunn, C.J., *Change and Continuity: Rural Settlement in North-East Lincolnshire*, 1991, HMSO for RCHME
Field, N. and Hurst, H., 'Roman Horncastle', in *Lincolnshire History and Archaeology*, 18, 1983
Fletcher, D., *British Mark I Tank 1916*, 2004, Oxford, Osprey New Vanguard series
Fletcher, D., *British Mark IV Tank*, 2007, Oxford, Osprey New Vanguard series
Foynes, J.P., *Battle of the East Coast 1939–45*, 1994, no place of publication
Garner, A.A., *Boston and the Great Civil War 1642–51*, 1992, Boston, Richard Kay
Gates, L.C., *The History of the Tenth Foot 1919–50*, 1953, Aldershot
Gaunt, P., *The Cromwellian Gazetteer*, 1987, Gloucester
Hall, C.E. (ed.), *Look, Duck and Vanish*, 1996, Heckington
Hall, G. and Feary, D., *Hagnaby, the Dummy Airfield*, c.1996, Spilsby
Halpenny, B.B., *Action Stations 2, the Military Airfields of Lincolnshire & the East Midlands*, 1981, Sparkford
Hancock, T., *Bomber County*, 3 volumes, 1978, 1985 and 2004, Lincoln
Harden, G., *Medieval Boston & its archaeological implications*, 1978, Heckington
Hardy, C., *Grimsby at War*, 1989, Grimsby
Higham, R. and Barker, P., *Timber Castles*, 1992, London, Batsford
Hill, Sir F., *Medieval Lincoln*, 1948 reprinted 1990, Stamford, Paul Watkins
Hill, Sir F., *Tudor & Stuart Lincoln*, 1956 reprinted 1991, Stamford, Paul Watkins
Holliss, B., 'The Impact of the Royal Air Force', in Mills, D. (ed.), *Twentieth Century Lincolnshire*, 1989, Lincoln, History of Lincolnshire Committee
Holmes, C., *Seventeenth-Century Lincolnshire*, 1980, History of Lincolnshire Committee
Howes, A., and Foreman, M., *Town & Gun, the 17th Century defences of Hull*, 1999, Hull
Hurt, F., *Lincoln during the War*, 1991, Lincoln
Hutson, H.C., *Grimsby's Fighting Fleet*, 1990, Beverley
Kenyon, J., *Medieval Fortifications*, 1990, Leicester
Kenyon, J., *Castles, Town Defences & Artillery Fortifications in the United Kingdom & Ireland: a Bibliography 1945–2006*, 2008, Donington, Shaun Tyas
King, D.J.C. and Alcock, L., *Ringworks of England and Wales*, in *Chateau Gaillard lll* (1966), ed. Taylor, A.J., 1969, Chichester
King, D.J.C., *Castellarium Anglicanum*, 1983, New York
Knapp, M., *Grantham, the War Years 1939–45*, 1995, Lincoln
Liddiard, R., *Castles in Context*, 2005, Macclesfield
Lincoln Engineering Society, *Made in Lincoln: Industrial Heritage Trail*, 2000, Lincoln
Lindley, P. (ed.), 'The Early History of Lincoln Castle', 2004, Lincoln, *Lincolnshire History & Archaeology*, Occasional Paper 12
Loveday, J., *Square-bashing by the Sea, RAF Skegness 1941–1944*, 2003, Norwich
Mahany, C., *Stamford Castle and Town*, 1978, Heckington, S Lincs. Archaeology Unit
May, J., *Prehistoric Lincolnshire*, 1976, Lincoln, History of Lincolnshire Committee
McCamley, N., *Cold War Secret Nuclear Bunkers*, 2002, Barnsley
Mills, D. (ed.), *Twentieth Century Lincolnshire*, 1989, Lincoln, History of Lincolnshire Committee
Morant, R., *The Monastic Gatehouse*, 1995, Lewes
Mould, P., *Wartime Schooldays in Boston*, 1996, Boston

Nalson, D., *The Poachers: the history of the Royal Lincolnshire Regiment 1685–1969*, 2003, Lincoln
National Trust, *Tattershall Castle*, 1974, London
Neave, D., *Anti-Militia Riots in Lincolnshire, 1757 & 1796*, 1976, SLH&A 11
Van de Noort, R., and Davies, P., *Wetland Heritage*, 1993, Kingston-upon-Hull, EH
Norton, J., *Gainsborough at War 1939–45*, 1995, Gainsborough
Olney, R. J., *Rural Society & County Government in Nineteenth Century Lincolnshire*, 1979, Lincoln, History of Lincolnshire Committee
Osborne, M., *20th Century Defences in Britain – Lincolnshire*, 1997, London, Brasseys
Osborne, M., *20th Century Defences in Britain – East Midlands*, 2003, Market Deeping
Osborne, M., *Defending Britain*, 2004, Stroud
Osborne, M., *Sieges & Fortifications of the Civil Wars in Britain*, 2004, Leigh-on-Sea
Osborne, M., *Always Ready, the drill halls of Britain's volunteer forces*, 2006, Leigh-on-Sea
Osborne, M., *Pillboxes of Britain and Ireland*, 2008, Stroud
Owen, A.E.B., *Louth before Domesday*, 1997, SLH&A, 32
Parker, C., *The Royal Observer Corps in Lincolnshire*, 1998, Lincoln
Pawley, S., *Grist to the Mill, a new approach to the early history of Sleaford*, 1988, LH&A, 23
Pevsner, N. (1964), Pevsner, N. and Harris, J. (1989), *Buildings of England: Lincolnshire* Harmondsworth, Penguin Books
Platts, G., *Land & People in Medieval Lincolnshire*, 1985, Lincoln, History of Lincolnshire Committee
Porter, S., *Destruction in the English Civil Wars*, 1994, Stroud
Pullen, R., *The Landships of Lincoln*, 2007 (2nd edition), Lincoln, Tucann Books
Rahtz, P., *Caistor, Lincolnshire, 1959, 1960, Ants. Journal*, XL
RCHM(E), *The Town of Stamford*, 1977, London, HMSO
Renn, D., *Norman Castles in Britain*, 1968 and 1973, London
Renn, D., *Burhgeat & Gonfanon*, in ed. Liddiard, R., *Anglo-Norman Castles*, 2003, Woodbridge
Reynolds, N., *Investigations in the Observatory Tower, Lincoln Castle*, 1975, in *Medieval Archaeology*, 19
Roberts, D. L., *Ayscoughfee Hall: the building of a great merchant's house*, 1975, *Lincolnshire History & Archaeology*, 10
Roffe, D., *Castles*, in Bennett, S. & Bennett, N., *An Historical Atlas of Lincolnshire*, 2001, Chichester
Rogers, A., *A History of Lincolnshire*, 1985, Chichester
Salter, M., *The Castles of the East Midlands*, 2002, Malvern, Folly Publications
Sansom, M., *The secret army: wartime underground resistance in Lincolnshire*, 2004, Lincoln
Sawyer, P., *Anglo-Saxon Lincolnshire*, 1998, Lincoln, History of Lincolnshire Committee
Scott, S.A., *Scampton Revisited, Airfield Focus*, 15, 2002, Peterborough, GMS
Simmons, B., *Iron Age and Roman Coasts around the Wash*, in Bennett, S. and Bennett, N., *An Historical Atlas of Lincolnshire*, 2001, Chichester
Smith, T.P., *Hussey Tower, Boston: a Late Medieval Tower-House of Brick*, 1979, *Lincolnshire History & Archaeology*, 14
Stocker, D. (ed.), *The City by the Pool*, 2003, Oxford
Swallow, S.C., collected papers on Yeomanry, Militia, Volunteers etc lodged in Lincolnshire Archives, 1990s, unpublished
Thompson, M.W., *Excavation of two moated sites at Cherry Holt near Grantham and at Epperstone near Nottingham*, Lincolnshire Architectural & Archaeological Society Report 6, 1957
Thompson, M.W., 'The Origins of Bolingbroke Castle and Further Work at Bolingbroke Castle, 1966 & 1969' in *Medieval Archaeology*, X and XIII

Thompson, M.W., *Tattershall Castle*, 1974, National Trust official guidebook
Turner, J., *'Nellie' The history of Churchill's Lincoln-built Trenching Machine*, 1988, Lincoln, Occasional Papers in *Lincolnshire History & Archaeology*, 7
Turner, J., 'Cold War remains in Lincolnshire', 2004, Lincoln, *Lincolnshire Past & Present*, 55
Turner, J., 'Prisoner of War Camps in Lincolnshire', 2004/5, Lincoln, *Lincolnshire Past & Present*, 58
Walker, A. (ed.), *Lincoln's West End: A History*, 2008, Lincoln, Survey of Lincoln
Walls, J. and Parker, C., *Aircraft Made in Lincoln*, 2000, Lincoln, *SLHA*
Ward, A., The Lincolnshire Rising 1536, 1996, Louth
Weir, A., Katherine Swynford, 2007, London
Whitwell, J.B., *Roman Lincolnshire*, revised edition 1992, Lincoln, *SLHA*
Wight, J., *Brick Building in England from the Middle Ages to 1550*, 1972, London
Wildman, G.A., *This Turbulent County, Lincolnshire in the Civil War 1642–46*, not dated
Wilkinson, M.C., *Skegness at War*, 2007, Skegness
Wilson, D.M. and Hurst, D.G., *The Templar Preceptory at South Witham*, 1967 in *Medieval Archaeology*, Xl
Wood, D., *Attack Warning Red*, 1976/1992, Portsmouth
Wright, N., *Lincolnshire Towns & Industry 1700–1914*, 1982, Lincoln, History of Lincolnshire Committee
Wynn, H., *RAF Nuclear Deterrent Forces 1946–69*, 1994, London, HMSO

Index

All locations are in Lincolnshire unless otherwise indicated. Page references in **bold** indicate illustrations

Agriculture 142, **223**, 224-225
Anti-Aircraft defences 133-4, 156-159, **158**, 213-215
Alford 109, 110, 115, 117, 159, 212, 218
Anarchy (1135-54) 28-31
Ancaster defended Roman town 14, 19
Ancaster Heath, Civil War action 94
Anglo-Saxon and Danish fortifications 21-4
Armoured trains & railway guns 180
Ashby de la Launde Preceptory 47
Aslackby Preceptory and 'castle' 35, 47, 49
Axholme, Isle of 46, 96-7

Bardney former RAF airfield 165, 167, 234, 245
Barkston Heath RAF & 9th USAAF airfield 12, 165, 167, 169, 200, 207, 229
Barons' Revolts, 1214 and 1265 45-6, 46-7
Barrow-upon-Humber earthwork castle 26, 31, **34**
Barton-upon-Humber 83, 117, 211, 215, 218
    possible Thegn's fort 24, 25
    Castledykes village enclosure 53
    St Peter's church tower 21, **23**, 26
Bassingham moat 62
Belleau moat 62
Belton House and Park 84, 85, 101, 115, 134, **135**, **136**, 137, 143, 144, 176, 189, 208
Belvoir Castle (Rutland) 87, 88, 89
Binbrook former RAF airfield 12, 150-1, **154**, 155, 201, 229, 230, **231**
Bishops of Lincoln
    Alexander 28, 29, 31, 32, 41
    Chesney 43
    Grosseteste 35, 55
    Henry Burghersh 43, 55
    Hugh 43
    Hugh of Wells 43, 45
    Oliver de Sutton 55
    Remigius 36
    William Alnwick 43
Blankney Hall 170, 210
Blyton former RAF airfield 165, 167, 176, 229
Bombing decoys 218-220, **219**
Boothby Pagnell manor-house 41-3, **43**
Boston 52-3, 54, 72, 81, 90, 93-4, 102, 109, 110, 159, 162, 163-4, 180, 183, 193, **198**, 212, 242
    Hussey Tower 74
    Rochford Tower, Skirbeck 74, **75**
    drill halls 115, 116-117
    town ditch 50
    Boston Haven defences 179, **179**, 180, **198**, 205
Bourne 46, 53, 54, 101-2, **102**, 123, 143
    possible Roman fort 20
    earthwork castle rebuilt in stone 32, 40, **42**
    abbey gate 57
Bracebridge Heath, No 4 Aircraft Acceptance Park 12, 127, **131**, 132, 144, **168**
Bracebridge Heath, A V Roe workshops 165, 229
Brackenborough Hall 183, 204
Brigg 83, 91, 102, 104, 226, 245
British Army (regular army units)
    60th Field Regiment Royal Artillery 159, 178

10th Foot, later Royal Lincolnshire Regiment 98, 112, 118-9, 134, 156, 177, 245
   17th Light Dragoons, later 17th Lancers 98, 178
   Machine Gun Corps 119, 137
   Manchester Regiment 11, 137, 139
   Royal Anglian Regiment 12, 245
British Resistance Organisation (Auxiliary units) 210-211
Brocklesby 102, 110, 116, 120, 211
Buckden Towers (Cambridgeshire) 73-4
Bullington *see* Goltho
Burgh le Marsh 20, 121, 198-9, 211
Burghley House (Cambridgeshire) 22, 88, 89-90
Burton Pedwardine earthwork castle 33

Caistor 14, 19, 32, 79
Caistor former RAF airfield 165, 234
Cameringham *see* Ingham
de Camville, Lady Nicholaa 45, 46
Canwick 183, **184**, **185**
Careby ditched enclosure 13
Castle Bytham earthwork castle, rebuilt in stone 26, **26**, 40-1, 46, 58
Castle Carlton   earthwork castle and village 26, 32, 35, 53, 68
Civil Defence 212, 220-222, **221**, 235
Civil War fortifications 87-88
Cleethorpes 100, 133, **133**, 134, 139, 187, 208, 212
Coast defence 111, 117-118, 120-3, **123**, 178-183, **179**, **186**, 187-189, **187**, **192**, **198**
Coleby Grange former RAF airfield 12, 165, **167**, 169, 234, **234**
Colsterworth late Iron Age ditched settlement 14
Coningsby RAF station 12, 150-1, 155, 170, 229, 230, **231**, **232**
Corby Glen earthwork castle 32
Cranwell RAF College and airfield 12, 125-6, 147, 148, 150, **151**, 169, 176, 230
Cressy Hall, Gosberton, moat 62, 84
Cromwell, Oliver, Lord Protector 85, 89-90, 96
Cromwell, Ralph, Lord Treasurer 45, 69-73
Crowland Abbey & town 47, 49, 57, 88-9, 242

Dalby castle (Partney) & Hall 32, 210, **211**
Deepings, the 57, 101, 102, 126, 199, **221**
Defence of airfields & VPs 199-204, **200**, **202**, **203**,
Defence Lines, World War II 188, 189-193, **191**
Defence of nodal points, World War II 193-199
Dewy Hill earthwork castle *see* Old Bolingbroke
Digby/Scopwick, RAF Station 12, 127, 147, 150-1, 155, 156, **157**, 165, 200, 201, **202**, 219, 233
Donna Nook 147, 176, 177, 216-217, 229
Dunholme Lodge former RAF airfield 165, 167, 237
Dymoke family of Scrivelsby, Champions of England 68, 76, 80, 98

Eagle Preceptory 47, 67
Earls and Countesses of Lincoln 35
   Countess Lucy 29, 36, 62
   William de Roumare 29, 31, 33
   Gilbert de Gant 29, 32
   Gilbert de Gant II 46
   Ranulf, 6th Earl of Chester, great grand son of Lucy 46
East Kirkby former RAF airfield 11, 165, 167, 169, 201
Edward I King of England 49, 55, 57
Elsham and Elsham Wolds former RFC/RAF airfields 126, 150-1, **153**
Eresby/Spilsby earthwork castle 55, 61

Faldingworth former RAF airfield 12, 165, 169, 233, 245
Falklands conflict 12, 235
Fiskerton former RAF airfield 165, 167, 241
Fleet earthwork castle 32
Flixborough defended settlement 21
Folkingham 101, 102, 165
Folkingham Castle 32, 46, 61, 71
Folkingham former RAF & 9th USAAF airfield 12, 207
Foss Dyke 24, 54, 87
Fosse Way 14, 20, 67
Freiston Shore coast battery 179, **179**, **198**, 205
Fulbeck Hall 183, **185**, 207-208

Index

Fulbeck former RAF airfield 12, 165, 167

Gainsborough 22, 76, 84, 85, 94, 95, 97, 99, 104, 115, 117, 126, 140, 142, 159, 195, 212
Gainsborough/Thonock earthwork fort and castle 14, 21, 26, 31, 33
Gainsborough Old Hall 78
Gibraltar Point 176, 179, 182, 205
Goltho (Bullington) Thegn's fort 21, 22, 25
Goltho (Bullington) earthwork castle 33, **34**, 35
Goxhill 98, 150
Goxhill moats 61, 62
Goxhill former RAF & 8th USAAF airfield 12, 165
Grantham 47, 49, 76, 84, 94, 96, 102, 109, 110, 112, 116, 140, 157, 159, 195, 212, 245
Grantham, Alma Park 176
Grantham Manor-house 61
Grantham militia barracks 107-9, **108**
Grantham, St Vincents, RAF & 8th USAAF HQ 147, **148**, 170
Grantham, Spitalgate airfield/TAC 27, 147, **149**, 155, 165, 169, 170, 176, 201, 218, 229, 242, 245
Grimsby 14, 45, 67, 80, 94, 98, 99, 103, 110, 111, 120, 121, 179, 180, 183, 212
Grimsby castle and town defences 45, 50
Grimsby drill halls **114**, 115, 116, 117, 157-9, 208, 215, 245
Grimsby, Royal Navy & fishing fleet 12, 118, 123, 161, 162-3, 164, 227
Grimsby, RAF Waltham former airfield 155, 167, 169
Grimsthorpe castle and Park **59**, 61, 80, 89, **175**, 176

Halstead Hall 78-9
Hanby Hall, Welton-le-Marsh earthwork castle 33
Harlaxton former RFC and RAF airfield 12, 127, 165, 167, 201, **203**
Harlaxton Manor 208
Hemswell/Harpswell RFC/RAF airfield 12, 127, 150-1, **152**, 155, 169, 218, 234
Henry IV (Bolingbroke) King of England 44, 62, 68
Heydour earthwork castle rebuilt in stone 41

Heynings Priory gate 57
Hibaldstow probable Roman fort 14
Hibaldstow former RAF airfield 165, 167, 169, 201
Holbeach 41, 147, 159, 165, 176, 229
Home Guard **197**, 208-212, **209**, **211**, 227
Honington Camp ditched enclosure 13
Horncastle 79, 90, 102, 110, 115, 117, 159
Horncastle defended Roman town 14, **17**, 19-20, 32
Hospitals 142-143, 225, 229
Hougham moat 41, 85, **86**
Hough-on-the-Hill possible Thegn's fort and earthwork castle 24, 32
Hull (East Yorkshire) 83, 94, 97, 101, 111, 162
Humber estuary, defences 111, 118, 121, **136**, 137, 138, 160, 161, 215

Immingham Port 12, 118, 124, 159, 161, **163**, 164, 183, 242, 244
Ingham (Cameringham) former RAF airfield 12, 165, 167, 169
Ingoldsby possible ditched enclosure 13
Iron-Age settlements 13-14

John of Gaunt, Duke of Lancaster 44, 62, 63, 67
John King of England 45

Kelstern former RAF airfield 165
Kettlethorpe moat 62, 85
Killingholme 121, 133
Killingholme, Admiralty fuel tanks and RNAS seaplane base 118, 124-5, 128, 244
Kingerby earthwork castle/moat 26, 32
Kirkstead Abbey gate 57
Kirmington settlement & Roman fort 11, 13, 14
Kirmington former RAF airfield (Humberside Airport) 11, 165
Kirton-in-Lindsey former RAF airfield 12, 126, 150-1, 156, 165, 242, 245
Kitchener's New Armies 119-120, 134
Knights Hospitaller 49
Knights Templar 47, 57
Kyme Tower **60**, 61, 71, 76

Langtoft 216, 217, 235, **236**
Lea moats 61
Licences to Crenellate 31, 55, 57, 61, 63, 64
Lincoln 45-6, 47-8, 49, 54, 68, 79, 81, 82, 90, 91-3, 159, 183, 212, 222-223
Lincoln barracks and drill halls 101, 107-9, 111-117, **113**, 157, **158**, 159
Lincoln Bishop's Palace 43, 55, 57, 73, **92**
Lincoln cathedral precinct walls and gates 55, 62, 63-4, **64, 65**, 66
Lincoln city and castle in Civil War 81, 82, 90, 91-3, **91**, **92**
Lincoln city walls and gates **30**, 50
Lincoln defences in World War II 193-195, **194, 196, 197**, 210, 211
Lincoln earthwork castle rebuilt in stone 11, 25, **27**, 31, **36**, 35-7, **38, 39**, 58, **91**
Lincoln munitions production: tanks aircraft, etc 128-132, 139-142, **141, 143**
Lincoln Roman legionary fortress and walled *colonia*; 16-19, **16, 17, 18**
Lincoln St Mary's Churches: le Wigford, Crackpole, Cathedral 32
Lincoln siege castle outside Castle's West Gate 32
Lincoln Thorngate castle 32, 50
Lincoln West Common aircraft acceptance park **130**, 132
Lincolnshire Rising 1536 79-80
Lovell's Rebellion 1486 79
Louth 45, 79, 102, 110, 115, 116, 117, 121, 170, 180, 183, 204, **209**, 214
Louth possible Roman fort 14, 20
Ludford Magna former RAF airfield 165, 167, 169, 234

Mablethorpe 62, 90, 91, 163, 177, 179, 180, 211, 212, 215
Manby former RAF airfield 12, 150-1, **154, 155**, 155, 169, 218, **230**, 230
Mareham-le-Fen, Birkwood Hall moat 62
Market Rasen 102, 159, 242
Mere preceptory 47
Metheringham former RAF airfield 12, 165, 167, 169, 170, **171, 172**
Militia, organisation and accommodation 100-101, 106-9, 112, 116
 (8th) Royal North Lincolnshire 100, 101, 106

 (29th) Royal South Lincolnshire 100, 101, 106
Missile systems 233-234, **234**, 237, **238**
Moated sites 61-63
de Montfort, Constable of Lincoln Castle 46
Moulton, Kings Hall Park earthwork castle rebuilt in stone 41
Munitions Industry (World War I) 128-132, **129**, 139-142, **141, 143**
Munitions Industry & depots (World War II) 222-224
Munitions Industry & depots (Cold War) 244-245

Nettleham palace 55, 57, 79
Newark-upon-Trent (Nottinghamshire) 29, 31, 41, 84, 85, 88, 91
Newhouse (maybe Newsham Priory, Brocklesby) earthwork castle 32
Norman earthwork castles 25-28, **26**, **27**, 31-35
Norman stone castles 35-43
North Coates former RAF airfield 147, 150, 165, 169, 177, 214, 218, 237
North Killingholme former RAF airfield 12, 165, **168**, 169
North Witham former RAF and 9th USAAF airfield 12, 165, 167, 169, 170
Nuclear attack, dangers and precautions 235-237, 241-244

Old Bolingbroke, Dewy Hill earthwork castle 32, 33
Old Bolingbroke stone castle 35, 44-5, **44**, 58, 68, 90, 91
Old Sleaford possible tribal *oppidum* 13
Old Winteringham Roman fort 14
Owston/Kinards Ferry earthwork castle 26, 31, 32, 33

Peterborough (Cambridgeshire) 12, 24, 37, 76, 89, 127, 242
Pillbox designs and tactics 122, **123**, 187, **186, 187**, 190, **192, 193**, 200-3, **202**, 204-8
Polygonal castles 44-5
Polish airmen & Polish troops 12, 180
Prisoner of War camps 144, **225**, 226

Radar and electronic warfare 156, 170, 173, 215-7, **217**, 218, 235, **236**, 241-4, **243**
Raithby-cum-Maltby Preceptory 47
Ranulf, Earl of Chester 31, 35, 36
Redbourne earthwork castle 32
Richard II, King of England 67
Riby Gap, Civil War action 94
Riby Park (Grove) 11, 137
Rifle Volunteer Corps 109, 110, 134
Roman fortifications 14-20, **16**, **17**, **18**
Royal Air Force 147-156, 162, 164-76, 227-9
Royal Air Force Regiment 176-7, 200, 234-5
Royal Australian Air Force 12
Royal Canadian Air Force 12
Royal Flying Corps 126-128
Royal Naval Air Service 124-126, 159
Royal Navy, RNR and Fleet Air Arm 122, 123-4, 165, 220, 227
Royal New Zealand Air Force 12
Royal Observer Corps 156, **206**, 207, 217-8, 235, 237-241, **239**, **240**

Sandtoft former RAF airfield 12, 165, 167
Scampton RAF Station 12, 126, 127, 150-1, **153**, 155, 219, 229, 230, 233, **233**, 235
Scrivelsby moated house 78, **78**
Scunthorpe 117, **117**, 208, 220, 224
Skegness 81, 100, 115, 121, 155, 156, 177, 179, 180, 183, 187, 205, 208, 211-2, 214
Skegness possible Roman shore fort 20
Skegness, HMS *Royal Arthur* 12, 164
Skegness, No 11 RAF Recruit Training Centre 173, **174**, **175**, 176
Skellingthorpe former RAF airfield 165, 167
Skendleby 183, **184**, 216, 235, **236**
Sleaford 52, 80, 90, 109, 159, 208
Sleaford Castle 29, 41, 58
Sleaford Old Place 61, 90
Somerton castle 55, **56**, 61
South Carlton RFC airfield 127
South Kelsey Hall 79, 84, 95
South Kyme Tower *see* Kyme
South Ferriby 13
South Witham Preceptory 47, 49
Spalding 45, 101, 102, 109, 115, 117, 159, 183, 193, 199

Spalding Castle 41
Spalding, Ayscoughfee Hall 74
Spalding Priory 57, 62
Spilsby (moat *see* Eresby) 110, 115, 117, 121, 159, 165, 169, 199
Stainby earthwork castle 32
Stallingborough 98, 111, 118, 121, 214
Stamford 45, 76, 84, 85, 101, 109, 159, 199, 210
Stamford *burhs* and possible Thegn's fort 21, 22, 25
Stamford castle 35, 37, 40, **40**
Stamford town walls 50, **51**
Stamford Greyfriars & White Friars gatehouses 57-8
Stow earthwork castle and palace 35, 57
Strubby former RAF airfield 165, 167, 169, 230
Sturgate former RAF airfield 165, 167
Sutton Bridge former RAF airfield 12, 147, 150, 200, 201
Swinderby former RAF airfield 150, 170, 176, **200**, 201, 230
Swineshead earthwork castle 26, 33, 35
Swynford, Katherine 62-3

Tattershall Castle 11, 44, 68, 69-73, **70**, 78, 90, 98
Tattershall Thorpe ditched enclosure 13
Temple Bruer Preceptory 47, **48**, 49, 57
Territorial Army 1920-39, 1947-present 156, 157, 227, 245
    Royal Lincolnshire Regiment (TA Bns) 157, 159, 177
    46th North Midland Division 159
Territorial Force 1908-20 107-8, 116-7, 121, 134, 137
    1st North Midland Brigade, Royal Field Artillery 116
    North Midland Divisions (46th & 59th) 116, 119, 137
    North Midland Mounted Brigade 116, 119
    Lincoln & Leicester Infantry Brigade 116
    Royal Lincolnshire Regiment (TF Bns.) 116, 119-20
    4th Northern General Hospital RAMC 116

Tetney Beam Station 160, **160**
Theddlethorpe 165, 176, **186**, 205
Thonock *see* Gainsborough
Thorganby Hall, Caistor 83
Thornholme Priory gate 57
Thornton Abbey 57, **57**, 58
Thorpe Camp, Tattershall Thorpe 12, 201, **238**
Torksey possible Danish fort and laager 21, 24
Torksey Manor **86**, 87
Tothill earthwork castle 35
Town defences 50-53, **51**
Tupholme Abbey gate 57

Ulceby 13, 235
8th United States Army Air Force (USAAF) 12, 165
9th United States Army Air Force (USAAF) 12, 165, 170, 207

Waddington RAF Station 12, 127, 150-1, 155, 164-5, 170, 219, 229, 230, **232**, 233, 235, 241, 245
Wainfleet-All-Saints 90, 176, 189, 211, 229
Wake family, of Bourne 40, 46-7, 57

Waltham airfield *see* Grimsby
Wars of the Roses 76-9
Welbourn earthwork castle rebuilt in stone 26, 41
Wellingore Hall 210
Wellingore former RAF airfield 165, 167, 200, 201
Wickenby former RAF airfield 165, 167, 169, 201
William of Normandy, the Conqueror 25, 37
Willoughton Preceptory 47
Winceby, Battle of, 1643 83, 90-91, 93, 94, 95
Withern earthwork castle 35
Woodhall Spa Tower-on-the-Moor 73
Woodhall Spa RAF Station 12, 165, 170, 201, 237, **238**, 245
Wrangle, Kings Hill earthwork castle 26, 35
Wykeham (Weston) moat 62

Yarborough Camp ditched enclosure 13
Yeomanry Cavalry 101-103, 104-6, 110, 115-6, 119, 121
    Lincolnshire Yeomanry 119, 137